mustsees
Hawaiian Islands

Manele Bay Tidepools/Lanai © Leslie Forsberg/Michelin

mustsees **Hawaiian Islands**

Editorial Director	Cynthia Clayton Ochterbeck
Editor	Gwen Cannon
Contributing Writer	Eric Lucas
Production Manager	Natasha G. George
Cartography	Peter Wrenn
Photo Research	Nicole D. Jordan
Layout	Nicole D. Jordan, Natasha G. George
Interior Design	Chris Bell, cbdesign
Cover Design	Chris Bell, cbdesign, Natasha G. George

Contact Us

Michelin Travel and Lifestyle North America
One Parkway South
Greenville, SC 29615, USA
travel.lifestyle@us.michelin.com
www.michelintravel.com

Michelin Travel Partner
Hannay House
39 Clarendon Road
Watford, Herts WD17 1JA, UK
www.ViaMichelin.com
travelpubsales@uk.michelin.com

Special Sales

For information regarding bulk sales, customized
editions and premium sales, please contact us at:
travel.lifestyle@us.michelin.com
www.michelintravel.com

Michelin Travel Partner
Société par actions simplifiées au capital de 11 288 880 EUR
27 cours de l'Ile Seguin - 92100 Boulogne Billancourt (France)
R.C.S. Nanterre 433 677 721

© Michelin Travel Partner
ISBN 978-2-067197-40-4
Printed: May 2014
Printed and bound in Italy

MIX
Paper from
responsible sources
FSC® C015829

Note to the reader:
While every effort is made to ensure that all information printed in this guide is correct
and up-to-date, Michelin Travel Partner accepts no liability for any direct, indirect or
consequential losses howsoever caused so far as such can be excluded by law. Admission
prices listed for sights in this guide are for a single adult, unless otherwise specified.

Welcome to the Hawaiian Islands

Introduction

Must See

p 22

p 155

p 104

TABLE OF CONTENTS

★★★ATTRACTIONS

Unmissable attractions awarded three stars in this guide include:

Hawaii Tourism Japan

Bishop Museum and Planetarium, Oahu p 119

Hawaii's Big Island Visitor Bureau

Hawaii Volcanoes National Park, Hawaii p 29

©Gavin James/Bigstockphoto.com

Kalalau Hiking Trail, Kauai p 96

©Stephan Hoerold/iStockphoto.com

Kaunaoa Beach, Hawaii p 26

MUST KNOW

Hana Highway, Maui p 65

USS Arizona Memorial,
Pearl Harbor, Oahu p 125

Hulopoe Beach, Lanai p 147

Haleakala National
Park, Maui p 62

Na Pali Coast, Kauai p 85

★★★ATTRACTIONS

Unmissable Hawaiian Islands sights

For more than 75 years people have used the Michelin stars to take the guesswork out of travel. Our star-rating system helps you make the best decisions on where to go, what to do, and what to see.

★★★	Unmissable
★★	Worth a trip
★	Worth a detour
No star	Recommended

★★★Three-Star

Bishop Museum and
  Planetarium (OAH) *p 119*
Haleakala NP (MAU) *p 62*
Hana Highway (MAU) *p 65*
Hanalei Bay Beach (KAU) *p 82*
Hawaii Volcanoes NP (HAW) *p 29*
Hulopoe Beach (LAN) *p 147*
Iolani Palace (OAH) *p 124*
Kalalau Hiking Trail (KAU) *p 96*
Kaunaoa Beach (HAW) *p 26*
Kilauea Volcano (HAW) *p 30*
Lanikai Beach (OAH) *p 109*
Na Pali Coast (KAU) *p 85*
North Shore (KAU) *p 90*
Pearl Harbor (OAH) *p 125*
Poipu Beach Park (KAU) *p 83*
Polynesian CC (OAH) *p 122*
Puuhonua O Honaunau
  NHP (HAW) *p 42*
Southeast Shore (OAH) *p 114*
USS Arizona Memorial (OAH) *p 125*
Waikiki Beach (OAH) *p 109*

★★Two-Star

Ala Moana Shopping (OAH) *p 139*
Aloha Stadium (OAH) *p 139*
Chinatown (OAH) *p 138*
Aloha Tower (OAH) *p 105*
Chain of Craters Road (HAW) *p 37*
Crater Rim Drive (HAW) *p 35*
Diamond Head (OAH) *p 112*
East End Drive (MOL) *p 157*
Halemaumau Crater (HAW) *p 35*
Hanauma Bay NP (OAH) *p 113*
Hapuna Beach SRA (HAW) *p 26*
Hawaii Tropical BG (HAW) *p 40*
Highway 44 (LAN) *p 149*

Hilo (HAW) *p 23*
Honolulu (OAH) *p 105*
Iao Needle (MAU) *p 64*
Iao Valley State Mon. (MAU) *p 64*
Kaanapali Beach (MAU) *p 60*
Kailua Beach Park (OAH) *p 110*
Kalalau Valley (KAU) *p 97*
Kalaupapa NHP (MOL) *p 160*
Kilauea Point NWR (KAU) *p 100*
Kilauea Visitor Center (HAW) *p 30*
Kokee SP (KAU) *p 86*
Lahaina (MAU) *p 57*
Laupahoehoe (HAW) *p 27*
Limahuli Garden (KAU) *p 93*
Maui Ocean Center (MAU) *p 73*
Mauna Kea (HAW) *p 32*
McBryde and Allerton BG (KAU) *p 93*
Mission Houses Mus. (OAH) *p 122*
Munro Trail (LAN) *p 150*
North Shore Beaches (OAH) *p 111*
Oheo Gulch (MAU) *p 64*
Polynesian Cul. Center (OAH) *p 122*
Sea Life Park (OAH) *p 134*
Senator Fong's Plantation (OAH) *p 118*
Shipwreck Beach (LAN) *p 147*
Waimea Canyon (KAU) *p 87, p 89*
Waimea Canyon Drive (KAU) *p 89*
Waimea Canyon SP (KAU) *p 87*
Waimea Valley (OAH) *p 130*
Waipio Valley (HAW) *p 22*
World Botan. Garden (HAW) *p 41*

★One-Star

Ala Kahakai National Historic
  Trail (HAW) *p 43*
Aloha Tower M'place (OAH) *p 140*
Akaka Falls SP (HAW) *p 33*
Battleship Missouri M. (OAH) *p 127*

MUST KNOW

ACTIVITIES

Look for the Michelin Man to find the top activities on the Islands.

Nightlife

Restaurants

Gardens

Shopping

Kids

Spas

Tours

Recreation

STAR ATTRACTIONS

CALENDAR OF EVENTS

Listed below is a selection of Hawaii's most popular annual events.
Please note that the dates may change from year to year.
*For more information, contact the Hawaii Visitors and Convention
Bureau (800-464-2924; www.gohawaii.com).*

January
Lunar New Year
808-536-4621
Chinatown, Honolulu, Oahu
www.chinatownhi.com

February
Waimea Town Celebration
808-338-1332
Waimea, Kauai
www.wkbpa.org
Pro Bowl
808-483-2500
Aloha Stadium, Honolulu, Oahu
www.nfl.com

March
Maui Whale Festival
808-249-8811, Lahaina, Maui
www.mauiwhalefestival.org

April
Merrie Monarch Festival
808-935-9168
Hilo Civic Center, Hilo, Big Island
www.merriemonarch.com
Celebration of the Arts
808-669-6200
Kapalua, Maui, www.
kapaluacelebrationofthearts.com

May
Big Island Film Festival
808-883-0394
Kohala Coast, Big Island
www.bigislandfilmfestival.com
**Molokai Ka Hula Piko
Hula Festival**
808-553-5221
Kaunakaikai, Molokai
www.kahulapiko.com

Puna Music Festival
800-800-6886
Puna district, Big Island
punamusicfestival.com

June
Kapalua Wine & Food Festival
800 KAPALUA
Kapaulua Resort, Kapalua, Maui
www.kapalua.com
King Kamehameha Celebration
808-586-0333
All islands
ags.hawaii.gov/kamehameha
Maui Film Festival at Wailea
808-579-9244
Wailea, Maui
www.mauifilmfestival.com
**Ki Hoalu Slack Key Guitar
Festival**
808-226-2697
Maui Arts & Cultural Center
Kahului, Maui
www.slackkeyfestival.com
**Puuhonua O Honaunau
Festival**
808-328-2326
Puuhonua O Honaunau National
Historical Park, Big Island
www.nps.gov/puho

July
Lanai Pineapple Festival
Dole Park, Lanai City
www.lanaipineapplefestival.com
Ukulele Festival
808-732-3739
Kapiolani Park
Waikiki, Oahu
www.ukulelefestivalhawaii.org

MUST KNOW

Koloa Plantation Days
808-652 3217
Koloa, Kauai (various locations)
www.koloaplantationdays.com

August
Establishment Day Festival
808-882-7218
Puukohola Heiau NHS
Kawaihae, Big Island
**Hawaiian International
Billfish Tournament**
808-836-3422
Kailua-Kona, Big Island
www.hibtfishing.com
Kaanapali Fresh Food Festival
Kaanapali Resort, Maui
kaanapalifresh.com

September
Parker Ranch Rodeo
808-885-7311, Parker Ranch,
Waimea, Big Island
www.parkerranch.com
Aloha Festivals
800-483-0730
All islands
www.alohafestivals.com
**Na Wahine O Ke Kai Molokai
to Oahu Canoe Race**
808-259-7112
Hale O Lono Harbor, Molokai
www.nawahineokekai.com
Kauai Mokihana Festival
808-651-1868
Various sites: Kauai
www.maliefoundation.org

October
Ironman World Championship
Kailua-Kona, Big Island
808-329-0063
www.ironman.com
Molokai Hoe Canoe Race
808-676-4272
Hale O Lono, Molokai
www.OHCRA.com

**Hawaii International
Film Festival**
808-792-1577
Regal Dole Cannery theater,
Honolulu, Oahu
www.hiff.org

November
**VANS Triple Crown Surfing
Championships** (Nov–Dec)
North shore of Oahu
www.triplecrownofsurfing.com
**World Invitational Hula
Festival**
808-753-2476
Honolulu, Oahu
www.worldhula.com

December
**Anniversary Commemoration
Pearl Harbor**
USS *Arizona* Memorial
808-422-3300
Honolulu, Oahu
www.arizonamemorial.org
Honolulu Marathon
808-734-7200
Honolulu, Oahu
www.honolulumarathon.org
Waimea Christmas Parade
808-241-6500
Waimea, Kauai
www.wkbpa.org
**Holiday Lighting of the
Banyan Tree**
808-667-9194
Lahaina, Maui
www.visitlahaina.com

September: Aloha Festivals float

© Hawaii Tourism Authority (HTA) /
Tor Johnson

PRACTICAL INFORMATION

WHEN TO GO

There is no bad time to travel to the Hawaiian Islands. The busiest time is mid-December through March, when mainlanders rush to the islands to cure their winter blues. Generally, you'll find the best lodging discounts from late September to mid-December. Weather is consistently warm throughout the year, with night-time temperatures about 10 degrees lower than during the day. The average water temperature is 74°F (23.3°C), with a summer high of 80°F (26.7°C).

Environments on each island are diverse: misty tropical rain forests, cool mountaintops, arid deserts, and sunny beaches—all within a few miles of each other. The major difference between **winter** (Nov–Apr) and summer (May–Oct) is the surf. The biggest waves form on the north and east shores in winter, the most popular time for surfers to head to Hawaiian beaches. Bigger swells reach southern shores in summer. The wettest months are November through March; most of the rain falls in the mountains and valleys on the windward (northeastern) side of the islands.

What to Pack
Casual is the rule here, but if you plan to dine in high-end restaurants, pack dressy resort wear. Bring a rain jacket and a sweater; it's cooler in the high country, and sudden showers are common. No need to bring big sports gear, like surfboards; rentals are available.

KNOW BEFORE YOU GO

Before you go, contact the following organizations to obtain maps and information about sightseeing, accommodations, travel packages, recreational opportunities, and seasonal events.

Tourism Offices
Hawaii Visitors and Convention Bureau
2270 Kalakaua Ave., Suite 801, Honolulu (Oahu)
800-464-2924
www.gohawaii.com
Big Island Visitors Bureau/Hilo
68-1330 Mauna Lani Dr., Kohala Coast. 800-648-2441
www.gohawaii.com/big-island
Kauai Visitors and Convention Bureau
4334 Rice St, Suite 101, Lihue
800-262-1400
www.kauaidiscovery.com
Maui Visitors Bureau (Maui, Molokai, Lanai)
1727 Wili Pa Loop, Wailuku
800-525-6284
www.gohawaii.com/maui
Oahu Visitors Bureau
2270 Kalakaua Ave., Suite 801, Honolulu
877-525-6248
www.visit-oahu.com

International Visitors

Visitors from outside the US can obtain information from the Hawaii Visitors and Convention Bureau on Oahu (*800-464-2924; www.gohawaii.com*) or from the US embassy or consulate in their country of residence. For a complete list of American

MUST KNOW

Average Seasonal Temperatures in Hawaii				
	Jan	**Apr**	**July**	**Oct**
Avg. high	79°F/26°C	82°F/28.9°C	88°F/31°C	87°F/30.6°C
Avg. low	64°F/17.8°C	66°F/18.9°C	70°F/21°C	69°F/20.6°C

consulates and embassies abroad, visit the US State Department Bureau of Consular Affairs listing on the Internet at *http://travel. state.gov/links.html*.

Entry Requirements

Travelers entering the US under the Visa Waiver Program (VWP) must have a machine-readable passport.

Any traveler without a machine-readable **passport** will be required to obtain a visa before entering the US.

Citizens of VWP countries are permitted to enter the US for general business or tourist purposes for a maximum of 90 days without needing a visa. Visitors from VWP countries must obtain clearance from the US Customs before arriving in the US by obtaining an ESTA authorization; see www.cbp.gov/ esta. Requirements for the Visa Waiver Program can be found at the Department of State's Visa Services website: http://travel. state.gov/vwp.html.

All citizens of non-participating countries must have a visitor's visa. Upon entry, non-resident foreign visitors must present a valid passport and round-trip transportation ticket. Naturalized Canadian citizens should carry their citizenship papers.

US Customs

All articles brought into the US must be declared at the time of entry. Prohibited items include plant material; firearms and ammunition (if not for sporting purposes); meat or poultry products. For more information, contact the US Customs Service (*1300 Pennsylvania Ave. NW, Washington, DC 20229; 202-354-1000; www.cbp.gov*) or the Hawaii Department of Agriculture (*808-973-9560; www.hawaii.gov/hdoa*). Because rabies doesn't exist in Hawaii, all animals entering Hawaii must be held for four months at the quarantine facility on Oahu. Hawaiian officials won't let you enter with live plants, animals, fresh fruits, or vegetables of any kind. Due to restrictions on taking fruits, plants and animals out of Hawaii, all baggage bound from Hawaii to the US mainland is subject to pre-flight inspection by the Hawaii Department of Agriculture. You can bring only pre-packed and pre-inspected fruits to the US mainland.

GETTING THERE
By Air

Hawaiian Airlines *(www.hawaiian airlines.com)* and Alaska Airlines *(www.alaskaair.com)* offer the most flights to Hawaii, largely from West Coast airports. United, Delta, American and Air Canada also offer flights. Japan Airlines flies to the islands from Asia.

Important Phone Numbers

Emergency (Police/Ambulance/Fire Department, 24hrs)	☏ **911**
Police (non-emergency, Mon–Fri 9am–6pm)	
Honolulu Police	☏ 808-529-3111
Kauai Police	☏ 808-241-1711
Big Island	☏ 808-326-4646 ☏ (Hilo) 808-935-3311
Maui and Lanai	☏ 808-244-6400
Poison Control	☏ 800-222-1222
Medical Referral:	
Queen's Medical Center Referral Program, Oahu	☏ 808-538-9011
Hilo Medical Center, Big Island	☏ 808-932-3000
Maui Memorial Hospital, Maui	☏ 808-244-9056
Lihue Wilcox Memorial, Kauai	☏ 808-245-1100
Lanai Community Hospital, Lanai	☏ 808-565-8450
Dental Emergencies: Dental Hotline	☏ (Oahu) 808-944-8863
24-hour Pharmacies: Long's Drugs in downtown Honolulu	
1330 Pali Hwy.	☏ 808-536-7302
2220 S. King St.	☏ 808-949-4781
Coast Guard Search and Rescue	☏ 800-552-6458
To report an injured turtle, dolphin, or whale	☏ 800-853-1964

Oahu – Honolulu International Airport (HNL) (*808-836-6413; www.honoluluairport.com*), on Oahu, located about 3 miles west of downtown Honolulu, is the airport where the majority of visitors to the Hawaiian Islands land. (Airports on the other three main islands are also seeing more direct traffic from the mainland these days.) From the Honolulu airport, you can hop on flights to the other major islands *(see p15)*. Airport Waikiki Shuttle (*808-544-0004; www.shuttlewaikiki.com*) provides 24-hour transportation from the airport to any hotel in

Waikiki for $20 round-trip. TheBus *(see p16)* runs from the airport to major stops in Waikiki Beach and downtown Honolulu. Taxis and rental cars *(see p16)* are available at Honolulu International and at all the airports listed below. **Big Island – Kona International Airport** (KOA) at Keahole is located about 7 miles north of Kailua-Kona (*808-327-9520; www.hawaii.gov/koa*), and is reached by numerous direct flights from the mainland. **Hilo International Airport** (ITO) is located 2 miles east of Hilo on the Big Island's eastern shore (*808-961-9321; www.hawaii.gov/*

ito), and serves inter-island traffic only. SpeediShuttle (*877-242-5777; www.speedishuttle.com*) offers service to Big Island resorts. (Also serves Maui, Kauai, and Oahu.) There is no public bus service from Kona airport, and hotel shuttles are limited. Several cab companies operate on the Big Island, but fares are not cheap *(see p16)*.

Maui – Kahului Airport (OGG) is located on the northern edge of the valley between Haleakala and the West Maui Mountain Range on Maui (*808-872-3830, www.hawaii. gov/dot/ogg*), just east of Kahului proper, and like Kona, is reached by numerous direct flights from mainland airports. SpeediShuttle *(above)* offers shuttle services from the airport to resorts. Commuter airlines also serve Kapalua airport (JHM) in West Maui, about 15 minutes north of Lahaina.

Kauai – Lihue Airport (LIH) is located about 1.5 miles east of Lihue, on the southeast coast of Kauai (*808-274-3800; www. hawaii.gov/lih*). A few airlines fly direct from the mainland to Lihue. SpeediShuttle *(above)* offers services from the airport. Bus service on Kauai is limited, so many visitors use rental cars to get around.

Lanai – Tiny Lanai Airport (LNY) is located about 3 miles southwest of Lanai City (*808-565-7942; www.hawaii.gov/lny*). Its single runway serves primarily scheduled interisland and commuter traffic. The two major resorts on the island provide shuttle service from the airport.

Molokai – Molokai Airport (MKK) is located about 4 miles west of Kualapuu on Maunaloa Highway (*808-567-9660; www.hawaii.gov/ mkk*). The airport has two runways that accommodate commuter/air taxi and general interisland flights.

By Cruise Boat

Norwegian Cruise Line (*800-327-7030; www.ncl.com*) offers cruises that begin and end in Honolulu; longer itineraries from Los Angeles, or including the French Polynesian islands, are available from other cruise lines. Major cruise companies include **Princess** (*800-PRINCESS; www.princess.com*); Carnival (*800-CARNIVAL; www.carnival.com*); **Holland America** (*800-724-5425; www. hollandamerica.com*); and **Royal Caribbean** (*866-562-7625; www. rccl.com*). Small-ship cruises are offered by **Un-Cruise** (*www.un-cruise.com*) on 36-passenger yachts.

GETTING AROUND
Island Hopping

Hawaiian Airlines (*800-367-5320; www.hawaiianairlines.com*) offers convenient and frequent interisland flights. **Island Air** (*800-652-6541; www.islandair.com*) also offers interisland flights from Oahu and Maui to the other islands, except Kahoolawe and Niihau.

By Car

Having a car on the islands offers convenience, but traffic in Honolulu can be heavy. The following rental-car companies are located on Oahu, Maui, the Big Island and Kauai. **Budget** (*800-526-6408; www.budget.com*), **Dollar** (*800-367-5171; www.dollar. com), Hertz (800-654-3011; www. hertz.com*), **National** (*800-227-7368; www.nationalcar.com*), and **Thrifty** (*800-847-4389; www.*

thrifty.com). Dollar is the only national affiliate that operates on Lanai. **Alamo** (*800-651-1223; www.alamo.com*) and National are located on Molokai.

Honolulu is a big city with busy streets and traffic jams. On some of the other islands, you'll find plenty of narrow, twisty dirt roads, one-lane bridges, and blind curves. On Lanai and Molokai, you may want to rent a four-wheel-drive vehicle to traverse the muddy dirt roads that cover much of the island.

Driving in the US – Visitors bearing a valid **driver's license** issued by their country of residence are not required to obtain an International Driver's License. Drivers must carry vehicle registration and/or rental contract, and proof of automobile insurance at all times. Gasoline is sold by the gallon (1 gal=3.78 liters). Vehicles in the US are driven on the right-hand side of the road. **Note:** The use of hand-held electronic devices while driving is against the law in Hawaii. Use of seat belts is mandatory for driver and passengers.

By Public Transportation

On Oahu, **TheBus** (*808-848-5555; www.thebus.org*) operates routes that cover the entire island and the airport; its fleet includes a number of hybrid vehicles. Look for well-marked bus stops and bus terminals near all major attractions and hotels in downtown Honolulu and Waikiki Beach, and in cities, neighborhoods and towns across the island. Fares are $2.50 for adults (one-way), $1.25 for children (ages 6–17). Fare for the Big Island's **Hele-On Bus** (*808-961-8744; www.heleonbus.org)* is $2.

By Taxi

You'll find taxis lined up at the major airports; some are readily available at large hotels and resorts. Generally you must call a cab when you need one. Rates on the islands are about $4 for the first 1/8-mile (1mile = 1.6km), 40¢ for each additional 1/8-mile, and 40¢ for each 45 seconds of waiting time. Here's a list of Hawaii's major cab companies. **Note:** There is no taxi service on Lanai.

Oahu – TheCab (*808-422-2222; www.thecabhawaii.com*) and Charley's Taxi (*808-233-3333; www.charleystaxi.com*).

Maui – Maui Pleasant Taxi (*808-344-4661; www.maui pleasanttaxi.com*) and Royal Taxi (*808-874-6900; www.royal taximaui.com*).

Big Island – Laura's Taxi (*808-326-5466*) and C&C Taxi (*808-329-6388*).

Kauai – Akiko's Taxi (*877-970-5305; www.akikostaxikauai.com*) and North Shore Cab (*808-639-7829; www.northshorecab.com*).

Molokai – Molokai Off-Road Tours and Taxi (*808-553-3369; www.molokai.com/offroad*).

ACCESSIBILITY
Disabled Travelers

Federal law requires that businesses provide access for the disabled, devices for the hearing impaired, and designated parking spaces. For further information, contact the **Society for Accessible Travel and Hospitality** (SATH) (*212-447-7284; www.sath.org*). All national parks have facilities for the disabled, and offer free or discounted passes; contact the National Park Service (*202-208-3818; www.nps.gov*).

Book hand-controlled rental cars in advance with the rental company.

Local Agencies – Contact the following agencies for detailed information about access for the disabled in Hawaii:

Disability and Communication Access Board publishes Hawaii Travelers Tips, including accessibility information at the five major airports (*available free; 808-586-8121; www.hawaii.gov/health/dcab*).

Access Aloha Travel specializes in providing travel services for disabled travelers in Hawaii (*808-545-1143 or 800-480-1143; www.accessalohatravel.com*).

Local Transportation – On Oahu, **The Cab** (*808-422-2222; www.thecabhawaii.com*) and **TheBus** (*808-848-4500; www.thebus.org*) provide public transportation services for the disabled.

The **Hawaii County Mass Transit Agency** (*808-961-8744*) provides wheelchair-accessible buses on the Big Island.

Maui Bus (*808-871-483*8) offers wheelchair-accessible buses.

The Kauai Bus, run by the **County of Kauai Transportation Agency** (*808-241-6410*), offers accessible public transportation on Kauai.

Equipment Rentals – For beach wheelchairs and other equipment rentals on Oahu, contact **Hawaiian Islands Medical** (*808-597-8087; www.himed.cc*).

Contact **Gammie** (*808-877-4032 or 808-632-2333; www.gammie.com*) for equipment rentals on **Maui and Kauai.**

Scootaround (*888-441-7575; www.scootaround.com*) offers wheelchair and scooter rentals on the Big Island.

Senior Citizens

Many hotels, attractions and restaurants offer discounts to visitors aged 62 or older (proof of age may be required).

The AARP offers discounts to its members (*601 E St. NW, Washington, DC 20049; 888-687-2277; www.aarp.org*).

ACCOMMODATIONS

For suggested lodgings on all the major islands, see Hotels at the back of this guide.

Hotel Reservation Services: RSVP Hawaii – *800-663-1118; www.rsvphawaii.com*.

Maui Dream Vacations – *808-871-8085; www.mauidreamhawaii.com.*

Condos and Villas – Available by the night, week or longer, condominiums and villas are found on every major island except Lanai and Molokai. They provide more space than hotel rooms, have comparable or better rates, and are usually within developments that offer pools, barbecues and other amenities. Having a kitchen allows visitors to enjoy fresh fruits, vegetables and seafood. Units with two or more bedrooms are perfect for families and friends to share vacation time, and costs. The premier vacation rental company in the islands is **Aston** (*www.astonhotels.com*), with dozens of properties on Oahu, Kauai, Maui and the Big Island; shoulder season rates can be very advantageous. Numerous smaller booking agencies handle rentals for individual condo owners; consult the visitor information sites for each island. And real estate agencies on the four main islands also represent vacation homes for rent—often spectacular homes in memorable settings, for those with more expansive budgets.

Hostels – A no-frills, inexpensive alternative to hotels, hostels are a great choice for budget travelers and students. Amenities vary from private rooms to dorm-style lodgings, on-site restaurant and kitchen, TV and Internet access. For listings of hostels throughout Hawaii, visit *www.hostelz.com* or *www.hostels.com*.

BASIC INFORMATION
Business Hours

Stores are generally open between 10am and 5pm, but many open earlier; some remain open until 9pm or later. Bank hours are 9am–5pm (or 6pm); some open Sat 9am–noon.

Discounts

Go Oahu – *www.smart destinations.com/oahu*
Other enterprises on each island offer booklets with discounts for entry to major attractions, a variety of tours, and also for many activities; look for the booklets when you arrive at the airport.

Electricity

Voltage in the US is 120 volts AC/60 Hertz. Foreign-made appliances may need AC adapters (available at specialty travel and electronics stores) and North American flat-blade plugs.

Internet

Free wireless Internet access is available across Hawaii; see www.wififreespot.com/ha.html to find the nearest Wi-Fi spot to you. Most cafes and restaurants provide free Wi-Fi to customers.

Hawaiian Words

Shaka (pinkie and thumb of the right hand is up, while the other fingers curl under, shaken side to side) is a greeting that can mean "way-to-go," "nice-to-see-you," or "be cool."

Aloha (ah-LOH-ha): Used for nearly everything good—hello, goodbye, love
Hale (ha-leh): House or building
Haole (how-leh): Foreigner
Kane (KAH-nay): Man
Keiki (kay-kee): Children
Mahalo (muh-HA-low): Thank you
Ohana (oh-HA-nah): Family
Ono (oh-noh): Delicious
Pupu (poo-poo): Appetizer
Wahine (wah-HE-nay): Woman

Money and Currency Exchange

The unit of currency in the Hawaiian Islands is the US **dollar** ($) comprising 100 cents. Coin denominations are 5¢, 10¢, 25¢, 50¢. Banknote denominations are $1, $2, $5, $10, $20, $50, $100 and higher. Currency can be exchanged at most banks. Currency-exchange services are also available at Honolulu International Airport, but not at the other island airports. Some major stores in Waikiki will accept Japanese Yen.

For cash transfers, **Western Union** (*800-325-6000; www. westernunion.com*) has agents throughout the Hawaiian Islands. Banks and some hotels accept travelers' checks with photo identification. To report a lost or stolen credit card: American Express® (*800-528-4800*); Diners Club® (*800-234-6377*); MasterCard® (*800-627-8372*); Visa® (*800-847-2911*).

Newspapers

Oahu's main daily newspaper is the *Honolulu Star-Advertiser*, with a calendar of weekend events in Friday's editions. The alternative *Honolulu Weekly* covers local happenings. Other daily newspapers include the *Hawaii Tribune-Herald* and *West Hawaii Today* on the Big Island; *Maui News* on Maui; and *The Garden Island* on Kauai. The *Molokai Dispatch* is a weekly newspaper. All of these newspapers offer online editions. You can pick up a copy of *101 Things To Do*, which is published for Oahu, Maui, Kauai and the Big Island, at most resorts and large shopping centers. *This Week* magazine has travel tips and discount coupons and is available free throughout the islands.

Smoking

Smoking is prohibited in enclosed or partially enclosed facilities, including airports, restaurants, clubs, within 20 feet of doorways, windows, and ventilation intakes, and in seating areas of sports arenas, stadiums, and amphitheaters. Hotels may designate smoking rooms, though they are rare; specify one when making your reservation. Smoking is also banned on many beaches, including Waikiki Beach.

Taxes and Tipping

Prices displayed in Hawaii do not include the state sales tax of 4% which is not reimbursable (1% sales-tax discount is given to citizens age 85 and older), or the hotel tax of 9.25%. County and municipal sales taxes may be added on top of the state's rate. It is customary to give a small gift

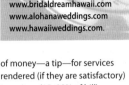

Getting Married in Hawaii
Marriage license applications can be downloaded from www.hawaii.gov/doh. For more information:
www.gohawaii.com/weddings
www.bridaldreamhawaii.com
www.alohanaweddings.com
www.hawaiiweddings.com.

of money—a tip—for services rendered (if they are satisfactory) to waiters (15–20% of bill), porters ($1-$2 per bag), hotel housekeeping staff ($1-$2 per day) and cab drivers (15% of fare).

Telephones

To call between the islands, dial 1 + 808 + seven-digit number. To dial from Hawaii to different area codes on the mainland, dial 1 + area code + seven-digit number. It's not necessary to use the area code to make a local call. Area code for all the Hawaiian Islands is 808.

Time Zone

Lying east of the International Date Line, Hawaii has its own time zone: Hawaiian Standard Time (HST). HST is 2 hours behind Pacific Standard Time (California) on the mainland, 5 hours behind Eastern Standard Time (New York), and 10 hours behind Greenwich Mean Time. Hawaii does not observe Daylight Saving Time. From the second Sunday in March to the first Sunday in November, add another hour to the time difference. Hawaii also falls an extra hour behind GMT during British Summer Time.

PEARLS OF THE PACIFIC

Rising from the floor of the Pacific Ocean, some 3,000 miles west of Mexico, the Hawaiian Islands form an archipelago of eight major islands and countless smaller ones that are actually the tops of a huge mountain range. Created over millions of years by magma flowing from a volcanic "hot spot" in the earth's crust, the islands were settled by Polynesians, explored by Europeans, and eventually annexed by the US. Today they draw millions of tourists to their glorious shores.

Revealed in ancient chants, dances and stories passed down through the centuries, Hawaii's history is rich with tales of the master sailors, kings, queens and powerful gods of this isolated edenic locale.
The **Polynesians** who first came here from the Marquesas and Tahiti around AD 400 were keenly attuned to the rhythms of the sea and sky, navigating more than 2,000 miles in large canoes. They brought pigs, taro, bananas, sweet potatoes and breadfruit. They called their new world *aina* (the land), as opposed to *kai* (the sea). Although British captain **James Cook**, the first European to visit the islands, was killed by Hawaiians in 1779 *(see p46)*, missionaries, whalers and colonists arrived in the 19C to "civilize" the inhabitants and turn the islands' natural riches into a thriving economy.

The island of Hawaii was the home of **King Kamehameha I** (c.1758–1819), who united the islands as he conquered other rival chiefs. Yet the monarchy lasted less than a century before armed insurrection by sugar planters, traders and Protestant missionaries overthrew the last native monarch, **Queen Liliuokalani**. Briefly a republic (1893-98), Hawaii was annexed as a US territory in 1898 during the Spanish–American War. Generations of influx by Chinese, Japanese, Portuguese, Filipinos and others blended into a unique ethnic mix that author James Michener labeled "Golden Man."
In 1941 the Japanese bombing of **Pearl Harbor** propelled the US directly into World War II. When the war ended, tourism on Waikiki Beach exploded; later other islands, notably Maui and the Big Island, joined in the boom. With tourism, sugar and pineapple dominating its economy, Hawaii became the 50th US state, in 1959.
Today each major island has its own character. Home of Honolulu, the only large city in the state, **Oahu** has a cosmopolitan feel. **Kauai**, the "Garden Isle," is the place many people envision when they think of Hawaii, thanks to movies such as *Blue Hawaii* and *South*

Getting Bigger All the Time

More than 80 volcanoes have bubbled from this mid-Pacific hotspot over the last 44 million years. Since it began its present round of eruptions in 1983, Kilauea has added 500 new acres to the Big Island. Today, 20 miles off the coast of Hawaii, a new island is being born. Called Loihi, this nascent islet is erupting in a red-hot flow beneath the sea; it's projected to reach the ocean's surface in 30,000 years.

Waikiki Beach with Diamond Head in background

© Hawaii Tourism Authority (HTA) / Tor Johnson

Pacific. **Maui** is unique, a place where Native Hawaiian culture is enjoying a strong resurgence amid extensive resort development. With its surf and volcanoes, the rugged landscape of the **Big Island** exerts a palpable presence, especially its southeast corner, where Kilauea's ongoing eruption embodies the fire goddess, Pele. **Lanai**, once home of the world's largest pineapple plantation, draws luxury lovers to its posh hotels and manicured golf courses. Laid-back, undeveloped **Molokai** considers itself pure "Old Hawaii," not gussied up for tourists, a place where its extensive beaches are almost empty. No matter which island you choose, you'll feel far from the mainland US.

Spread like a lei across the blue Pacific, the Hawaiian Islands are farther from any other landmass than any inhabited place on earth. Their closest neighbors (though each is more than 2,000 miles away) are California and Tahiti. Despite its geographic isolation, Hawaii has cast its spell worldwide: who does not know about its volcanoes, beaches, surfing, hula and the lilt of a steel guitar? Indeed, its singular beauty and magical culture resound around the globe.

Fast Facts

- Seven of Hawaii's eight principal islands—with a total land area of 6,422 square miles—are inhabited.
- With 4,028 square miles, the largest and geologically youngest is the Island of Hawaii, popularly known as "The Big Island."
- Kahoolawe is an uninhabited former bombing range; Niihau is a private island occupied by a couple hundred Native Hawaiians.
- Oahu, home of Pearl Harbor and the state capital of Honolulu, is by far the most heavily populated island, home to more than 975,000 of the state's nearly 1.4 million people.
- The Hawaiian word "aloha" can mean hello, goodbye, love or welcome.

PEARLS OF THE PACIFIC

HAWAII, THE BIG ISLAND★★

Far more than a typical palmy paradise, the Big Island—officially named Hawaii Island—is a land of contrasts—from the raw, primal beauty of **Hawaii Volcanoes National Park** in the south to the glitzy resorts and manicured golf courses of the **Kohala Coast**. Nature is on grand display here, encompassing at least 10 climate zones; the landscape ranges from subarctic mountain summits to eerie, lava-black deserts. To spend all your time here lazing on the beach would be missing the point—not that the beaches aren't wonderful. You could visit a different Big Island beach every day for a month and still not see them all. Even beach sand offers variety on this island; you can hop from black sand to gold to white, and even green. *Visitor information: 800-648-2441; www.gohawaii.com/big-island.*

Two volcanic mountains dominate the landscape. In the north, **Mauna Kea★★** (13,796 feet), long dormant, is home to several astronomical observatories. In the south, **Mauna Loa★** (13,677 feet) is considered active but is usually sleeping. More impressively, it is earth's biggest mountain, measured from seafloor base to summit—an astounding 56,000 feet. Meanwhile, the world's most active volcano, **Kilauea★★★**, has been a dramatic scene in recent years, with eruptions occurring with some regularity at Halemaumau crater on Kilauea's summit beginning in 2008.

Fast Facts

- **Island Capital**: Hilo
- **Landmass**: 4,028sq mi (nearly twice as large as all the other Hawaiian Islands combined). It's still growing: 500 acres have been added since 2008.
- **Population**: 190,000 residents
- **Livestock**: Hawaii Island has most of the Aloha State's cattle, more than 100,000 head, in fact.
- **Coastline**: 266 miles of coastline, (not to mention the world's most active volcano, **Kilauea**).
- **Annual Visitors**: 1.5 million.

Volcanic beach on the Big Island

© Brigitta L. House/Michelin

Hilo★★

Hilo, Hawaii, holds the record as America's wettest city, with more than 150 inches of rain each year. Nobody seems to mind, since there's so much to do here, and there are frequent periods of sunshine between showers. Tsunamis (aka tidal waves) are another story—this town has been ravaged twice (in 1946 and 1960) by towering walls of water. Many of the once-abandoned downtown buildings remain today, brightly painted Victorians dripping with funky charm; some are listed on the National Register of Historic Places.

The Hilo area is home to Lili'uokalani Gardens, **Hawaii Tropical Botanical Garden** (*see p 40*), Nani Mau Gardens and more. The classic Hilo sight, though, is **Rainbow Falls** (*see p 34*). Catch this 80-foot cascade in early morning or late afternoon, when the sun glints through the mango trees and creates prisms of color.

On the north coast, the spectacular one-mile-wide **Waipio Valley** (*accessible only by foot or four-wheel-drive vehicle*) wedges itself between 2,000-foot cliffs that funnel ribbon-like waterfalls onto a sandy ocean beach far below. Divers and snorkelers are drawn to the underwater world on the leeward side of Hawaii, where a watery landscape of caves, cliffs, and tunnels reveals colorful tropical fish and other marine life. Kayakers explore the island's 266-mile coastline, where pristine coves and inlets await. You can hike (or ride horseback) in a crater with an active volcano nearby, hunt for petroglyphs, hook a blue marlin, or catch sight of a rare bird or a migrating whale. And it's the only place on earth where you can drive up to a volcano *(see Kilauea, p30)*. The Big Island has its historic side, too. The great monarch, **Kamehameha I** (1758–1819), was born on the Kohala Coast, and these shores were his base for conquest and unification. Temples and ruins are tucked into the hillsides, often where you'd least expect them.

Volcano Viewing

Hawaii Volcanoes National Park recorded message: 808-985-6000. **Kilauea** eruption update: hvo.wr.usgs.gov; 808-961-8093. The Hawaiian fire goddess, **Pele**, knows how to put on a show. In March 2008, Kilauea's summit experienced its first explosive eruption since 1924. Active lava flows have recently been visible but only in extremely remote areas difficult to reach on foot.

© Brigitta L. House/Michelin

Waipio Valley

HAWAII, THE BIG ISLAND

23

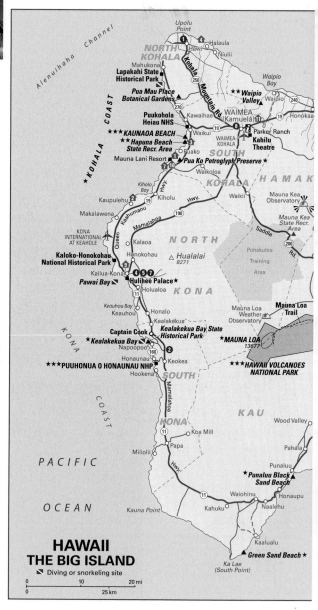

HAWAII
THE BIG ISLAND

◥ Diving or snorkeling site

| 0 | 10 | 20 mi |
| 0 | 25 km | |

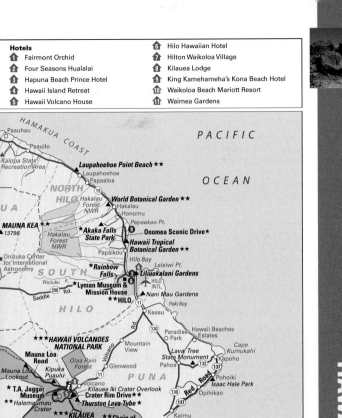

HAMAKUA COAST

PACIFIC

OCEAN

Paauhau
Paauilo
Kalopa State Recreation Area

Laupahoehoe Point Beach ★★
Laupahoehoe
Papaaloa

NORTH
HILO
Hakalau Forest NWR
Hakalau
Honomu

MAUNA KEA ★★
▲13796

Hakalau Forest NWR

World Botanical Garden ★★
Pepeekeo Pt.

★Akaka Falls State Park
Papaikou
Onomea Scenic Drive★
Hawaii Tropical Botanical Garden ★★

Onizuka Center for International Astronomy

SOUTH

Hilo Bay
Leleiwi Pt.

★Rainbow Falls

★Liliuokalani Gardens

Wailuku R.
★Lyman Museum & Mission House
★★HILO

Saddle (200) Rd.

HILO INTL.

HILO

Nani Mau Gardens

Poki Bay

Keaau

★★★HAWAII VOLCANOES NATIONAL PARK

Mauna Loa Road

Olaa Rain Forest

Mountain View

Paradise O Park

Lava Tree State Monument
Pahoa

Hawaii Beaches Estates

Cape Kumukahi
Kapoho

Mauna Loa Lookout

Kipuka Puaulu

Glenwood

PUNA

★T.A. Jaggar Museum
★★Halemaumau Crater

Volcano
Kilauea Iki Crater Overlook
Crater Rim Drive★★
Thurston Lava Tube ★

Pohoiki
Isaac Hale Park
Opihikao

★★★KILAUEA VOLCANO
★Chain of Craters Road

Kaimu

Kau Desert

Hilina Pali Overlook

Hilina Pali Road

★★★HAWAII VOLCANOES NATIONAL PARK

PACIFIC   OCEAN

HAWAII, THE BIG ISLAND

BEACHES

The Big Island is ringed with sandy stretches of gold, green, black and classic white. As on all the islands, they're open to the public, even at the most exclusive resorts. Stretch out your towel and say "ahhh!"

Kaunaoa Beach★★★

Hwy. 19, behind the Mauna Kea Beach Hotel, Kohala Coast.
Kaunaoa Beach is also known as **Mauna Kea Beach**. Despite the fact that beach authority Stephen P. Leatherman *(see box, right)* once crowned it "America's Best Beach," Kaunaoa is still less crowded than nearby Hapuna Beach. All of Hawaii's beaches are public, so no worries about pulling out a beach blanket here. This quarter-mile crescent of white sand contrasts nicely with its lava headlands. Beyond the beach rises a grassy slope and the manicured grounds of the **Hapuna Beach Prince Hotel** *(see Hotels)*. Thanks to the hotel, the beach is clean and well maintained. Rough water often makes it a better beach for boogieboarding and bodysurfing than swimming. Stick around to view the sunset; this sultry spot is a wonderful destination for watching the sun melt into the water.

Dr. Beach

Director of the Laboratory for Coastal Research at Florida International University, Stephen P. Leatherman, aka "Dr. Beach," is America's most-quoted authority on beaches. In 1991 the PhD. in Coastal Sciences premiered his list of America's Best Beaches, which has become an annual event ever since. Leatherman's accolades have become to tourism officials what the Oscars are to the movie industry (though his purpose is to promote shoreline conservation).

Hapuna Beach State Recreation Area★★

Hwy. 19, 12mi north of Waikoloa, Kohala Coast. 808-961-9540. www.hawaiistateparks.org. Open year-round daily dawn–dusk.
Hapuna, like most of the Big Island's white-sand beaches, is found on the Kohala Coast. (Look for black- and green-sand beaches on the south coast.) The best beach on the west coast (the dry side)

Hapuna Beach

© Hawaii's Big Island Visitor Bureau (BIVB)

MUST SEE

of the island, Hapuna's half-mile stretch of sparkling sand leads to cerulean water and the occasional lava-rock outcropping. Facilities include a picnic pavilion, a snack bar, and a less than stellar set of restrooms. Bring your own beach toys; there are no vendors here.

Laupahoehoe Point Beach★★

Hwy. 19, Laupahoehoe, 25mi north of Hilo. Follow signs from Hwy. 19. Open year-round daily dawn–dusk.

As long as you don't expect a wide, sandy beach, you'll love this spot. A grassy area opens up to a wonderfully craggy stretch of lava-rock coastline, with pounding surf and dazzling ocean views.

You can get some memorable photos on this beach plus a pleasant dose of serenity, since it's off the tourist track.

Camping is allowed here and the big picnic pavilion makes this spot a popular place with locals on Sunday afternoons. Purchase camping permits (*$6*) directly from the Department of Parks and Recreation (*101 Pauahi St., Suite 6, Hilo*) or online (*www.hawaii-county.gov*).

Touring Tip

The trailhead to Green Sand Beach is located at the base of Puuo Mahana cinder cone. Walk 2.5 miles to the top of the cliff, and then climb down the cliff to the beach. The unmarked trail begins at the rocky overhang here. Going over the edge of the cinder cone is the easiest way down; even then, it is a difficult and treacherous walk. Allow about 1hr to reach the beach.

Green Sand Beach★

3mi east of South Point (Ka Lae), Kau District. A 2.5mi drive by four-wheel-drive vehicle or an hour or so on foot.

You'll walk straight into the wind to get here, and once you do, the surf is fierce and dangerous, but how often do you get an opportunity to see a green-sand beach? The olive-green-colored "sand" is actually made up of a mineral called **olivine** that is created when basaltic lava cools. This semi-precious stone is also found in Iceland (the site of much geothermic activity) and on the moon.

© Hawaii's Big Island Visitor Bureau (BIVB)

Laupahoehoe Point

BEACHES

Punaluu Black Sand Beach

© Brigitta L. House/Michelin

Nearby **Ka Lae** is the southernmost tip of the United States, and is also believed to be the first landfall of the arriving Polynesians.

Take care, however, since the entire area is very fragile, so it's important to remain on the trails and to stay away from historical sites and artifacts. Endangered Hawaiian monk seals and hawksbill sea turtles also use the shoreline.

Green turtle on Punaluu Black Sand Beach

© Brigitta L. House/Michelin

Punaluu Black Sand Beach★

Hwy. 11, 5mi southwest of Pahala.
Lava from the Kilauea Volcano obliterated the world-famous Kalapana Black Sand beach in the 1990s, but there are other black-sand beaches to explore in Puna and Kau (KAH-oo), near Hawaii Volcanoes National Park. Fringed with coconut palms, Punaluu offers the choicest setting for a swim in impossibly blue water.

This picturesque stretch of shoreline is also a popular nesting spot for Hawaii's **green sea turtles**. To prevent the turtles' confusion, the Aloha State has a law that limits the lights along the shore. The islands are home to five species of sea turtles, including green, leatherback and loggerhead.

Color Me Sandy

Why do Hawaii's beaches come in so many colors? It's all about the raw material. White-sand beaches are composed of coral or quartz, pounded into a powder by powerful waves. Hawaii's black-sand beaches are, of course, made of lava rock—fairly coarse stuff that's hot to walk on and sticks like crazy to skin that's slathered with sunblock. The reddish-hued stuff at Red Sand Beach at Hana, on Maui, comes from the caldera of a cinder cone and is made up of finely ground red cinders. **Green Sand Beach** *(see p 27)* on the Big Island is a hidden gem with a gem-like color—an olive green, which contrasts nicely with azure sea and white surf.

PARKS AND NATURAL SITES

Hawaii's attractions include an active volcano (currently gushing steam and gas in a plume of white) and the most massive mountain on earth. With all that, who needs a theme park?

HAWAII VOLCANOES NATIONAL PARK★★★

Mamalahoa Hwy. (Hwy. 11), in Volcano, 28mi southwest of Hilo. 808-985-6000. www.nps.gov/havo. Open year-round daily. $10 per vehicle; pass good for 7 days.

A UNESCO World Heritage Site, this is the only national park—not to mention one of the few places in the world—where casual travelers can visit a live volcano. At this 520-square-mile park, the major attraction is the wildly active **Kilauea** volcano, and its simmering-but-sleepy neighbor, **Mauna Loa**. The park encompasses the summit calderas of both of these volcanoes, along with a rain forest, a desert, ancient petroglyphs, and the unique landscapes created by the force and drama of past eruptions. Unlike such deadly volcanoes as Mount St. Helens and Mount Pinatubo, Hawaii's shield volcanoes produce slow, quiet eruptions,

Touring Tip

Most people drive through the park and feel they've done it all—indeed, you can see a lot by driving the park's **Crater Rim Drive** *(see p 31)* and pulling off at key spots along the way. But the best way to really visit the park is to spend a couple of days hiking the weird lava landscapes or paths that snake through deserts, rain forests, and beaches (the park has 150 miles of trails). You can camp in the park *(for tent camping details, call 808-961-8311 or visit www.nps.gov/havo).*

not violent explosions. Rather than fleeing Kilauea's spectacular fireworks, people show up and bring a picnic! The show is really something at night, when red-hot sparks splatter against a backdrop of inky sky. Of course, lava flow has the potential to be dangerous; park

Offering to the volcano goddess Pele at Halemaumau Crater

© Hawaii Tourism Japan (HTJ)

PARKS AND NATURAL SITES

Eruption gases venting, Hawaii Volcanoes National Park

© PL3 - Fotolia.com

rangers continually change hiking-trail routes as the lava changes its course. For eruption updates, visit hvo.wr.usgs.gov.

Park Highlights

There's much to see in this vast park, but don't miss the following:

Kilauea Visitor Center★★

🅑 *on map p25. On Crater Rim Dr., .25mi from the park entrance, off Hwy. 11. Open year-round daily 8:45am–5pm. 808-985-6000.*
Here you'll learn the secrets of volcanoes and how to view the craters safely. Exhibits and a 25-minute film provide helpful background for your visit.
You can still dine or stay at the only hotel within the national park, **Volcano House** (*808-756-9625;*

www.hawaiivolcanohouse.com), adjacent to the visitor center. Built as a one-room shelter in 1846, it was rebuilt and enlarged in 1941 after a fire destroyed it. Remodeled in 2012, the rambling, wooden 33-room hotel sits on the rim of the Kilauea Caldera, at 4,000 feet elevation.

Kilauea Volcano★★★

Kilauea's Halemaumau crater, legendary home of **Pele**, the volcano goddess, has been active since 2008. Right now, while you can't see the lava lake bubbling below, you can see its plume of gas and ash from the **Jaggar Overlook** within Hawaii's Volcanoes National Park.
The floor of the Puu Oo crater vent collapsed in March 2011,

The Road Not Taken

The **Kau Desert** within Hawaii Volcanoes National Park is so similar to the moon's surface, NASA astronauts have trained for lunar landings here. To get a peek at this eerie moonscape yourself, check at the visitor center to see if access is open from Chain of Craters Road at the 2.2-mile marker. Few tourists take this route, so you'll enjoy grand vistas of cliff, sea and sky in solitude when the road ends at the Hilina Pali Overlook. Remember, this isn't Disneyland: whether you see a real show during the volcano's "downtime" is up to Mother Nature—or, rather, the goddess Pele (see p 32). For updates on volcanic activity, visit the Hawaiian Volcano Observatory website (www.hvo.wr.usgs.gov), or call the park's hotline (808-985-6000).

after a spectacular five-day fissure eruption in a remote part of the park. While parts of the park have been closed due to dangerously elevated levels of sulfur dioxide in the air (mostly downwind of the crater, where the eruption occurred), there are great viewing places in several areas.

Given that this is an active volcano, conditions change daily, so you never know what you might see. The best place to monitor current conditions at Kilauea is the USGS Kilauea status update at www.nps.gov/havo.

Crater Rim Drive★★

The 11-mile Crater Rim Drive circles the great pit of **Halemaumau Crater★★**, which began erupting on March 11, 2008, with three gas explosions within the crater wall. Although much of the drive is currently closed due to sulfur dioxide fumes, open portions offer a look at the dramatic effects of volcanic activity, both past and present.

Stop at the **Thomas A. Jaggar Museum★** *(see Museums)* to see geological exhibits and readings taken from inside the volcano.

Touring Tip

Look for plumed Kalij pheasants, natives of Nepal that were brought to the island in 1962. Once you reach Mauna Loa Lookout, you'll appreciate the enormity of the mountain and, chances are, you'll feel very small. At the end of the road, the hiking trail begins.

Crater Rim Drive is currently closed past the Jaggar Museum due to volcanic activity.

Mauna Loa★

Mauna Loa Road starts 2mi west of the entrance to Hawaii Volcanoes National Park, off Hwy. 11.
The road climbs 3,000ft to the Mauna Loa Lookout, 13.5mi from Hwy. 11. Mauna Loa Trail begins where Mauna Loa Rd. ends, 14mi north of Hwy. 11. Call 808-965-6000 for maps and details.

At a mere 13,677 feet, Mauna Loa comes up short compared with Mauna Kea, the highest peak in the Pacific. It is, however, the most massive mountain on earth, 100 times the size of Mount Rainier. Rising 56,000 feet from

Plants growing on the lava shield by Chain of Craters Road

© Hawaii Tourism Japan (HTJ)

PARKS AND NATURAL SITES

the floor of the Pacific Ocean, this perfectly shaped shield volcano is considered active, but last erupted in 1984. There are two ways to see it: by car or on foot.

Mauna Loa Road – The road climbs up 6,662 feet from Highway 11 and gives you a good sense of the mountain. You'll drive through a curtain of rain forest to reach the **Mauna Loa Lookout**, taking a turn-off to see the lava trees. The phantom forest was created when lava flows engulfed trees and fossilized them.

You'll also see **Kipuka Puaulu**, a forest grove that has escaped Mauna Loa's 37 eruptions unscathed. This is a quiet beauty of a spot, teeming with native plants, birds and insects, surrounded by fields of lava.

Mauna Loa Trail – This trail requires miles of perhaps what is the toughest hiking in Hawaii. It ascends from the Mauna Loa Lookout to a cabin at Red Hill, then continues 12 miles up to the Mauna Loa summit cabin at 13,250 feet. It's a 7,000-foot-high, steep route up, through a moonscape of lava flow. This is a serious trip, for those in excellent condition—only experienced hikers need apply. Expect to spend four days tackling

the mountain, along with some advance planning (pre-registration is required). The climate is subarctic up here, with whiteouts and overnight temperatures below freezing year-round; snow in July is even possible. Altitude sickness is another issue and most hikers spend the night at the cabin at Red Hill to acclimatize themselves. Talk to the rangers at the park visitor center for more details. Hikers can also access Mauna Loa by starting at the Mauna Loa Weather Observatory, via Saddle Road.

Mauna Kea★★

Map p25. 1hr drive northwest from Hilo or southeast from Waimea to the Onizuka Center for International Astronomy (808-961-2180; www.ifa.hawaii.edu; open daily 9am–10pm).
The drive to the summit takes 30-45 minutes. Take Saddle Rd. (Hwy. 200) from Hwy. 190, 19mi to Mauna Kea State Recreation Area. Go 9mi to the Summit Rd. turn-off at mile marker 28. A four-wheel-drive vehicle is recommended to get to Observatory Hill.

You'll feel as though you're at the top of the world here. Certainly, you're close—when measured from its base on the ocean floor, Mauna

---

Pele

The goddess of fire and volcanoes, Pele arrived in Hawaii by canoe, looking for a fiery dwelling place. As the legend goes, Pele moved south along the island chain, quickly fleeing the islands as her sister Namakaokahal, the goddess of the sea, attempted to destroy them. Ultimately, Pele found the perfect digs in the Halemaumau Crater of the Kilauea Volcano, where she resides to this day. Pele's love affairs and rivalries are the stuff of legend and literature here. Locals say Pele appears to this day as a lovely woman dressed in red, or as a wizened crone who hitchhikes along the roadway. If you pass her by, you'll be cursed with car trouble. If you pick her up, she will vanish when you turn around to gaze at her.

Kea reaches an amazing 32,000 feet (13,796 above sea level). Set out in the Pacific, with clear skies and no light pollution, Mauna Kea is among the best places on earth to stargaze *(see p 48)*. No wonder that 11 nations have set up infrared telescopes here to peer into space. Prepare for a serious drive, in low gear. The 6-mile road climbs from 9,000 feet to nearly 14,000 feet. Guard against altitude sickness— the elevation gain is extreme. Once you arrive, you'll see the twin **Keck Telescopes**—the world's largest—and 360-degree **views★★★** that defy description. You might also see **Lake Waiau**, an alpine tarn sacred to Hawaiians and subject to severe fluctuations in level during droughts. Avoid entering or even touching the lake waters.

Akaka Falls State Park★

North of Hilo. Hwy. 220, 3.6mi southwest of Honomu. 808-974-6200. Open year-round daily 24hrs.
An easy-going, quarter-mile loop trail will bring you to some of Hawaii's prettiest **waterfalls★**. Hike through a rain forest, along bamboo- and ginger-lined trails and past banks of wild orchids to arrive at the observation point of 442-foot Akaka Falls and its little sister, 100-foot **Kahuna Falls**.

Akaka Falls

©Rmarmion/Dreamstime.com

Touring Tip

On weekends, free summit tours depart from the Mauna Kea visitor center at 1pm. Participants must be 16 years of age or older, in good health, and have a four-wheel-drive vehicle. Stargazing is offered at the visitor center nightly *(6pm–10pm, free)* following an astronomy lecture. Dress warmly. Families are welcome (if all family members are aged 16 or older). The trip takes approximately 30 minutes each way.

PARKS AND NATURAL SITES

Pua Ko Petroglyph Preserve

© Hawaii's Big Island Visitor Bureau (BIVB)

temples in Hawaii and a sprinkling of prehistoric **petroglyphs**, and you'll get a sense of the reason this region exudes such a special power.

Admire more than 1,000 ancient rock paintings via a short hike just north of the Fairmont Orchid *(see Hotels)*; pick up a free map and brochure at the hotel.

Rainbow Falls★

Waianuenue Ave., Hilo (next to the hospital). Open year-round daily 24hr.

Nestled amid a riot of colorful blooms, this waterfall tumbles 80 feet into a round natural pool. It gets its name from the play of early-morning sunshine on the waterspray, which creates thousands of tiny rainbows.

Pua Ko Petroglyph Preserve★

On the northwest tip of the Big Island, Kohala Coast, off Hwy. 19, north of the Fairmont Orchid hotel.

Kamehameha the Great was born here on the Kohala Coast, which is as impressive as it gets in these parts. Add some of the oldest

Rainbow Falls

© Hawaii Tourism Authority (HTA) / Kirk Lee Aeder

Cool, Clear Water

Big Island visitors flying in and out of Kona International Airport often notice a strange collection of ponds and buildings south of the airport, near the shore. What's this, in the middle of a lava plain? Decades ago, during the first energy crisis in the 1970s, engineers conceived a plan to draw up cold ocean water from deep offshore—2,000 feet or so—and use the temperature difference to make electricity. That scheme never came to fruition, but it turned out the cold, rich water is good for something else: aquaculture. So here, at NELHA, the National Energy Laboratory of Hawaii, enterprising farmers grow vast amounts of cold-water shellfish, algae and other "crops." When you see "Kona lobster" on local menus, it's from here. *For more information, visit friendsofnelha.org.*

SCENIC DRIVES

You've got to love a place where the scenery includes ancient lava fields, tumbling waterfalls, dense tangles of jungle, and Mother Nature's fireworks—an active volcano.

Crater Rim Drive★★

Off Hwy. 11, in Hawaii Volcanoes National Park (28mi southwest of Hilo). $10/vehicle; pass good for 7 days. For individual sight descriptions, see Parks and Natural Sites.

Though much of this 11-mile road is closed due to dangerous fumes, its many sights remain unparalleled. How often do you get to peer into craters, walk on glossy black lava, and see the steaming vents of active volcanoes? It's still worth several hours to take in the amazing lunarlike landscape of lava-rock hillsides to peer into steam vents, stroll through the lush fern forest and perch on the rim and watch the main vent pour gas clouds into the sky.

❯ *See map p25. Start at the Kilauea Visitor Center (on Crater Rim Dr., .25mi from the park entrance off Hwy. 11) and continue southwest on Crater Rim Drive.*

Touring Tip

Plan on one to three hours to cover Crater Rim Drive, depending on where and how long you stop. Start early in the day (the **Kilauea Visitor Center★★** opens at 8:45am) if you plan to hike Devastation Trail, walk through the lava tube, and do the longer (but well worthwhile) 4-mile hike at **Kilauea Iki**. Add another 2-3 hours to drive **Chain of Craters Road★★** *(a 38mi round-trip; see p 37)*, longer if you plan to hike the end of Chain of Craters Road. Wear hiking boots or other closed-toe shoes near lava.

You can see the steam vents from the car, but the small **Thomas A. Jaggar Museum★** *(3mi west of Volcano House; see Museums)* is worth a stop to get a sense of the science of volcanology.
Next up: **Halemaumau Crater★★**, the site of the most recent

The road cutting through the lava plain

© Hawaii Tourism Japan (HTJ)

Overlooking Halemaumau crater

© Hawaii Tourism Authority (HTA) / Tor Johnson

eruption, and the most action over time. Typically, you can park and walk to the crater, but the viewing area is currently closed due to heavy content of sulfur dioxide in the air. Please check with the **Kilauea Visitor Center**, near the park entrance off Hwy. 11, for current conditions.

Along Crater Rim Road, you'll see blacker lava from a September 1982 eruption that looks like a torn-up road, with chunks of rock an inch thick. As you drive along, note the signs marking when lava flows occurred.

You'll want to pop out of the car to stroll the **Devastation Trail**, a half-mile path through a forest that was destroyed by the eruption of Kilauea Iki in 1959.

This boardwalk trail looks fresher and greener than its name implies; back in 1959, lava, ash, and hot gases roared into the sky from this tranquil spot, gushing some 1,900 feet into the air and turning the forest to cinders. Now, vegetation has sprouted up and softened the bleak landscape here.

If you continue along Crater Rim Drive, don't miss a stop at **Thurston Lava Tube**★ *(2mi east of Volcano House; see p 52)*.

Across the street is the **Kilauea Iki Crater Overlook**, where you can peer into an enormous "frozen" lava lake, still steaming from the 1959 eruption. Want to get closer? There's a terrific hike that descends 400 feet through native rain forest into the crater, where you can wander across the lava lake. It took about 35 years for all of the molten rock trapped beneath the surface of the lava lake to crystalize, scientists say. Even now, the rocks are still hot to the touch, and there are steam vents all along the crater floor. For fast hikers it's a two-hour loop, but most visitors find it to take closer to three hours. So allow yourself plenty of daylight to complete this hike.

Even if you don't go all the way down to the lake, it's worth hiking the beginning of this trail; it's a pretty rain-forest romp, with lovely views—a cool respite on a hot day.

Touring Tip

In the national park, the two main roads, **Crater Rim Drive**★★ and **Chain of Craters Road**★★, are paved, two-lane roads, suitable for cars.

Hiking Hawaii

Be flexible and be prepared. Those instructions are key when you're hiking in Hawaii. Weather and conditions can change abruptly—one minute, it's fine to swim in the pools along the waterfall; the next minute, high waters fed by rain squalls far above make creeks dangerous. Count on a sudden cloudburst, and bring a raincoat and a waterproof pack for your camera, even if it's sunny when you leave. Fog is common, especially in the rain forest. Pack snacks, and bring more water than you think you'll need. Stay on the trail, even if it's muddy; loose soil off-trail can send you sliding down a ravine. Land managers close trails if conditions are dangerous, so be flexible with your itinerary. There's always another lovely trail to explore!

Chain of Craters Road★★

See map p25. Connects with Crater Rim Drive at Devastation Trail, Hawaii Volcanoes National Park. Allow at least 3 hours for a round-trip. For current lava conditions, call 808-985-6000 or check at the Kilauea Visitor Center.

This 38-mile road is one of the most spectacular drives in the world. The two-lane blacktop curves through a vast landscape of lava fields, descending 3,700 feet to the coast. At times, the hillsides are rust-colored, where orangey lava and spiky vegetation slope toward the sea. In other places, fields of ropy pahoehoe lava are glossy and black, like dark chocolate syrup poured over a hot-fudge sundae.

Take a Hike – Park the car along the road, grab a bottle of water, put on a hat and sturdy shoes (lava can be cracked, uneven and slippery), and follow the path. Here, lava flows from several hundred years ago meet recent flows, and **petrogyphs** (images etched in lava) are numerous; look for the oft-photographed, half-buried highway sign.

Though there have been no lava flows here in recent years, the landscape still drives home the impression of vast geological forces at work.

© Hawaii Tourism Japan (HTJ)

Chain of Craters Road seen from the hardened lava

Onomea Scenic Drive★
See map p25. Off Hwy. 19,
4mi north of Hilo.

This little jog is worth a trip if you're heading from Hilo to Volcano Village or vice versa. The 4-mile detour features wonderful views of lava-rock coastline along Onomea Bay, waterfalls and fragrant jungle. Stop for a fruit smoothie at **What's Shakin'** (*27-999 Old Mamalahoa Hwy.; 808-964-3080*), then follow the narrow road that winds alongside rain forest and ocean. Twisty vines fall like fringe from the roadsides, bridges are barely one lane—and traffic is two-way, so beware. Dense vegetation eventually falls away to a backdrop of sapphire blue. Stops along the way include **Hawaii Tropical Botanical Garden** (*27–717 Old Mamalahoa Hwy.; see p 40*), and, just beyond, the spectacular **Onomea Overlook**, where you can pull over to park and peek through the foliage for gorgeous vistas of too-blue-to-be-true Onomea Bay. A short walk from the overlook leads to the **Onomea Foot Trail**, where you can walk along the shoreline and stretch your legs.

Mauna Loa Road
See map p25. Off Hwy. 11,
4mi west of Volcano Village.

At nearly 14,000 feet, Mauna Loa is not the highest—but is the most massive—mountain on earth. Its summit caldera stretches three miles long; it last erupted in 1984. While the trip to the top is a rigorous, four-day hike, the drive up (to 6,662 feet) provides a sense of the grandeur of this volcano. Stands of stately koa trees line the roadway, where you might catch a glimpse of the **Kalij pheasant** (*see sidebar p 31*)—an invasive,

Touring Tip

Bring a picnic; there are tables at the base of the trail to Mauna Loa's summit.

Onomea Falls, Hawaii Tropical Botanical Garden

© Michael Ireland/ Fotolia.com

non-native bird, unfortunately. At **Kipuka Puaulu**, or Bird Park, where an eruption 400 years ago resulted in pockets of untouched forest set within a sea of lava, a 1.2-mile loop meanders through this enchanted environment, whose air is filled with birdsong.

Red Road
See map p25. Hwy. 137, 27mi south of Hilo.

You'll feel like a local when you take a jaunt down this 14.6-mile-long old coastal road, originally paved with red lava. The stretch from Kalapana to Paradise Park features natural pools fed by volcanic springs, basalt cliffs, coconut groves and black-sand beaches. A string of beach parks lines the shore; a local favorite is **Isaac Hale Park** at Pohoiki, where everyone goes on Sunday afternoons to fish, swim and picnic.

Nearby, check out **Lava Tree State Monument**, off Highway 132, with its lava-wrapped koa trees *(808-961-9540; www.hawaii stateparks.org; open year-round daily dawn–dusk)*.

Touring Tip

Wouldn't it be nice to scoop up that cool black lava rock and take it home as a souvenir? Don't even think about it! According to Hawaiian legend, removing rocks is disrespectful to the goddess Pele and brings bad luck. It is illegal to remove rocks, stones or any living thing from park properties. Hawaiian parks and post offices receive returned rocks each year, with tales of the woe they provoked. It's best to leave stones unturned.

Say What?

Here's the meaning of some place names you may encounter on highway signs. Remember to pronounce every vowel, and you'll get the hang of it.

Hilo	To twist or braid; also, the name of a famous Polynesian navigator
Kaupulehu	Roasting oven of the gods
Kealakekua	Pathway of the gods
Kona	Whispering sea
Laupahoehoe	Smooth, flat lava
Mauna Kea	White mountain
Waikoloa	Strong wind
Waimea	Red water

Kohala Mountain Road
See map p24. Hwy. 250, north of Waimea.

Most visitors miss this drive, which is a shame because it's very scenic. Heading north from Waimea through the **Waipio Valley★★**, you'll reach Upolu Point, where a lookout offers great views of Mauna Loa and Kea, and Hualalai, plus the gorgeous Kohala coastline. Miles and miles of lush grassy pasture descend the mountain slopes. The road ends in Hawi, home to a string of galleries and restaurants and the center of a burgeoning grass-fed cattle industry. Stretch your legs and then continue on to **Mookini Heiau★** and King Kamehameha's Birthplace. Follow the road to Pololu Valley, where you can descend a steep trail to a dazzling black-sand beach (great for exploring but dangerous for swimming). Head back south along stunning coastal Highway 270.

GARDENS

Impressively massive though it may be, the island of Hawaii has lush pockets of tropical foliage, roadsides where wild impatiens and ginger grow in a riot of color, and botanical gardens that dazzle beholders.

Hawaii Tropical Botanical Garden★★

Map p25. Off Hwy. 19 along Onomea Scenic Drive, Onomea Bay (8mi north of Hilo). 808-964-5233. www.htbg.com. Open year-round daily 9am–4pm. Closed Jan 1, Thanksgiving Day, & Dec 25. $15.

Getting here is half the fun: The 4-mile **Onomea Scenic Drive★** *(see p38)* is a rain-forest-lined twist of roadway, skirting cliffs that tumble to the sea. You'll cross one-lane wooden bridges and get tantalizing glimpses of aqua waters as you follow the serpentine drive that leads, 1.5 miles in, to this tropical paradise set on Onomea

Touring Tip

Mosquitoes thrive at **Hawaii Tropical Botanical Garden**, too. Happily, the garden staff provides bug repellent for visitors. Allow about two hours for a leisurely visit.

Touring Tip

Look for **two-for-one admission coupons** for many gardens and other island attractions in local tourist brochures like *101 Things to Do on the Big Island*, which is widely available in island visitor centers, hotels and many shops.

Bay. Onomea means "good feeling," and you'll certainly pick up that vibe here.

Set in a 40-acre valley that slopes to the sea, this tamed jungle displays a variety of orchids, heliconias, gingers, bromeliads, and other plants—more than 2,000 species at present, some rare and exotic. The garden's collection of **palm trees** (some as tall as 100 feet) boasts some 200 species, ranging from sago and wanga to betel nut and date palms. A three-tiered **waterfall** and natural streams add to the serenity of the setting. Wander through a torch-ginger

Hawaii Tropical Botanical Garden

© Brigitta L. House/Michelin

forest, where some gingers stand sentry-like on 12-foot stalks. Then meander through a banana grove. The golden bamboo grove positively thrums when breezes whistle through it.

In addition to serving as a sanctuary for plants, the garden acts as a living seed bank and study center for tropical trees and plants. Plan time to visit the **Amy B.H. Greenwell Ethnobotanical Garden**, run by the Bishop Museum (*www.bishopmuseum. org/greenwell*), in the town of Captain Cook, on the Kona Coast

World Botanical Garden★★

Map p25. Off Hwy. 19 near mile marker 16 in Umauma, Honomu. 808-963-5427. www.wbgi.com. Open year-round daily 9am– 5:30pm. Closed major holidays. $13.

Hawaii's largest botanical garden (300 acres) features some 5,000 species and other pleasant diversions, such as a children's hedge maze. Among the nice touches here are free samples of juice from garden fruits in season, and a wheelchair-accessible rain-forest nature walk.

At the end of the bloom-edged trail, the view of 300-foot **Umauma Falls** is a treat. Check out the Hawaii wellness garden, displaying medicinal endemic plants, and a garden planted with trees and plants arranged according to when they first appeared on earth.

Liliuokalani Gardens

Map p25. Banyan Dr., Hilo. 808-961-8720. Grounds open daily 24hr.
Named after Hawaii's last queen, Lili'uokalani, this 30-acre park is

the largest formal Japanese garden east of the Orient. The garden is located on Banyan Drive on the Waiakea Peninsula, where the towering trees have their own stories: many were planted in the 1930s by famous folk such as Babe Ruth and Amelia Earhart. Japanese features include koi ponds, pagodas and a moon bridge. Cross the bridge to Coconut Island for views of Hilo Bay with a backdrop of mountains.

Pua Mau Place Botanical Gardens

Map p24. 10 Ala Kahua St., Kawaihae, Kohala Coast. 808-882-0888. www.puamau.com. Open year-round daily 9am–4pm. Donation requested.

This enchanting 45-acre desert garden rises over the ocean, with fine views of Maui across the Alenuihaha Channel. Fun features at this family-friendly spot include giant bronze insect sculptures, wandering peacocks, and a hibiscus maze with more than 200 varieties.

Umauma Falls, World Botanical Garden

© Michael DeFreitas/Photoshot

HISTORIC SITES

From ancient idols and ruins to a lavish palace built of lava rock and coral, the island of Hawaii is an enchanting place to get an overview of the fascinating history of this island chain.

Puuhonua O Honaunau National Historical Park★★★

Hwy. 160, Honaunau, 22mi south of Kailua-Kona. 808-328-2288 www.nps.gov/puho. Open year-round daily 7am–8pm. Visitor center open year-round daily 8am–5pm. Closed state holidays. $5 (pass good for 7 days).

One of the most magical places in the islands, these quiet bayside grounds hark back to simpler times. In the 16C, defeated warriors and *kapu* (religious taboo) violators found refuge at this lava-black place by the sea. Places of refuge (*pu'uhonua*) were found on every island in ancient times. A lawbreaker who reached one of these sacred sites was purified by a priest; at that point, he could not be harmed by his pursuers, even after he left. Puuhonua o Honaunau is especially important because it holds the bones of

Touring Tip

A great time to visit the historical park is in August, when a cultural festival called **Establishment Day** is celebrated here. The event features crafts, music, hula and community net fishing. This is one of the best places on the island to get a sense of traditional Hawaiian ways. Bring a picnic and have lunch at one of the tables near the beach under a fringe of coconut palms. Later, walk the mile-long **trail** that leads along the coast past archaeological sites where temples and houses once stood.

23 high chiefs. Here are other highlights of a visit:

Great Wall – An impressive, 1,000-foot-long rock wall marks the location of Puuhonua O Honaunau. Look for its reflection in the

Great Wall, Puuhonua O Honaunau National Historical Park

Statues at Puuhonua O Honaunau National Historical Park

© Brigitta L. House/Michelin

fishpond—a wonderful place to take a photo of a Hawaiian sunset.

Self-guided Tour – Take a 30-minute walk around the 180-acre property and see the thatched huts, burial sites, temple, ancient idols and ruins, and canoes made in the old way—lashed together with coconut fiber. En route, you might see local canoe builders, wood carvers and other traditional craftspeople at work.

Ala Kahakai National Historic Trail★

Portions of the trail can be accessed in the four national parks on the island—Hawaii Volcanoes National Park, Puuhonua O Honaunau, Kaloko-Honokaohau National Historical Park, and Puukoha National Historic Site. Other sections can be accessed via state and county lands. Mostly unmarked, the trail runs from Upolu Point at the northwest tip of the island, around the South Point (Ka Lae), to Wahalula Heiau on the east side of the Big Island. 808-326 6012. www.nps.gov/alka; www.hawaiitrails.org.

Part of the National Park Service trail system, this 175-mile corridor links sites of historical and cultural significance. The trail follows the coastline along ancient fishermen's trails and old Hawaiian Kingdom roads that have merged, over time, into a single route.

The trail passes through public and private lands, and connects with numerous beaches and resorts. The Ala Kahakai also traverses some of the most pristine shoreline in the state of Hawaii, including rare and protected ananchialine ponds (home to tiny red shrimp.) As you wander, you'll take in beautiful coastal views, see native plants, and encounter bits of ancient Hawaiian history, including *heiau* (temples), kahua (house site foundations), fishponds, fishing shrines, petroglyphs and more. Assuming you want to hike the trail in sections, not all at once, public **access points** include Spencer County Beach Park (from Highway 270), Hapuna State Beach Park, Holoholokai Beach Park, Waikoloa Beach Marriott, Hilton Waikoloa Village Resort, and the Puako Boat Ramp (all off Highway 19.) Parking, toilets and water are available at most locations.

Hulihee Palace★

75-5719 Alii Dr., Kailua-Kona. 808-329-1877. www.daughtersof hawaii.org. Open year-round Mon–Sat 9am–4pm; Sun 10am–4pm (last tour at 3pm). Closed major holidays. $10.

Once the most elegant residence on the Big Island, Hulihee Palace was built in 1838 by the island's governor, John Adams Kuakini. Made of lava rock and coral mortar, the house served as the summer

HISTORIC SITES

Ranchlands

© Brigitta L. House/Michelin

Horseback Rides

Kahua Ranch and **Ponoholo Ranch** are working horse and cattle ranches. Horseback rides at both feature breathtaking scenery on and from Kohala Mountain, the island's northernmost volcano. *For prices and times, visit kahuaranch.com and www.panioloadventures.com/theranch.htm.*

home of Hawaii's *ali'i* (royal family). You'll see koa furniture, Hawaiian quilts and 19C artifacts; docent-led tours are available.

The palace suffered major damage in the October 2006 earthquake; a full restoration was completed in 2009.

Try to plan your visit during one of the palace's frequent **concerts** of Hawaiian music and hula, typically held here the last Sunday of the month (call or go online for a schedule).

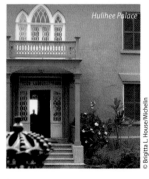

Hulihee Palace

© Brigitta L. House/Michelin

Lyman Museum & Mission House★

276 Haili St., Hilo. 808-935-5021. www.lymanmuseum.org. Open year-round Mon–Sat 10am– 4.30pm. Closed major holidays. $10/person, $21/family.

Mark Twain slept here. That's one of the claims to fame of the Lyman House, built in the 1830s by missionaries David and Sarah Lyman. Located in Hilo, the mission house is the oldest wooden structure on the Big Island, and one of the oldest in the state. The house served as a boarding school for young Hawaiian men, as the Lyman family residence and as guest quarters for several notables, including Twain and many members of the Hawaiian *ali'i* (royal family).

Exhibits feature furniture, tools, and household items, plus collections of seashells, minerals, ancient Chinese art and Hawaiian art, as well as temporary exhibits.

H.N. Greenwell Store Museum

Mamalahoa Hwy., 14mi south of Kailua-Kona. 808-323-3222. www.konahistorical.org. Open Mon & Thu 10am–2pm. $7.

Constructed by Englishman Henry Nicholas Greenwell in 1875, and operated by his wife Elizabeth, the oldest surviving store in Kona sold everything from salted salmon to saddle soap, poi to parasols. It is run by the Kona Historical Society.

Kaloko-Honokohau National Historical Park

Hwy. 19 (Queen Kaahumanu Hwy.), 3mi south of Kona International Airport, Keahole. 808-326-9057. www.nps.gov/kaho. Open year-round daily 8:30am–4pm. Closed state holidays.

Set at the base of the Hualalai Volcano on the Kona Coast, this 1,160-acre site marks an ancient Hawaiian settlement stretching

Settlement, Lapakahi State Historical Park

© Hawaii's Big Island Visitor Bureau (BIVB)

from mountain to sea. Wander past fishponds, *kahua* (house site foundations), *ki'l pohaku* (petroglyphs), *holua* (stone slides), and *heiau* (religious sites). On the recreational side, there are hiking trails and good snorkeling in the crystalline waters of Honokohau Bay. Look for shore birds, sea turtles and perhaps, an Hawaiian monk seal basking in the sun.

Lapakahi State Historical Park

Akoni Pule Hwy., N. Kohala. 808-327-4958. www.hawaii stateparks.org. Open year-round daily 8am–4pm. Closed state holidays.

From the 14C through the 19C, this site was a fishing village. Self-guided walking paths feature interpretive signs describing what it was like to fish the traditional way, with salt-making pans, nets and fishing gear. You'll also stroll

---

Touring Tip

Snorkeling is permitted just off the coral beach at **Lapakahi State Historical Park**. Throw some clothes on over your swimsuit if you decide to come back and visit the site, though; they frown on visitors wearing bathing attire at the park facilities.

HISTORIC SITES

Captain Cook

No name is more synonymous with exploration in the Pacific Ocean than that of Captain James Cook. He made three voyages between 1767 and 1779, and is credited with mapping the coasts of Australia and New Zealand, in addition to "discovering" numerous islands, including Tonga, New Caledonia, and Easter Island. Cook failed in his third voyage (1776–79) to find a northern passage from the Pacific to the Atlantic, though he traced the west coast of North America from Oregon to the Arctic Ocean. When he arrived in Hawaii, the natives welcomed him warmly, perhaps mistaking him for the peripatetic god Lono. But Cook and several of his men were later killed by Hawaiians in a skirmish over a stolen boat at **Kealakekua Bay★**. A town on the island's west coast bears his name.

Captain Cook Monument, Kealakekua Bay

© Russ Bishop / age fotostock

past thatched huts and fishing shrines, and visit an overlook where fishermen played a game similar to checkers while they waited for schools of fish to show up.

Puukohola Heiau National Historic Site

62-3601 Kawailhae Rd., 2mi north of the intersection of Hwys. 19 & 270, Kawaihae. 808-882-7218. www.nps.gov/puhe. Open year-round daily 7:45 am–5pm. Closed state holidays.

Ancient archaeological sites mark the windswept coastline of north Kohala. Puukohola Heiau was built as a temple around 1550 and reconstructed in 1791 by Kamehameha I, who treacherously murdered his last Big Island rival here to dedicate the temple and make himself supreme chief. As British sailor John Young looked on, the king built the temple himself, along with his chiefs and commoners—men, women, and children.

A rival was sacrificed, so the war god Ku would be pleased. Today Hawaiian cultural and craft demonstrations are offered throughout the week.

Each August, the site hosts the **Hawaiian Cultural Festival**, with crafts, dance, traditional Hawaiian games and music.

Interpretive programs for children are a highlight here; kids can take a hike, play ancient Hawaiian games and become a Junior Ranger.

Touring Tip

Use Puukohola Heiau park as an access point for hiking the Ala Kahakai National Historic Trail. A short-but-sweet option: the 3/4-mile walk to Mau' umoe Beach.

MUSEUMS

The Island of Hawaii isn't exactly Museum Central, but the Jaggar Museum is worth a peek (and a good spot to volcano-watch). If coffee is your addiction, the Kona tour will be your cup of tea... um, java.

Thomas A. Jaggar Museum★

In Hawaii Volcanoes National Park, on Hwy. 11 (28mi southwest of Hilo). 808-985-6000. www.nps.gov/navo. Open year-round daily 8:30am–7:30pm. $10 (park entrance fee). See p 35.

Though it's a bit old and cramped, this venerable facility—named for the professor who founded the **Hawaiian Volcano Observatory** next door *(closed to the public)*—offers a worthy vantage on volcanoes. The entry affords views of the **Halemaumau Crater★★**, a half-mile across and 1,000 feet deep; look west to see **Mauna Loa★★** in the distance. Seismometers and other things, enable you to "see" every tiny earthquake on the island (there are several hundred tremors a day here). Videotapes show footage of spewing volcanoes. **Rock samples** depict the types of igneous stone, including the two basic Hawaiian lava types, a'a and pahoehoe.

Imiloa Astronomy Center

600 Imiloa Pl., Hilo. 808-969-9703. www.imiloahawaii.org. Open Tue–Sun 9am–5pm. $17.50 (includes one planetarium show).

This newly expanded facility (part of the University of Hawaii at Hilo) is basically a state-of-the-art planetarium. The highlight is a thought-provoking explanation of the importance ancient Hawaiians placed on observing the heavens for guidance and navigation. Information is presented in both English and Hawaiian, and other exhibits include Hawaiian voyaging canoes, a recounting of the history of hula, and an exploration of Hawaiian musical development. Astronomy exhibits explore the nature of the cosmos.

Make Mine a Cuppa Kona

Kona coffee is recognized worldwide as among the very best. Grown only on a narrow, 20-mile-long strip of land on the mountain slopes above Kailua-Kona, it is noted for its rich flavor and high quality. It's considered "shade-grown" because of the persistent mauka clouds that hover over the growing district. The first trees, a variety of Arabica from Ethiopia, were planted here more than 175 years ago. The combination of rich, volcanic soil and the region's distinctive weather worked like magic; now the Big Island is the best-known place in the US where coffee beans are grown commercially. Numerous farms in the Kona District offer tours and tastings and the chance to roast your own beans, perhaps even pick some. *For more information visit www.konacoffeefarmers.org.*

MUSEUMS

FOR FUN

Big fun on the Big island almost always involves an outdoor pursuit, say, snorkeling with rays or stargazing on the summit of a volcano. And if golf is your passion, check out one of the island's 18 courses.

Stargaze on Mauna Kea★★

The 13,796-foot summit of Mauna Kea offers amazing stargazing. Dress in winter clothing (it's chilly at the top) and head up the narrow, winding, unpaved Saddle Road *(Hwy. 200)*. Check weather report before you go, because Mauna Kea is off limits in bad weather. First stop at the visitor information station at **Onizuka Center for International Astronomy** (located part-way up the mountain, at 9,300 feet), so you can become acclimatized to the thin air and altitude. Up top, as darkness falls, you'll stand in the midst of the largest collection of telescopes anywhere, at **Mauna Kea Observatory.** The stargazing here is unparalleled; the air above the mountain is exceptionally dry, cloud-free and unpolluted, and there is little artificial light to compete with the heavens above.

Touring Tip

Each October **Kailua-Kona** on the Big Island is home to the toughest multisport event around: the **Ironman Triathlon World Championship**. Nearly 1,800 elite athletes, from all 50 states and some 50 countries, compete in a 26-mile marathon, a 2.4-mile ocean swim, and a 112-mile bike ride. Spectators line up along the seawall on **Alii Drive** to see the 7am start. Competitors have 17 hours to finish the race. www.ironman.com.

Hawaii Forest & Trail company offers **guided trips** at sunset *(7-8hrs)* to the world's tallest volcano (*808-331-8505; www. hawaii-forest.com; $179; ages 16 and up*). The trip includes pick-up (from Waikoloa hotels), a picnic and parkas.

Gemini Telescope on the summit of Mauna Kea at sunrise

© Hawaii Tourism Authority (HTA) / Kirk Lee Aeder

HAWAII, THE BIG ISLAND

MUST DO

Swim with Rays★

Rays can be found, most days, from as far north as Keahole Point down to Keauhou Bay. To dive and snorkel with the rays, contact one of these Kona-based companies: Jack's Diving Locker (808-329-7585; www.jacksdivinglocker.com), Fair Wind Ocean Guides (www.fair-wind.com) and Kona Honu Divers (808-324-4668; konahonu divers.com).

The Big Island's **Kona Coast** is the place to swim with amazing underwater acrobats, manta rays. More than 150 manta rays have been identified here.

Related to sharks, manta rays have no teeth and no tail stingers. (Note: this is not the kind of ray that killed Crocodile Hunter, Steve Irwin.) They rely on speed and aerodynamic design to outwit predators. The first thing you'll notice is, they're huge! The shy, typically harmless fish have triangular wings with spans that reach up to 20 feet across. The best way to find rays is to join a **diving trip** (participants must be certified divers); dive-boat captains know where these intriguing fish are known to gather. They also arrange night dives and snorkel excursions to see manta rays. Divers must keep their distance, so these flying fish have plenty of room to maneuver.

The mantas and other sea life come to feed on plankton at night (plankton are attracted to dive lights). Mantas may sometimes follow divers back to the boat, and perform a farewell loop-de-loop!

Rundown on Rays:

♦ Manta rays *(Manta hamiltoni)* are the largest type of ray; they can weigh up to 3,000 pounds.

♦ In Hawaiian, rays are called *hahalua*; the name manta is Spanish for "cloak."

♦ A ray's mouth is located on the underside of its body.

♦ Females give birth to one to two babies at a time; each infant ray can weigh up to 25 pounds.

♦ Manta rays have been reported to jump 15 feet out of the water.

Watch for Whales

Captain Dan McSweeny's Whale Watch offers 3-hour tours departing from Honokohau Harbor in Kona Dec–Apr. 808-322-

Manta ray

© Hawaii Tourism Japan (HTJ)

FOR FUN

Touring Tip

For a great aerial overview of the islands, and a look at places you wouldn't otherwise be able to see, a helicopter tour is your best bet. You'll peer into craters and see hidden valleys dripping with waterfalls. **Sunshine Helicopters** *(808-270-3999; www.sunshinehelicopters.com)* operates flights on Maui, Oahu, Kauai, and the Big Island. Tip: A helicopter tour is an excellent way to get a bird's-eye view of the ongoing eruptions near Hawaii Volcanoes National Park.

0028 or 888-942-5376. www.ilovewhales.com. $110.
Each year, from November to May, hundreds of **humpback whales** cruise the warm waters of the islands to give birth and care for their young before heading back to Alaska. These gentle giants are so large, you can see them from shore, but boat-borne excursions offer closer viewing along with interpretive narration. Whale-watch boats are crewed by marine scientists; some are equipped with a hydrophone so you can listen to whalesong underwater. Watch for a "spout"—the whale's exhalation—and the smaller "puff" that means a baby is nearby. Then, a big black tail might rise up and smack the water's surface. The spectacle everyone looks for (even veteran whale watchers) is a **breach**—the whale leaps out of the water and falls back in with a huge splash.

Hike Kilauea Iki

Once you get a look at the sunken lava lake at the Kilauea Iki Crater Overlook at **Hawaii Volcanoes National Park★★★** *(Hwy. 11, in Volcano)*, you'll want to get closer. It's possible—and well worth it—if you're willing to hike about 3hours. **The Hike** – The 4-mile loop begins at the parking area for Kilauea Iki Crater Overlook (across the street from Thurston Lava Tube, about 1.5mi from the Kilauea Visitor Center off Hwy. 11). Bring water and a windbreaker on this challenging hike; it's cool in the crater. You'll start out with a breathtaking view of what's ahead, and then descend about 400 feet through dense rain forest.

Humpback whale
©Dale Walsh/iStockphoto.com

The trail is pretty easy to follow, if somewhat steep at the beginning. As you get to the crater floor, look for *ahu* (rock piles) that mark the way. You'll pass the Puu Puai cinder cone and return along the crater's rim.

Snorkel at Kealakekua Bay State Historic Park

Some call this the best snorkel spot in the entire state. Located on the Big Island's west coast, this underwater marine preserve is a prime snorkeling destination. Schools of paintbox-hued tropical fish swirl amid delicate fingers of pink and lavender coral and chunky pillow lava. Plus, the water is normally calm and clear, perfect for kids and first-timers. There are two ways to do it: on large catamarans and on small, rubber rafts. The former are great for families, since the powerboats offer onboard restrooms, food, a snorkeling lesson, and flotation rings.

- **Fair Wind Cruises** – Catamaran snorkel cruises depart from Keauhou (*808-322-2788; www.fair-wind.com; $75–129*).
- **Captain Zodiac Raft Expeditions** – Raft trips to Kealakekua Bay depart from Honokohau Harbor (*2.5mi north of Kailua on Hwy. 19; 808-329-3199; www.captainzodiac.com; $97*).

Take a Surfing Lesson

The Hawaiian Islands are known for their immense waves, ideal for daring surfers, though not for beginners. While surfing in Hawaii was once reserved solely for royalty, today on the Big Island there are plenty of opportunities to watch the sport from shore or ride your own wave.

Kealakekua Bay

© Hawaii's Big Island Visitor Bureau (BIVB)

Touring Tip

Here's another snorkeling fave on the west coast. Set between Honokohau Harbor and Kailua Bay, Pawai Bay is accessible only by boat, and is a great spot to see dolphins, rays and sea turtles. Boats that offer trips to Pawai Bay include **Kona Honu Divers** (*808-324-4668; www.konahonudivers.com; $80*) and **Body Glove Cruises** (*808-551-8911; www.bodyglovehawaii.com; $78–$120*), who specialize in first-time snorkelers. Trips depart from the marina at Honokohau Harbor (*2.5mi north of Kailua on Hwy. 19*).

Beaches like Banyans in Historic Kailua VIllage (Kailua-Kona), Pine Trees Beach north of Kona Airport or Kahaluu Beach in Keauhou are suitable for beginners. It's best to reserve private lessons in advance. Here are two companies that give surfing lessons on Big Island:
Hawaii Lifeguard Surf Instructors (*808-324-0442; www.surflessonshawaii.com*)
Kona Boys (*808-328-1234; www.konaboys.com*).

FOR FUN

51

FOR KIDS

Kids who love adventure will be delighted by Thurston Lava Tube, a short but intriguing underground hike. Not your thing? See the cute (and free) Pana'ewa Rainforest Zoo & Gardens (www.hilozoo.com), where 80 kinds of animals inhabit the 12-acre facility, including Bengal tigers and giant anteaters, just south of Hilo.

Thurston Lava Tube★

At Hawaii Volcanoes National Park, on Hwy. 11. 808-985-6000. www.nps.gov/havo. Park open year-round daily 24hr. $10/vehicle (park admission). See p 36.

At this theme-park excursion designed by Mother Nature, hike through a fern-bedecked rain forest, with sound effects provided by native birds, before reaching the giant hole-in-the-ground. The lava tube is dark with gnarly tree roots hanging down like

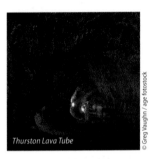

Thurston Lava Tube

© Greg Vaughn / age fotostock

bizarre chandeliers. Bring a flashlight and poke around.

PERFORMING ARTS

For a list of what's happening, visit www.gohawaii.com/arts. If you can swing it, plan your trip for the Merrie Monarch Hula Festival, the big kahuna of all the Big Island's events (week following Easter Sunday).

Kahilu Theatre

67-1186 Lindsey Rd., Waimea-Kamuela Box office: 808-885-6868. www.kahilutheatre.org. Box office opens one hour prior to performances, whose times and ticket prices vary. Arrive one hour early for best seating.

Hula, Hawaiian music groups and international stars take center stage here, at the "cultural heart" of the Big Island in Waimea. Acts have included Ladysmith Black Mambazo, Keali'i Reichel, and the Brothers Cazimero, a contemporary Hawaiian musical duo—along with fashion shows, musical theater, and opera. Kahilu appeals to children with its Youth

Touring Tip

For pre-concert dining, try **Merriman's** restaurant, featuring local farmers' ingredients and innovative Hawaiian regional cuisine, such as the delicious *opakapaka* (local Hawaiin pink snapper) served with a tropical apricot sauce. As for post-concert dining, forget about it—this is *paniolo* (cowboy) country—cowboys go to bed early and wake up with the cows. No late-nights for them!

Live Performance Series and summer arts program.

SHOPPING

Island shopping centers on resort areas such as Waikoloa—whose Kings Shops is a small mall—and small boutiques and galleries in Waimea-Kamuela. Check out Sig Zane for stylish duds by a local designer, Big Island Candies, a local institution, and Waimea General Store (fun kitsch).

Hilo Farmers' Market
400 Kamehameha Ave. at Mamo St., Hilo. 808-933-1000. www.hilofarmersmarket.com. Open Sat–Thu 7am–4pm (Wed & Sat 6am–4pm).

The oldest, biggest and fans believe, best farmers' market in the islands is a key facet of island life for residents. More than 200 vendors set up shop here, offering fresh flowers, vibrant produce (including exotic fruits and vegetables), handicrafts, warm baked goods, fish sausage, soursop, and puka-shell ankle bracelets "from dawn 'til it's gone."

Mountain Thunder Coffee Plantation
72-1027 Henry St., Kailua-Kona. 808-325-2136. www.mountain thunder.com.

The aroma of this high-elevation farm and processor will send java lovers to heaven—as will the actual taste of award-winning Kona coffee. Located on the slopes of Hualalai, this family-owned plantation grows regular and organic Kona coffee. **Free tours** include coffee tastings, and cover the coffee-growing process from bean to cup. On a longer "VIP tour" *(fee applies)* visitors learn about picking, processing and roasting the famous beans. One tour concludes with customers roasting and taking home their own beans. The gift shop has coffee-themed items, like chocolate-covered coffee beans and body cream made with Kona coffee.

Volcano Art Center
In Hawaii Volcanoes National Park, next to Kilauea Visitor Center. Mamalahoa Hwy. (Hwy. 11), Volcano (28mi southwest of Hilo). 808-967-7565. www.volcanoartcenter.org. Open daily 9am–5pm.

Does living near an active volcano inspire some primal creative spirit? Decide for yourself at the Volcano Art Center where changing exhibits in the gallery feature the works of more than 350 artists. Paintings, woodcrafts, jewelry, and more are housed in the 1877 **Volcano House**, the original hotel in Hawaii Volcanoes National Park. Volcano Art Center's Niaulani Campus is nestled in a native Hawaiian rain forest in Volcano Village. The non-profit arts and educational organization offers art lectures, readings, concerts, workshops and much more.

©Volcano Art Center
Volcano Art Center

NIGHTLIFE

Though there are few mainland-style nightclubs, many major resorts on the Big Island often feature local musicians—usually performing slack-key or other Hawaiian styles—in their casual restaurants a few nights a week.

Sunset Family Luau

At Waikoloa Beach Marriott Resort & Spa, 69-275 Waikoloa Beach Dr., Waikoloa. 808-886-6789. www.waikoloabeachmarriott.com. Held Wed and Sat at sunset. $98; $50 for ages 6-12.

OK, traditional *luaus* can seem a bit corny, but this one aims for "cute", since *keiki* (kids) take center stage. Before the show begins, little ones can try hands-on cultural activities like *pu* (conch shell) blowing, *'ulu maika* (stone bowling), and coconut husking. They also learn how to do an authentic hula dance, so they can perform the opening act at the *luau* show (and even take a bow.) Of course, the crowd goes wild. Other elements of the evening include a tour of the ancient Hawaiian fishponds at the resort, a conch shell-blowing contest, Hawaiian crafts and storytelling, and the traditional ceremony to unearth the *umu* (underground oven) and the kalua pig that will be served for dinner. Expectedly, there's live Polynesian music and dance, including that ultimate

crowd-pleaser, the Samoan fire knife dance. The food—never a highlight at these events—isn't bad, and a special *keiki*-friendly buffet is offered.

Blue Dragon Restaurant

61-3616 Kawaihae Rd., Kawaihae. 808-882-7771 www.bluedragonrestaurant.com.
Located across from Kawaihae Harbor, this club (formerly the Blue Dolphin) features live music nearly every night of the week. Hawaiian music is the theme on Thursdays. On Surfin' Saturdays, local pop music, R&B, reggae, and surf bands take to the stage. Thanks to an open ceiling, you can dance under the stars.

Huggo's on the Rocks

75-5828 Kahakai Rd., next to Royal Kona Resort, Kailua-Kona. 808-329-1493. www.huggos.com.
Now this is a beach bar! Perched on the sandy edge of Kailua Bay, Huggo's is as close to the ocean as you can get without getting wet.Listen to the waves crash and order the Kiluaea, a concoction for two that arrives in a bowl spouting a pool of fire and sip—with caution—from two-foot-long straws. Live entertainment is on tap every night.

Palace Theater

38 Haili St., Hilo. 808-934-7010. www.hilopalace.com. The Palace is a Neo-classical gem showing first-run movies and art films, plus staging concerts and theater performances.

SPAS

Resort spas are fabulous, but if they're not quite in your budget, here's a tip: locals go for pampering to Mamalahoa Hot Tubs & Massage in upcountry Kealakekua (www.mamalahoa-hottubs.com).

Hualalai Sports Club and Spa

Four Seasons Resort Hualalai, 100 Kaaupulehu Dr., Kaaupulehu-Kona. 808-325-8000. www.fourseasons.com.
Choices range from a lava-rock snorkeling pond to an open-air gym. Water-related fitness activities are so numerous that the resort offers guides to direct you.
For a body treatment, try the Island Glow sugar scrub, with Hawaiian cane sugar, coconut oil, organic vanilla beans, and island honey, or the green tea and ginger body wrap.

Kohala Spa

Hilton Waikoloa, 69-425 Waikoloa Beach Dr., Kohala. 808-886-1234. wwwhiltonwaikoloavillage.com.
Hilton's massive Big Island resort spa is oriented outdoors. Many treatments are done outside in lush landscapes. Salt scrubs and soaks, lomilomi massage and other Polynesian treatments are on tap,

and surroundings bless the visitor with profound relaxation.

Spa Without Walls

The Fairmont Orchid, 1 N. Kaniku Dr., Kohala. 808-885-2000. www.fairmont.com.
Imagine enjoying the long, rhythmic strokes of a *lomilomi* massage in an open-air cabana, surrounded by waterfalls, orchids and coconut palms. Massage *hale* (houses) are set along the waterfront, or nestled within tropical flora. The signature treatment here is the Awa Earth & Fire, blending lomilomi massage with a compress of Hawaiian herbs.

Spa Without Walls, Fairmont Orchid

Fairmont Hotels and Resorts

Spa Terms—A Cheat Sheet

Here's a quick glossary of some you'll encounter in Hawaii:
Haipi – Haipi (Hawaiian for "pregnant") refers to a massage for expectant mothers.
Japanese furo bath – Uses gently bubbling water to relax and rejuvenate the body.
Lomilomi – A traditional Hawaiian massage technique employing a light, rolling motion. Lomilomi is said to restore the free flow of *mana*, or life force.
Noni/Nonu – This plant was used by ancient Polynesians to treat illnesses. Mineral-rich, it's now employed as a healing agent in facials and treatments.
Pohaku massage – Pohaku is Hawaiian for "stone." This is the local version of hot-stone therapy.

MAUI★★

For a dozen-plus years running, Maui has been voted one of the top islands in the world by an international travel magazine. Maui has great beaches, superb resorts and lively nightlife, so the Valley Isle's many fans certainly won't argue. *Visitor information: 808-525-6284; www.gohawaii.com/maui.*

Maui no ka oi! This local motto means "Maui is the best!" T-shirts that read "Eat, Drink, and Be Maui" seem to sum up the island's attitude. There's a young, vibrant ambience here, where locals seem to feel outrageously blessed by their good fortune of living on Maui; visitors tap into that feeling of goodwill. Of course, one has to make a living, even in paradise, and there's nothing low-key about tourism here. Local entrepreneurs have found a million and one ways to provide Island fun, from **ziplining** *(see p70)* through trees on the slopes of **Haleakala** *(see p70)* or tunneling through a lava tube in **Hana** *(see p68)* to riding horseback to the floor of a crater *(see p63)*. Well-heeled tourists find more than ample ways to spend their money on Maui, and also play a major role in supporting the burgeoning arts

Fast Facts
- At 48 miles long and 26 miles wide, Maui is the second-largest island in the Hawaiian chain.
- Less than 20 percent of Maui is inhabited.
- With 120 miles of shoreline and 81 accessible beaches, Maui has more swimmable beaches than the other Hawaiian Islands.
- Maui is home to the world's largest dormant volcano, Haleakala.
- Haleakala's peak, at 10,023 feet, occasionally receives snow.

community that draws inspiration from the island's glorious scenery and Hawaiian heritage. What attracts more than 3 million visitors to Maui each year? Certainly, the island's four marine preserves and spectacular coastline are strong draws, as is **Haleakala**, the

Lahaina Harbor

© Hawaii Tourism Authority (HTA) / Tor Johnson

Haleakala National Park

© Brigitta L. House/Michelin

island's mammoth volcano. Now dormant, Haleakala has left its mark on Maui's landscape. Haleakala ("House of the Sun") rises 10,023 feet, and boasts a moon-like crater surrounded by towering forests, waterfalls, and jagged sea cliffs. What else would you expect but powerful beauty from an island named for the Polynesian demigod Maui, who managed to capture the sun as it rose from Haleakala's crater?

Beautiful though it is, Maui is about more than good looks. Whether you're a surfer or a socialite, there's something about the place that dictates simple pleasures— the sheer bliss of running barefoot on a beach, or admiring the countryside on horseback. Maui is simply blessed by the gods.

Fun Fact
Two million years ago, Maui, Lanai, Molokai and Kahoolawe all formed part of one big landmass known as Maui Nui, or Big Maui. Six different volcanoes created this body; over the eons, rising sea levels separated the islands.

The Allure of Lahaina
There's nothing ordinary about the town of **Lahaina★★**, the hub of Maui's visitor scene: Lahaina is home to one of the biggest **banyan trees** in the US, shading almost an acre; it also boasts the biggest Buddha outside of Asia. Celebrated in James Michener's novel **Hawaii**, Lahaina exudes an atmosphere reminiscent of the 19C, when pious missionaries and rowdy whalers vied for the attentions—and affections—of Native Hawaiians. The whalers are long gone, but the whales remain an attraction. From November to May, the giant cetaceans play, mate, and give birth offshore here before migrating back to northern waters for the summer. Other highlights: loads of outdoor expeditions, great dining... everything but parking. Since 2 million people visit Lahaina each year, and there seem to be about 15 parking spots, using resort shuttles and local buses is a wise choice for visiting Lahaina.

MAUI

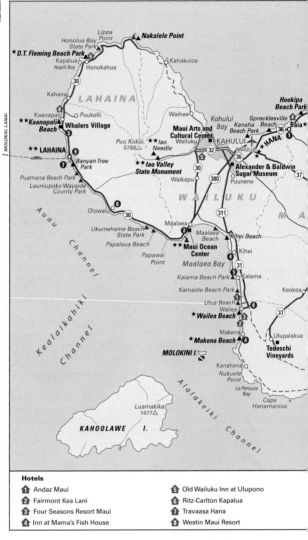

Hotels

1. Andaz Maui
2. Fairmont Kea Lani
3. Four Seasons Resort Maui
4. Inn at Mama's Fish House
5. Old Wailuku Inn at Ulupono
6. Ritz-Carlton Kapalua
7. Travaasa Hana
8. Westin Maui Resort

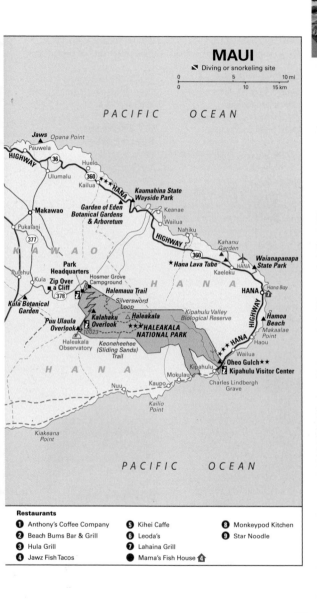

MAUI

◥ Diving or snorkeling site

0 — 5 — 10 mi
0 — 10 — 15 km

PACIFIC   OCEAN

Jaws Opana Point
Pauwela
HIGHWAY (36)
Huelo
Ulumalu
Kailua
(360) ★★ **HANA**
**Kaumahina State
Wayside Park**
Keanae
**Garden of Eden
Botanical Gardens
& Arboretum**
Wailua
Nahiku
HIGHWAY
Kahanu
Garden
★ **Hana Lava Tube**
Makawao
Pukalani
(360)
Kaeleku
**Waianapanapa
State Park**
(377)
K A W A O
**Park
Headquarters**
Hosmer Grove
Campground
HANA
HANA Hana Bay
Rulehu
Kula
**Zip Over
a Cliff**
(378) 7
Halemauu Trail
Silversword
Loop
**Kula Botanical
Garden**
**Puu Ulaula
Overlook**
**Kalahaku
Overlook**
△ Haleakala
★★★ **HALEAKALA
NATIONAL PARK**
Kipahulu Valley
Biological Reserve
**Hamoa
Beach**
Makaalae
Point
Haleakala
Observatory
10023
Keoneheehee
(Sliding Sands)
Trail
Haou
★★ **HANA**
H A N A
Mokulau
Kipahulu
Oheo Gulch ★★
2 **Kipahulu Visitor Center**
Nuu
Kaupo
Charles Lindbergh
Grave
Kailio
Point
Kiakeana
Point

PACIFIC   OCEAN

Restaurants

1 Anthony's Coffee Company
2 Beach Bums Bar & Grill
3 Hula Grill
4 Jawz Fish Tacos
5 Kihei Caffe
6 Leoda's
7 Lahaina Grill
● Mama's Fish House 🏠
8 Monkeypod Kitchen
9 Star Noodle

MAUI

BEACHES

Maui's beaches are always fabulous, but arguably, they're best at sunset, when the sea turns to silver, sailboats appear in silhouette, and the south shore's three offshore islands catch the last rays of sun.

Kaanapali Beach★★

Map p58. Hwy. 30, 2mi north of Lahaina, in Kaanapali.

Selected America's best beach several times by Stephen Leatherman (aka Dr. Beach; *see box p26*), this long golden strand is excellent for swimming and snorkeling, especially near the Sheraton's "Black Rock" headland that fends off northeasterly trade winds. The three-mile-long beach backs up to a strand of resort hotels, as well as **Whalers Village**, home to waterfront restaurants and shopping. (**Tip:** Look for beach-only parking spots next to Whalers Village.) A concrete path runs from Black Rock to the Hyatt hotel.

Kaanapali's tumbling surf makes it good for boogieboarding, too. Stay late to catch the sunset. You might luck into an empty lounge chair where you can get cozy and watch night fall.

D.T. Fleming Beach Park★

Map p58. Off Hwy. 30 on Napili Bay in west Maui, Kapalua.

Another one of Stephen Leatherman's picks for Best Beach in the US, this mile-long crescent of white sand is the unofficial beach of the Ritz-Carlton hotel, but, as with all Hawaiian beaches, is public. Staffed, by lifeguards, Fleming Beach is great for body- and boardsufing.

Makena Beach★

Map p58. Off Hwy. 31, Shoreline Rd., Makena.

Set in Southwest Maui, Makena Beach (aka Big Beach) is the largest undeveloped white-sand beach on the island. To locate the beach, a good landmark is **Jawz** taco stand, across the street; to the right you'll find a parking lot. The surf can be rough, but the views are great. Locals set up tent villages here on Sunday and make a day of it.

Wailea Beach★

Map p58. Off Hwy. 31, just south of the Shops at Wailea, in Wailea.

A favorite of Stephen Leatherman, Wailea is located in South Maui, behind the Grand Wailea and Four Seasons hotels. Long and wide, this white-sand strip features high dunes, a sandy ocean bottom,

---

Touring Tip

During the winter months, waves deliver 4- to 20-foot faces at Hookipa, Honalua Bay, and Hamoa Bay. Then there's **Jaws**, the huge, rideable waves located in Peahi Bay, east of Paia. These awesome waves rarely break, and faces can be big enough to fit a bus in, so Jaws is recommended for experts only. For a gentler ride, seek out Maui's south shores: Maalaea Harbor, Big Beach, and the string of beaches between Lahaina and Maalaea, including Papalaua, Ukumehame, and Launiupoko Wayside park.

Whale of a Time

Come November, thousands of humpbacks arrive in the Hawaiian Islands to mate, having come 2,600 miles from Alaska. They birth their two-ton babies in the warm waters, then head north again in April, to their North Pacific feeding grounds. Large numbers of humpbacks congregate in the channel between Maui, Lanai and Molokai. Maui has the largest whale-watching fleet in the islands *(for details, check online at www.gohawaii.com/maui or contact the Pacific Whale Foundation, which sponsors cruises out of Lahaina Harbor Dec–mid-May; 808-249-8811; www.pacificwhale.com).*

and a shallow drop-off into deeper water. It's calm enough for snorkeling, a popular activity here.

Hamoa Beach

Map p59. Haneo'o Rd., 2mi south of Hana.

Novelist James Michener compared this swath of sand favorably with the beaches of the South Pacific. Named one of America's best beaches in 2010 by Dr. Beach, Hamoa is great for bodysurfing. Park on the road; stairs lead to the beach. The view of Mauna Kea across the channel is breathtaking.

Hookipa Beach Park

Map p58. Hwy. 36, 6mi east of the intersection of Haleakala & Hana Hwys., about 2mi east of Paia.

North Maui's Hookipa Beach (*Hookipa* means "hospitality" in Hawaiian) is Windsurfer Central. Thanks to strong trade winds and consistent surf, Maui is a paradise for board sailors, and Hookipa is the real deal. It's the most-photographed windsurfing site on the planet. Kite-surfers also take advantage of the amazing conditions at Hookipa, especially in winter, when the big north-shore waves roll in. Powerful rip currents, exposed reefs and snaggle-toothed lava rock make this one the perfect match for more experienced surfers. There are several places on the island to rent equipment. Windsurfers show up at 11am or so. The beach borders a coral reef, creating a shallow area that's great for kids. Beyond the reef, the northern swells churn up big, surfable waves.

Windsurfing, Hookipa Beach Park

© Hawaii Tourism Authority (HTA) / Tor Johnson

BEACHES

PARKS AND NATURAL SITES

Most visitors take in Maui's premier natural site, Haleakala Volcano, by car, at sunrise. Early-morning traffic doesn't make for a peaceful escape. For a less crowded volcano experience, go at sunset (as residents do), or hike the crater, or see it all by horseback.

HALEAKALA NATIONAL PARK★★★

Map p59. 36mi southeast of Kahului via Haleakala Hwy. (Rte. 37) to Rte. 377 to Rte. 378. 808-572-4400. www.nps.gov/hale. Park open year-round daily 24 hours. Visitor Center open year-round daily 8am–3:45pm. $10 per vehicle (pass is good for 3 days).

The word Haleakala (Huh-LAY-uh-ka-lah) means "house of the sun" in Hawaiian. According to myth, the god **Maui** climbed to the top of the Haleakala Volcano and lassoed the sun to force it to move more slowly across the Hawaiian sky. In turn, **La**, the sun god, agreed to slow his pace for half of the year so that people could enjoy longer days in summer.

Haleakala, now a dormant volcano, completely dominates the landscape in east Maui. The spectacular desolation of its enormous crater valley—7.5 miles long, 2.5 miles wide and 3,000 feet

© Hawaii Tourism Authority (HTA) / Ron Dahlquist

Nene Bird

The endangered nene (pronounced neh-nay), also known as the Hawaiian goose, is Hawaii's state bird. Once hunted to near extinction, nene have been successfully bred in captivity and released back into the wild. You'll find wild nene populations in Maui's Haleakala National Park, in Hawaii Volcanoes National Park and Mauna Loa on the Big Island, and along the Na Pali Coast on Kauai.

deep—has been compared with the mountains of the moon. Pastel hues of red, yellow, and orange, as well as gray, purple, brown, black, and pink, accent cliffsides and cinder cones. To truly experience

Haleakala National Park

© Brigitta L. House/Michelin

Stalking the Elusive Silversword

Also known as *ahinahina*, or gray-gray, silversword is among the rarest of plants. So rare is this relative of the common sunflower that it grows only above 7,000 feet on the Haleakala Volcano on Maui. Another variety grows on the high slopes of Mauna Kea and Mauna Loa on the Big Island. Bursting from the ashy cinders of the volcano, the silversword erupts into bloom *(Jun and Oct)*, sprouting a stalk 3 to 9 feet tall. Pinecone-shaped, the plant is covered with purple blossoms that emerge from the center of silvery, swordlike leaves. Look but don't touch: these plants are a threatened species.

© Brigitta L. House/Michelin

the wonder of it, time your visit so you can watch the sunset from Haleakala's 10,023-foot summit. (Sunrise brings hordes of visitors, and traffic. Skip it.)

Along the Haleakala Highway, the scenery changes from lush vegetation at the base to lurid lavascape at the top—over a span of 40 miles.

Park Highlights

Maximize your experience by visiting the following places.

Kalahaku Overlook

This is a good place to spy sprouts of silversword (*see box, above*). Silverswords bloom just one time

per human generation, and then the plant promptly dies.

Puu Ulaula Overlook

Get to this viewpoint at sunset to take in the sweeping views. It's located near the visitor center.

Visitor Centers

You'll find maps and information at the park's three visitor centers:

◆ **Park Headquarters** – *Near park entrance on Rte. 378. 808-572-4400. Open year-round daily 8am–3:45pm.*

◆ **Haleakala Visitor Center** – *11mi south of the park headquarters at Puu Ulaula summit. Open daily dawn–3pm.*

Touring Tip

Thirty miles of trails crisscross the crater floor. Only experienced hikers should attempt these, and it takes twice as long to get out as it does to go in. The park service leads guided hikes weekly, and an outfitter runs **horseback rides** to the floor of the caldera *(Pony Express Tours; 808-667-2200; www.ponyexpresstours. com; 4 hrs; $182)*. If you're prepared for changeable conditions—rain, cold, and wind—you're the type of camper who will enjoy sleeping near a volcano! **Hosmer Grove Campground** *(no permit required)* is located at 6,800 feet elevation, and connects with **Hosmer Grove Nature Loop**, a half-mile nature trail that meanders though a cloud forest. Campsites have grills, picnic tables, water, and accessibility to toilets. The **Kipahulu Campground**, located about 1/8mi south of the Kipahulu Visitor Center, overlooks ocean cliffs and is a short walk from Oheo Gulch. The park also offers primitive campsites *(available by permit, issued at park headquarters)* and wilderness cabins.

- **Kipahulu Visitor Center** –
  *10mi south of Hana on Hana
  Hwy., at the east end of the park.
  808-248-7375. Open year-round
  daily 9am–5pm.*

Iao Valley State Monument★★

*Map p58. Iao Valley Rd. (Hwy. 32),
5mi west of Wailuku. 808-984-8109.
www.hawaiistateparks.org. Open
year-round daily 7am–7pm.
$5/car parking fee.*

Ancient Hawaiians carried their
royal dead into this verdant valley
for secret ceremonial burials. Now,
the bright green cliffs and gurgling
stream at the eroded core of an
age-old volcano have made it a
popular picnic and hiking venue.
The 6.2-acre park is laced with
hiking trails and offers beautiful
vistas. The highlight here is **Iao
Needle★★**, a basaltic spire that rises
1,200 feet above the valley floor.
A 1.5-mile trail meanders beneath
cliffs that spout spectacular
waterfalls after heavy rains.

Iao Needle directional marker

Oheo Gulch★★

*Map p59. On Pulaui Hwy., 10mi
south of Hana. 808-248-7375.
www.nps.gov/hale.*

One of the highlights along
the famed **Hana Highway★★★**
(see p 65) is Oheo Gulch, set in the
Kipahulu District of **Haleakala
National Park★★★** *(see p 62).*
At this picturesque spot, a series
of waterfalls tumbles from the
southeast flank of Haleakala,
feeding from one pool to another.
These are the two dozen famous
Pools of Oheo. The lure to dive in
and enjoy the water is powerful,
but the stream is dangerous,
frequently flooding in response to
rain squalls high above.
The simple marble grave of
celebrated aviator **Charles
Lindbergh** (1902–74) rests on
a promontory at the Palapala
Hoomau Hawaiian Church,
1.2 miles past Oheo Gulch.

Nakalele Point

*Map p58. Follow Hwy. 30 (Hana-
Honoapiilani Hwy.) 7mi north of
Kapalua.*

Set on Maui's northern coast,
Nakalele Point is an otherworldly
scene of twisted lava and hissing
ocean. In stark contrast to its lush
surroundings, the point is marked
by a US Coast Guard lighthouse.
Hike down the hill to the awesome
blowhole below the beacon, where
water erupts like a geyser, rising
100ft or more. There's a labyrinth
here at Nakalele Point. On a sunny
plateau overlooking the coastline,
chunks of white coral are laid out on
the green grass in a classic design.

© Hawaii Tourism Authority (HTA) / Max Wanger

SCENIC DRIVES

Local grocery stores sell T-shirts that read "I Survived the Road to Hana", though the dangers are mild these days; the road's narrow curves and blind corners have been improved greatly and signed extensively. The south side road, from Hana to Ulupalakua, is a more rugged experience still. Drive it once, and you'll understand it. White knuckles aside, this is one of the prettiest drives in the world.

Hana Highway★★★

Map pp58-59. The road begins as Rte. 36 at Kahului Airport; it then becomes Rte. 360. 52mi.

If you aren't inclined to the careful driving and endless curves of this road, there are many tour companies that will be more than happy to handle the task, while you sit and ogle *(for information, contact the Maui Visitors Bureau; see top p 56)*. Narrow curves and narrow bridges snake past rainforested tangles of countryside that will make you feel as if you're driving through a botanical garden. You'll cruise at about 10mph around approximately 600 curves, flanked by great walls of bushy, Dr. Seuss-like trees in some spots, skinny bamboo and drippy waterfalls at others.

The (barely) two-lane road is now in good condition after being first paved in 1984; it was truly a slice of Old Hawaii before it was modernized. Don't go too slowly, or you'll annoy the locals who use this as a commuting road. Do not film video while driving—that will bring you trouble from many quarters. And be sure to honk your horn at the hairpin turns to warn oncoming traffic; whoever gets to the stop sign first has the right of way.

Along the Highway

Garden of Eden Botanical Gardens & Arboretum – *Mile marker 10½. 808-572-9899. www.mauigardenofeden.com. Open year-round daily 8am–3pm. $15.* Scenes from *Jurassic Park* were filmed here. Walk the trails, have a picnic, and enjoy views of jungly hillsides and rocky coast.

Kaumahina State Wayside Park – *Mile marker 12.* Alas, the access to Puohokamoa Falls has been closed due to a property dispute, but you'll want to stretch your legs here, where gardens burst

© Hawaii Tourism Authority (HTA) / Tor Johnson

Waterfall along Hana Highway

Touring Tip

They warn you to gas up and pack snacks before you attempt the Hana Highway, and the gas part is true. There are no gas stations past **Paia★** *(see p75)* until you reach Hana town. At one of several fruit stands along the way, try some fresh coconut, banana bread or homemade fruit smoothies. Start out early in the morning, as the highway tends to become more trafficked as the day goes on. Keep in mind that you must yield to oncoming traffic on the one-lane bridges. It's best to have two drivers on this exhausting route; you'll want to switch so each of you can enjoy the views. And finally, plan your trip so you're not driving the Hana Highway after dark.

with torch and shell gingers. An unmarked trail meanders within a eucalyptus forest. Admire sweeping views of the ocean, just a short walk to the left of the parking lot.

Waianapanapa State Park – *Mile marker 32. 808-248-4843. Open year-round daily dawn–dusk.* Considered one of the must-stops on the Hana Highway, this park gets busy, but it's worth a visit. Attractions include a black-sand beach, caves, and cave pools for swimming. Hike the short ancient lava rock footpath for views of sea caves and the shoreline.

Hana – *At the end of Rte. 360.* Hana (population 1,235) is home to the deluxe **Hotel Travaasa Hana**, the Hana Coast Gallery, the Hasegawa General Store and a gas station. Stop at the **general store** for items that you didn't know you needed, like flip-flop socks and Spam sushi. Just south of town, follow the signs to Hamoa Beach *(see p61)*. A hike up to Fagan Memorial Cross reveals the best views of Hana town and the beautiful coastline.

Road to Hana

MUSEUMS

Talk about raising cane. At one time, Hawaii held 80 sugar plantations; now there are 2. The valley between Haleakala and the West Maui Mountains is still almost entirely planted in cane.

Alexander & Baldwin Sugar Museum

3957 Hansen Rd., Puunene. 808-871 -8058. www.sugarmuseum.com. Open year-round daily 9:30am– 4pm. Closed major holidays. $7. Smelling pleasantly of molasses, this museum chronicles the interplay of geography, water and people in growing sugar cane and producing sugar. Immigrant workers arrived in the mid-19C; their presence helped make Hawaii the melting pot it is today.

GARDENS

This picture-pretty spot in upcountry Maui features native plants, an aviary with nene geese, and great views of western mountains.

Kula Botanical Garden

638 Kekaulike Ave., 1mi from junction of Hwys. 377 & 37. 808- 878-1715. www.kulabotanical garden.com. Open year-round daily 8am–4pm. Closed major holidays. $10. For a sense of what Hawaii might have looked like before the Polynesians arrived (bringing their own plants and animals by canoe), take a look at the collection of native plants here.

This 8-acre site, perched at an elevation of 3,300 feet, features orchids, proteas, bromeliads, poisonous plants, native fauna, even the mighty koa tree, a broadleaf evergreen that can reach heights of 100 feet.

HISTORIC SITES

The lively seaport town of Lahaina was the first capital of the Kingdom of Hawaii (the center of government for the Hawaiian monarchy), and also a busy whaling port and plantation settlement.

Lahaina Historic Trail

Pick up a guide to historic trail sites at the Lahaina Visitor Center in the **Old Lahaina Courthouse**, between the famous banyan tree and Lahaina Harbor. Get a snapshot of Maui history on the Lahaina Historic Trail, a self-guided walking tour of 62 historic sites. Bronze plaques along Front Street mark points of interest. Highlights include **Baldwin House** (home of Protestant missionaries in the mid-1830s), **Hale Paahoe** (a jail for rowdy sailors), **Wo Hing Temple**, and the **Lahaina Jodo Mission**, featuring one of the largest statues of Buddha outside of Asia (it's 12ft high and weighs 3.5 tons).

FOR FUN

For the adventurous, nothing says "fun" like wriggling through a lava tube—unless it's biking down a volcano. Looking for a more mellow pursuit? Sample some pineapple or passionfruit wine.

Bike Down a Volcano

Several companies offer guided bike tours down Haleakala. Some companies specify a height or minimum age requirement (call to check before you go—see p 69 for outfitters to contact). Tour prices start at about $80 and up. (Look for online discounts.)

Imagine biking down the slopes of a volcano with a backdrop of fiery sunrise. Biking down Haleakala ("House of the Sun" in Hawaiian) is a true Maui adventure. While numerous accidents led the park service to suspend bike tours from the volcano's 10,000-foot summit, you can still join a tour group and begin your ride at 6,500 feet. Choose a tour that goes from Haleakala to the beach town of **Paia** (28 miles) or to an upcountry winery (20 miles). Not a bad way to spend a morning! Tour guides will take you up the volcano by van,

provide gear, and ride with you as you glide down the mountain. Average speed is 15–20mph, slowing down for turns and curves. Expect some wild belly-flips as you career down the mountain! The following **outfitters** will get you rolling:

♦ **Haleakala Bike Company** – *888-922-2453. www.bikemaui.com.*
♦ **Maui Sunriders** – *808-579-8970. www.mauibikeride.com.*
♦ **Maui Downhill Volcano Rides** – *808-871-2155 or 800-535-2453. www.mauidownhill.com.*

Head into a Lava Tube

205 Ulaino Rd., Hana (turn onto Ulaino Rd. at mile marker 31, and drive .4mi to cave). 808-248-7308. www.mauicave.com. Self-guided tours daily 10:30am–4pm. $12.

Don a hard hat and a flashlight and head into the **Hana Lava Tube★**, one of the world's largest

Biking down Haleakala

©Sheldon Kralstein/iStockphoto.com

© Hawaii Tourism Authority (HTA) / Tor Johnson

Free Hula for You-la

You might luck into a free Hawaiian dance performance in Lahaina's **Banyan Tree Park** *(off Front St. in downtown Lahaina)* if you visit during one of the many annual festivals *(see pp 10–11)*. You'll discover that hula isn't the hip-shaking extravaganza as depicted by Hollywood in *Blue Hawaii*; it's a serious art form. Hula Kahiko (traditional) is performed mainly with percussion instruments, while Hula Auana (contemporary) typically features ukuleles, acoustic and steel guitars and bass. Grass skirts, by the way, are non-Hawaiian, and scorned by traditional practitioners.

volcanic lava tubes.

No tight passages here (except the optional tiny chamber), so it's an easy walk into an underground lavascape of **stalactites, stalagmites,** and **flowstone.** The flowstone looks like chocolate syrup in some spots, and like candy kisses in others. Interpretive signage describes how the cavern was formed.

Also on the grounds is the **Red Ti Botanical Maze,** which is worth a meader through, if you're not in a hurry.

Learn Stand-up Paddling

Maria Souza's Stand-Up Paddle Surf School, 185 Paka Pl, Kihei. Mon–Fri 9am and 10am. 808-579-9231. www.standuppaddlesurfschool.com. Ages 7 and up. 90-minute lesson, $165. You must know how to swim to participate.

Stand-up paddle boarding (aka SUP), a fusion of surfing and paddling, is one of the fastest-growing sports in the world. It originated in Hawaii, some say, making this a dandy place to learn. You'll be in good hands with self-described "extreme water woman" Maria Sousa, a windsurfer, kite-surfer and SUP surfer, who can get you up and paddling in flat water in just 30 minutes. Go home with the ultimate souvenir: a new sport.

Taste Local Wine

Tedeschi Vineyards, Rte. 37 (Haleakala Hwy.), Ulupalakua. 808-878-6058. www.mauiwine.com. Free tours daily 10.30am and 1.30pm. Tasting room open daily 10am–5:30pm.

Located in upcountry Maui, on the slopes of Haleakala, these vineyards dot **Ulupalakua Ranch,** where cowboys still herd cattle.

FOR FUN

The pasturelands are beautiful, as are the views of the golden-sand-laced Kihei coastline below. Stroll the grounds, and sample some of the wines they make from grapes, pineapples and raspberries. The tasting room is housed in a renovated cottage; note the cool bar, cut from the trunk of a mango tree. Maui Blanc, made from pineapples, is a pleasant, and popular, wine. Maui Blush is sweetened by passionfruit. Most wines cost about $12 per bottle and up.

Take Pipiwai Trail

Follow the Hana Hwy. south to Haleakala National Park entrance at Kipahulu (10mi south of Hana). $10 park admission. Trail is located across the street from parking lot. This moderately strenuous 3.7-mile trail offers rewards aplenty, including a sweet-smelling guava forest, an eerily dark bamboo grove, and two sets of waterfalls, including 400-foot Waimoko Falls. Plan on three hours, so you can meander. Wear hiking shoes and prepare to get muddy.

Learn to Surf

Maui Waveriders meets at two locations: 133 Prison St. in Lahaina and 1975 S. Kihei Rd. in Kihei. 808-875-4761. www.mauiwaveriders.com. 2hour group lessons, $60 adults, $50 kids ages 8 and up. Private lessons, $140. Private lessons are available for kids under age 8.
"If you don't have fun, and you don't ride a wave, you don't pay," according to the Castleton family, who run **Maui Waveriders**—and so far, they say, only one person has asked for a refund. They say they can teach you to surf in one easy lesson—cowards and non-swimmers included. Classes are organized by age group and families; after the two-hour lesson, surfer wannabes can give it a try on their own if boards are available. As far as surfing on Maui goes, the south shore boasts some gentle breaks that are great for beginners, including the "fastest ride in the world" at **Maalaea Harbor**, north of Kihei on the west coast. **Honolua Bay**, on the northwest tip of the island, is famous for its winter waves, which can range in size from 4- to 20-foot faces. Then there's **Jaws** *(see box p60)*, the mother of all waves, in

Sliding Sands Trail

© Hawaii Tourism Japan (HTJ)

More Great Hikes on Maui
Halemauu Trail to Valley Rim is a pretty easy two-mile-plus round-trip walk through native shrubland to the rim of the 1,000ft Haleakala Crater *(in Haleakala National Park; trailhead is located on the road to Puu Ulaula Overlook).* If you're in good shape, try the strenuous **Keoneheehee Trail**, also called **Sliding Sands Trail** *(also in the park; trailhead is located near the visitor center parking lot).* It's a difficult half-day hike to the first cinder cone—an elevation change of 2,800 feet in 4 miles—but it's a once-in-a-lifetime experience of the breathtaking Mars-like landscape of red, orange, silver and blue cinder cones within the crater.

Molokini Island

Peahi Bay, where the enormous swells are truly jaw-dropping and for experts only.

Snorkel at Molokini Island★★

Excursions below depart from Maalaea Harbor, off Hwy. 30. Prices start at $89 and up; check websites for online discounts.

Three miles off Makena on Maui's west coast lies an enchanting crescent of Crater Rim known as **Molokini Island**. Eighteen-acre Molokini rises 160 feet above waters filled with coral heads and a dazzling array of tropical fishes. This protected area, a Marine Conservation District, is irresistible to snorkelers and divers. Molokini is also a seabird sanctuary, and a great place to see migrating whales in season *(Dec–May)*. Don't miss it! (Tip: Afternoon tours are typically cheaper, but the water is calmer in the morning, so tours are less likely to be cancelled.)

Boats run year-round from Maalaea and Lahaina. Companies who run trips to the island include **Trilogy Excursions** *(808-874-5649; www.sailtrilogy.com)*, **Pride of Maui** *(808-242-0955; www.prideof maui.com)*, and **Maui Classic Charters** *(800-736-5740; www.mauiclassiccharters.com)*.

Watch Whales

Few things are more thrilling to kids—and adults—than seeing a whale in the wild. Possibly the most graceful and amazing mammals of all, whales come to Hawaii by the thousands each winter—mostly humpbacks, but fin, blue and gray whales are occasionally seen. Whale season in Hawaii runs roughly from December through mid-May, before the massive cetaceans head back north to their Alaska feeding grounds. Respect for the whales is a big deal here; during whale season, personal watercraft and parasail boats are prohibited.

There's no lack of whale-watching excursions in Maui, but the most well regarded of these is operated by the **Pacific Whale Foundation** *(808-249-8811 or 800-942-5311; www.pacificwhale. org)*. This nonprofit group, a marine research and conservation organization, operates trips led by certified naturalists. They report a 99 percent success rate in seeing

Windsurfing in Maui

© Hawaii Tourism Authority (HTA) / Tor Johnson

whales; trips run from December through mid-May.
Cool feature: You can listen to whale song on underwater hydrophones. Trips depart from Lahaina and Maalaea Harbor *($33.95 adults, free for children ages 6 and under)*. Look for online booking discounts on their website.

Windsurf on Maui

People move to Maui just for the windsurfing—that's how awesome it is! Expert board sailors go airborne at **Hookipa Beach Park** *(Hwy. 36, 6mi east of the intersection of Haleakala & Hana Hwys.; see p61)*, taking advantage of the strong trade winds that blow in from the north. Everyone else heads to the gentler waters at **Spreckelsville** and **Kanaha** *(west of Hookipa Beach on the north coast)*, as well as **Kihei Beach** *(on the west coast at*

the junction of Hwys. 311 & 31) for lessons and practice. No need to plan ahead for lessons; windsurfing schools often set up shop on the beach. You can rent gear at one of the many sports shops in Paia, Wailuku and Kahului.

Zip Over a Cliff

Skyline Eco-Adventures, Hwy. 378 (Crater Rd.), Kula. 808-878-8400. www.zipline.com. $89. Also offered in Kaanapali (eight ziplines) and on Kauai and the Big Island; trip meets at the Fairway Shops. $113 (includes lunch).
Ziplining is catching on everywhere, and Maui is no exception. After a pretty, half-mile hike through a forest, you'll walk to the edge of the valley, get strapped into a harness, and soar over gulches, cliffs, and valleys on a zipline strung on the slopes of Haleakala. You can do this five times if you choose—since five ziplines are strung through this property on Haleakala Ranch. They've been doing ziplining here since 2002—and so far, so good! And, they promise, once you've done it, you will be thoroughly hooked (or perhaps they're just stringing us along). And if you get into the harness and decide, "Nah, not for me," no worries. This is Maui, after all!

See? Turtles.
If you're lucky enough, you'll go flipper-to-flipper with a **honu** while you're snorkeling or diving in Hawaii. A *honu* is a green sea turtle *(Chelonia mydas)*, an endangered species that feeds in coastal waters around the Hawaiian Islands. Adults can weigh up to 400 pounds, with a carapace (upper shell) around 3.5 feet long. Why are green sea turtles green? They feed mainly on algae. Revered by Native Hawaiians, they are protected by law—do not chase, harass or, heaven forbid, try to ride them. Yes, they can bite.

MUST DO MAUI

FOR KIDS

Teens and older kids thrill to Maui's wild outdoors scene, with its opportunities to surf, windsurf and snorkel at every turn. For little ones, nothing beats the chance to see wild creatures (from a safe distance).

Maui Ocean Center★★

192 Maalaea Rd., Maalaea. 808-270-7000. www.mauiocean center.com. Open Sept–Jun daily 9am–5pm (Jul & Aug until 6pm). $26 adults, $19 children (ages 3–12).

Though it's compact by mainland standards, this center is a match for much larger facilities elsewhere with its imaginative exhibits that reveal what lies beneath the waters just outside its walls. The state-of-the-art aquarium's centerpiece is a tunnel within its main tank, putting visitors in the center of a giant fishbowl, where sharks glide past and spotted eagle rays swoop through a 750,000-gallon tank. The **Living Reef** houses live corals and teems with moray eels, reef fish, sharks, octopuses and more. Outdoor pools are home to sea turtles, tide-pool creatures--some of which kids can touch--and stingrays, while the Marine Mammal Discovery Center lures kids with the eerie song of the humpback. At the **Bubble Net** exhibit, see what it feels like to be krill, in danger of being devoured by a gigantic humpback whale in Alaska bubble netting. **Hammerhead Harbor** brings kids (and parents) eye-to-eye with hammerhead sharks. The **Sea Jelly Gallery** is an awesome glimpse at the beauty of nature, as these intriguing creatures pulse and swirl in the tank's currents. Maui Ocean Center is also a key conservation

Touring Tip

You can see whales without spending a dime at **McGregor Point** *(mile marker 9 on Hwy. 30)* in Lahaina, in the shallow waters offshore. Look for the cetaceans as they migrate past the island's west coast. Want to learn more about these gentle giants? Take a peek at the **Whalers Village Museum** in Kaanapali to see whaling artifacts, weapons, ship models, scrimshaw, and a cool sperm whale skeleton *(2435 Kaanapalai Pkwy., in Whalers Village; 808-661-5992; www.whalers village.com/museum; open year-round daily 9:30am–10pm).*

organization, helping propagate green sea turtles for release to the ocean each winter.

Whale exhibit, Maui Ocean Center

© Hawaii Tourism Authority (HTA) / Tor Johnson

PERFORMING ARTS

With two theaters, gallery space and an outdoor stage, the Maui Arts and Cultural Center always has something going on. Maui is home to Hawaiian music's popular artists, such as Hapa and Keali'i Reichel, who have blended modern styles with ancient traditions.

Maui Arts & Cultural Center

1 Cameron Way, off Kahului Beach Rd., Kahului. Box office: 808-242-7469. www.mauiarts.org. Box office open Mon–Sat 10am–6pm.

Peter Frampton, the Larry Carlton Trio and New Shanghai Circus are among the mainland acts that have appeared at this state-of-the-art performance space/visual-arts gallery. It's known as a showcase for global as well as local talent.

Maui Arts & Cultural Center

© Brigitta L. House/Michelin

SHOPPING

The island has more than 50 galleries and a thriving community of artists. Discover cool finds (and delicious donuts) in Makawao.

⚓ Lahaina★★

Front Street, the main drag in downtown Lahaina, is chock-a-block with shops. Need a pair of rubber slippahs (local lingo for flip-flops), a plumeria-scented candle, or surfer gear? It's all here, and then some. Yes, there's a huge amount of cheesy stuff—loads of T-shirts,

Shop in Lanai

© Brigitta L. House/Michelin

and lots of questionable craft items made elsewhere—but if you're willing to put in some effort, you'll turn up some gems.

Maui Hands *(612 Front St.; also in Paia and Kaanapali)* boasts a collection created solely by Maui-based artists. Items range from Christmas ornaments to tables carved from koa wood (for a cool $10,000).

Makawao

From Route 36 (Hana Highway), take Route 365 South 5mi to Makawao.

Formerly a rough-and-tumble *paniolo* (cowboy) town, Makawao retains Western storefronts that are now home to galleries, shops and eateries. **Baldwin Avenue** is a fun shopping zone with a New Age tilt. Fortify yourself with one of the famous cream puffs from **Komoda Bakery**, and check out the Western-wear-with-attitude at **Aloha Cowboy** (including handbags made from cowboy boots). Good gallery stops include Viewpoints, David Warren, and Hot Island Glass. Art lovers, don't miss **Hui No' Eau** (*2841 Baldwin Ave.*), a two-story stucco building that houses Maui's most prominent arts organization. Check out art classes, demos, exhibits and a gift shop featuring work of local artists (*Mon–Sat, 10am–4pm*).

Paia★

Located 7mi east of the Kahului Airport on the Hana Hwy.

A former plantation town, Paia (say pah-EE-ah) has evolved into a bohemian beach hangout, a place with small boutiques and natural-food shops. The town makes a fun place to wander, even if the shops keep irregular hours. ("When the wind is right at Hookipa, everybody takes off," is the way locals explain it.) Fashionistas head directly to **Tamara Catz** (*83 Hana Hwy.*), a local designer whose lines of beaded skirts, bronze miniskirts, and embroidered sundresses have been featured in the pages of the *Sports Illustrated* swimsuit issue,

SELF, *Vogue*, *Lucky*, and *InStyle* magazines. Try **Paia Mercantile** (*corner of Hana Hwy. & Baldwin Ave.*) for pottery and art glass; **Nuage Bleu** (*76 Hana Hwy.*) for trendy girlie duds from Trina Turk, Ella Moss, Paige Denim, and Juicy Couture; **Maui Crafts Guild** (*69 Hana Hwy.*), a cooperative gallery featuring the work of 25 artists; and **Maui Girl Beachwear** (*12 Baldwin Ave.*), for the tiniest bikinis imaginable. Arrive hungry—the **Paia Fish Market** (*100 Baldwin Ave.*) makes some of the best fish and chips on Maui. They're positively *ono* (delicious)!

Takamiya Market

359 Market St., Wailuku. 808 244 3404. www.takamiyamarket.com. In Central Maui, this local supermarket is the go-to destination for great picnic fare. (Why pay for restaurant take-out when you can DIY?) Prepared foods are a specialty here. Plan a beachside feast (or take-along hiking lunch) featuring Takamiya's tasty kalua pork, *ahi/tako poke*, or a chilled fish salad.

Maui Swap Meet

Maui Community College parking lot, 310 W. Kaahumanu Ave., Kahului. Open Sat 7am–1pm. 808-244-3100. www.maui exposition.com. $.50.

Touring Tip

You'll find surf shops all over Maui. A couple of the best known are **Maui Tropix** (*261 Dairy Rd., Kahului; 808-871-8726; www.mauitropixsurfco.com*), the exclusive dealer of **Maui Built gear** (*boards, tees, sunglasses, etc.*), and **Neil Pryde Maui** (*400 Hana Hwy., Kahului; 808-877-7443; www.neilprydemaui.com*). Once a windsurfer shop, Neil Pryde has expanded into a water-sports superstore, catering to surfers and kiteboarders as well as the windsurfing crowd.

SHOPPING

The Shops at Wailea

© Brigitta L. House/Michelin

Forget the strip malls—do your shopping here, where you can find a fascinating assortment of trash and treasures. Two hundred-plus vendors offer everything from vintage muumuus to handmade jewelry to Hawaiian nose flutes made with Maui bamboo. (File that one under, "Things you didn't know you needed but must have.")

The Shops at Wailea

3750 Wailea Alanui Dr., Wailea. Open daily 9:30am–9pm. 808-891-6770. www.theshopsatwailea.com. Free shuttles run from most Wailea resort hotels to The Shops at Wailea.

Maui's most glamorous shopping address features more than 70 shops and restaurants, plus gallery receptions and live entertainment. Beyond the usual designer boutiques, interesting stops include **Celebrities Gallery of Celebrity Art** (where you can find artwork created by Slash, David Bowie, and John Lennon, among others) and **Dolphin Gallery**, where works include the stunning glass wave sculptures by David Wight. Here, **Tommy Bahama** coexists happily with **Tiffany & Co**, and you can even find an outpost of Hawaii's answer to a general store, **ABC Stores**, which stocks everything from Hawaiian jewelry to hula dolls for your dashboard *(www.abcstores.com).*

© Brigitta L. House/Michelin

Maui's Gallery Scene

Everybody knows about the island's wet-and-wild outdoor scene, but Maui isn't all surfer dudes and babes in bikinis. Surprise: the island has a high concentration of art galleries, more than 50 in all, and an active, thriving community of artists. Their work turns up in some surprising places, too, like outdoor fairs, upscale resort shopping villages, and artists' cooperatives in Paia and Makawao.

Always in Style: The Aloha Shirt

Say "Aloha" to Hawaii's favorite shirt. Even the stuffiest of offices observes "Aloha Friday" when the colorful shirts come out to play. Vintage models from the 1930s and 40s, with real coconut buttons, are collectibles, worth thousands of dollars. The earliest Hawaiian shirts were made for plantation workers, evolving in the 1920s into wild floral designs. With the birth of rayon, the dazzlingly hued, tropical-themed garments became a must-have souvenir for the cruise-ship crowd. Now, thanks to laser technology, those old designs are new again, and hotter than ever.

© Brigitta L. House/Michelin

Whalers Village

2435 Kaanapali Pkwy., Kaanapali (Lahaina). 808-661-4567. www.whalersvillage.com. Free shuttle to Whalers Village daily throughout the Kaanapali Beach resort area.

You can shop for surfer duds with sand between your toes—that's the beauty of Whalers Village, a real shopping destination set on Maui's most famous beach. There's a **whaling museum** here, too, with a giant whale skeleton as a centerpiece but, really, it's all about the shopping.

Some of these names, like **Coach** and **Louis Vuitton**, you can find elsewhere but, hey, you can't beat the ambience! For goods that are unique, check out the batik designs at **Blue Ginger** and **Blue Ginger Kids**, the 14K gold Hawaiian glass slipper (flip-flop) set with diamonds at **Na Hoku Jewelers**, the too-cute hula-girl tote bags at **Sand People**, and island-made koa bowls, Ni'hau shell jewelry, and more at **Totally Hawaiian.**

Special Events – Whalers Village is also the place to go for fun free events, like lei-making, hula lessons and dance performances, or one of the most-anticipated happenings, the **Maui Onion Festival** (May). Festivities include chef's demonstrations and a beer garden.

Whalers Village

© Brigitta L. House/Michelin

Touring Tip

Seek out the island's best ice-cream shop, **Roselani Tropics Ice Cream** *(918 Lower Main St, Waikulu)*. Run by the Nobriga family for as many years as anyone can remember, Roselani has creamy treats made with island ingredients such as mango, poha berry and coconut.

SHOPPING

NIGHTLIFE

Want to know who's playing where? Pick up a free copy of *Maui Time Weekly*, which provides loads of entertainment listings. Click on *"The Grid" (www.mauitime.com).*

MUST DO MAUI

Mulligan's on the Blue

100 Kaukahi St., Wailea. 808-874-1131. www.muligans ontheblue.com.

South Maui's premier party spot features live entertainment most nights, including "Jazz on the Blue" (live jazz acts) on Saturday, Irish music on Sunday, and a Rocking 80s Party every Monday. Mulligan's Happy Hour pupu platters are legendary, and the drink of choice (besides a perfectly-poured Guinness) is Mulligan's Mai Tai, topped with a float of Hana Bay dark rum.

Ambrosia Martini Lounge

1913 S. Kihei Rd., Kihei 808-891 1011. www.ambrosiamaui.com

Voted "best bar" by the readers of *Maui Time Weekly*, this posh lounge has style, expert mixologists, high-octane DJs and friendly ambience. The best drink deals are on Sunday and Martini Mondays.

Ulalena

Maui Theatre, 878 Front St., Lahaina. 808-856-7900. www.ulalena.com. $60-$80 adults; $30 children.

Blending the showy acrobatics of Cirque du Soleil with traditional Hawaiian legends, chants and dances, Ulalena is among the most authentic such shows in the islands—yet also hugely entertaining and modern. It shares its theater home with an Elvis presentation that, though obviously not Hawaiian, is also very popular.

Kimo's

845 Front St., Lahaina. 808-661-4811. www.kimosmaui.com.

Lahaina's Front Street is a bustling place at night, and Kimo's is one of the most popular live music venues on the street. Local musicians perform almost every night--covering genres that range from dance to Hawaiian to reggae--with Friday nights devoted to bigger name acts from around the islands.

Early Hawaiian Music

The first musical instruments on the islands were simple wooden drums, covered with sharkskin. Dancers held small stones between their fingers and clicked them, and they tied coconut shells to their arms and legs and tapped them with sticks to create percussion. The earliest wind instruments were bamboo flutes and conch shells. Storytellers chanted poems and myths while the music played.

© Hawaii Tourism Authority (HTA) / Tor Johnson

SPAS

It's amazing what can be done with coffee beans, volcanic clay and Hawaiian honey. Maui spas match those anywhere on earth for luxurious ease. Many feature treatments based on local materials and traditional Hawaiian techniques

Honua Spa

Hotel Travaasa Hana, 5021 Hana Hwy., Hana. 888-820-1043. travaasa.com/maui.

Named after the Hawaiian word for earth, Honua Spa takes tranquility to the next level—sheer bliss. Can't decide between a massage and a body wrap? You won't have to; the pink clay wrap and pohaku wela hot stone massage are both superb. Another popular treatment is the deep moisture facial, with layers of organic jasmine, papaya, jojoba and shea butter.

Spa Grande

Grand Wailea Resort, 3850 Wailea Alanui Dr., Wailea. 808-875-1234. www.grandwailea.com.

A typical spa experience here begins with a one-hour termé

Spa Grande
© Grand Wailea Resort

Wailea hydrotherapy session—meaning, you choose a pool, perhaps an aromatic soak, a cascading waterfall bath or a coconut milk soak.

Next comes the really hard part, selecting from more than 100 treatments. Many incorporate local ingredients: there's a seashell massage, a volcanic ash facial, and an awaphui (ginger) salt body glow, for example. The latter features a mixture that sounds (and smells) good enough to eat: fresh ginger root, lemon grass and Hawaiian honey, followed by an application of macadamia nut and coconut oil. Try the deep shiatsu barefoot massage, wherein a therapist walks on your back.

Willow Stream Spa

Fairmont Kea Lani Maui, 4100 Wailea Alanui Dr., Wailea. 808-875-2229. www.fairmont.com.

Suffering from the effects of too much sun? They know just what to do at Willow Stream: a gentle application of aloe and native ti leaves will remedy the problem. Facials are absolutely irresistible here, especially the Awapuhi-chai treatment that uses organic mud scented with gingered chai, and sure to leave you happily aglow. The new 9,000-square-foot facility includes a "mud bar" and soothing relaxation areas.

KAUAI★★★

This lush tropical island is home to rain forests, waterfalls, sparkling sand beaches, towering sea cliffs and 5,148-foot Mount Waialeale.
Visitor information: 800-262-1400; www.gohawaii.com/kauai.

Grand and diverse, Kauai is the beloved "auntie," to use a Hawaiian term, of the Islands, the oldest and fourth-largest of the main islands. Lush fields of greenery and thick rain forests spill down from **Mount Waialeale**, the island's central peak, earning Kauai the nickname, "The Garden Isle." The rain that falls on the 5,148-foot peak of Mt. Waialeale feeds seven rivers, including the state's only navigable river, and produces an ongoing show of gushing waterfalls. A deep cleft runs across the western end of the island, creating the impressive **Waimea Canyon★★**, nicknamed the "Grand Canyon of the Pacific" *(see p87)*. The stunning **Na Pali Coast★★★** *(see p85)*, with its 2,700-foot sea cliffs, lies on Kauai's northwest coast. Adventurers flock here to hike the strenuous, 11-mile **Kalalau Hiking Trail★★★**, considered one of the finest short hiking trails in the world *(see p97)*. If your idea of Hawaiian paradise is simply relaxing on tropical

beaches, don't despair. Kauai's southern and western sides are sunny and dry, and ringed with pretty stretches of warm, white sand. Though the North Shore sees frequent rain showers, it also has plenty of sunny interludes—and some of the most alluring beaches in the state. In fact, Kauai is home to 43 beaches—some 50 miles—

Fast Facts

- Kauai is home to some 70,000 people.
- The 533-square-mile island measures 33 miles long and 25 miles wide at its widest point.
- Most of Kauai's land— 97 percent—has been set aside for conservation and agriculture.
- Mount Waialeale, located roughly in the middle of the island, is one of the wettest spots on earth, with an average annual rainfall of 444 inches.
- Waimea Canyon plunges to depths of 3,000 feet in places.

Aerial view of fields in Kauai

©Jiang Chen/Bigstockphoto.com

KAUAI

≤ Diving or snorkeling site

| 0 | | 5 | | 10 mi |
| 0 | | | 15 km | |

Hotels
1. Grand Hyatt Kauai
2. Hanalei Bay Resort
3. Kauai Marriott Resort
4. Koa Kea Hotel
5. Koloa Landing
6. Outrigger Waipouli Beach
7. St. Regis Princeville Resort
8. Sheraton Kauai Resort
9. Waimea Plantation Cottages

Restaurants
1. Beach House
● Kaui Grill
2. Ono Family Restaurant
3. Red Salt
4. Roy's Poipu Bar & Grill
● Tidepools

more beach per mile of coastline than any of the other islands. And as on all the islands, all beaches are public. Most of Kauai's residents now live along the Coconut Coast on the east shoreline, including **Lihue**, Kauai's main town, **Wailua** and **Kapaa**. Tourist services cluster around three island resort areas: Lihue, sunny **Poipu** on the south shore, and the **Princeville** and **Hanalei Bay** areas on the north shore. The west side has quaint old-fashioned plantation-style towns, including charming Waimea and Hanapepe.

Fun Facts

- Kauai Coffee is the largest coffee plantation in the US (31,000 acres).
- Captain Cook made his first landing in the Hawaiian Islands at Waimea Beach on Kauai.
- Huleia National Wildlife Refuge is home to 31 species of birds.
- The Kilauea Lighthouse is one of the country's most intact historic light stations.

KAUAI

BEACHES

Kauai has more accessible beaches than any other Hawaiian island. As on all the islands, all beaches on Kauai, from broad swaths of white sand to tiny, hidden coves, are open to the public. Even private, fancy resorts provide public access walkways to the beach.

Hanalei Bay Beach★★★

North shore, off Hwy. 560.
Any road off Hwy. 560 will take you to the water.

This large, beautiful half-moon beach is one of the most popular on Kauai's north shore.

The curving crescent of white sand fronts the town of **Hanalei**, which lies at the base of picturesque mountains—some call it the most scenic beach in Hawaii. It's tough to argue the point. Hanalei Bay Beach, featuring a series of three beaches strung along a too-blue-to-be-true bay, offers a bit of everything. The western end harbors the calmest waters, while the center of the bay boasts the highest surf. You can walk the entire stretch; there are picnic areas, restrooms and showers along the way. **Hanalei Beach Park**, near the east end, is a good spot for relaxing sunset viewing.

Touring Tip

For your own private slice of sand head to **Secret Beach**. You'll share this golden stretch of sand with a handful of locals on a busy day; walk down the beach toward the Kilauea Lighthouse, and you'll have even more privacy. To get there, take Kalihiwai Road, off Highway 56, a half-mile west of Kilauea. Turn right onto the first dirt road and follow it to the parking lot. The trail to the beach is easy to spot. In back of the beach is a freshwater lagoon; a rope swing hangs in a tall tree here.

Poipu Beach Park★★★

South shore, off Poipu Rd.

Located on the sunny, dry side of Kauai, this hard-to-resist beach is consistently ranked as among the best in the nation. It has

Looking toward Hanalei

© Hawaii Tourism Authority (HTA) / Tor Johnson

MUST SEE KAUAI

Poipu Beach

© Hawaii Tourism Authority (HTA) / Tor Johnson

everything going for it: fine, white sands, tropical trade winds, and a range of water conditions to keep swimmers, snorkelers and surfers all blissfully content.

The beach consists of a string of three white crescents of sand, running from the Sheraton Kauai Resort east to Poipu Beach Park. Surfers and boogieboarders head to the rocky outcroppings to ride offshore breaks (rentals and lessons are available from small beachside concessions). Families and bathers stick to the east side of the rock jetty, where the relative absence of surf makes for calm waters. It's easy to make a day of it here; Poipu

Beach Park has showers, lifeguards and picnic areas. It's also one of the most-developed resort areas on the island, with a range of new lodging and dining choices, along with small shops and tour operators.

Spouting Horn★ – If you're in the Poipu Beach area, stop to see the Spouting Horn, Kauai's answer to western geysers. The frothy surf gushes into a lava tube, and then bursts up through a small opening at the surface. Sprays can reach up to 50 feet in the air, especially on windy days. At dusk, the rays of the setting sun paint the spray in a rainbow of colors.

Monk Seals

If you're lucky, you may walk out on the beach one morning to find a Hawaiian monk seal basking in the sand. The Hawaiian monk seal remains one of the most endangered species on earth; there are only about 1,200 left

that call the waters and beaches of Hawaii home. Stay at least 100 feet away; when taking photos, leave the flash off, and never shout or throw things at the seals in order to make them move. *For more information, visit www.kauaimonkseal.com.*

© Hawaii Tourism Authority/Pierce M Myers Photography

BEACHES

Kee Beach

© Hawaii Tourism Authority (HTA) / Tor Johnson

Kee Beach★

North shore, at the end of Hwy. 560.
The backdrop at Kee Beach—Na
Pali sea cliffs and tropical woods—
is hard to beat. Add a sandy bottom
and gentle waters, and you've
found a beachgoer's paradise.
It's one of the few **North Shore**
beaches that often has calm waters
during winter's high northerly swell
season. Tidepools are popular with
families who bring their kids to
poke around in the safe shallows.
Nestled at the end of the road on
Kauai's north shore, Kee sits near the
start of the famed **Kalalau Trail★★**
along the **Na Pali Coast★★★**.
Looming to your left, as you
approach the shoreline, is the
1,280-foot-tall sea cliff dubbed Bali
Hai, as it was known in the movie
South Pacific. Bring your snorkeling
gear; you'll spot tropical fish around
the reef at the right of the cove.

Polihale Beach★

West shore, off Hwy. 50.

○ *Take Hwy. 50 west from
Waimea to the end of the paved
road. Continue straight on the dirt
road to Polihale.*

The state park lies at the north end
of the beach. **Queen's Pond,** with
calmer waters for swimming, is at
the south end. Stand on this vast
beach, looking out into the wild
surf, and you'll think you've been
transported back in time. It's hard to
imagine beaches like this still exist
in America: miles of golden sand,
rugged dunes—and you won't have
to fight the crowds, if you're willing
to walk a little.
The isolated, golden beach,
stretching 17 miles, is the state's
longest and one of its most
serene. (**Warning:** the surf can be
dangerous.) Granted, Polihale Beach
is a bit difficult to get to, resting on
the westernmost point on the island
down a long, dirt road, but it's worth
the trek. According to Hawaiian
mythology, Polihale was the
gateway to the Afterworld, drawing
spirits and ghosts to its shores.
After resting, the spirits would
climb the towering sea cliffs and
leap off to get to Po, the offshore
Afterworld. Polihale means "House
of Po." **Polihale State Park** lies at
the northern end of the beach,
equipped with restrooms, showers
and picnic areas.

PARKS AND NATURAL SITES

Discover cloud-shrouded mountains, misty rain forests, sea cliffs, caves, blowholes, fern grottoes, canyons and more.

Na Pali Coast★★★

Begins at the end of the road at Kee Beach, on Kauai's northwest coast.

The 22-mile stretch of rugged and remote coastline along Kauai's northwest shores is arguably one of the most beautiful natural spots on earth. Known the world over, the Na Pali Coast, stretching from Kee Beach in the north to Polihale State Park in the west, has inspired poets, artists, and photographers for thousands of years. It's also been the backdrop for several movies *(see box, on right)*.

Some historians believe that this area was the first to be settled in Kauai by the early Hawaiians. Today, it is accessible only by the strenuous **Kalalau Hiking Trail★★★** *(see p97)*, guided boat or kayak trips (several outfitters offer Na Pali Coast excursions), or viewed from a helicopter *(see p95)*. No matter how you see the dramatic coastline—with its

Pretty as a Picture

It's no surprise that many people get an eerie sense of *déjà vu* when they land in Kauai; after all, the island has been a favorite of Hollywood filmmakers for decades. In all, Kauai has served as the backdrop for more than 60 major movies and television shows, including the beachy, island scenes in *South Pacific*, the wedding scene in *Blue Hawaii*, the opening waterfall shot in *Jurassic Park*, and the jungle scenes in *Outbreak*.

soaring sea cliffs, hanging valleys, gushing waterfalls, mysterious sea caves, lava tubes, and pristine beaches—you won't be disappointed.

Make sure that you have plenty of room on your camera and extra battery power for this excursion.

PARKS AND NATURAL SITES

© Hawaii Tourism Authority (HTA) / Ron Garnett

Na Pali Coast

View of Kalalau Valley

© Hawaii Tourism Authority (HTA) / Tor Johnson

Kokee State Park★★

Off Hwy. 550, 15mi north of Kekaha. 808-274-3444. www.hawaiistateparks.org. Open year-round daily dawn–dusk.

This cool, mountainous park on the far west end of Kauai offers the chance to visit one of the world's most intriguing "cloud forests," a place where nearly nonstop mist and rain create an otherworldly landscape. On your way there, you'll have several great views of Waimea Canyon.

Once in the park, there are not-to-be-missed lookouts across the deep Kalalau Valley, plunging to the remote Na Pali Coast. The 4,345-acre park features forests of koa and red-blossoming ohia lehua trees, and a spiderweb of rippling streams. On clear days, you may have views of rainy Mt. Waialeale and below to Alakai Swamp. **The Lodge at Kokee** *(see box below)* offers rustic cabins for overnight visitors.

Kokee Natural History Museum – *Located at mile marker 15. 808-335-9975. www.kokee.org. Open year-round daily 10am–4pm.* Stop by this tiny museum, located at the park headquarters, to check out the displays of ancient artifacts and local plants.

Hiking in the Park – There are 45 miles of trails to explore in Kokee State Park, from easy nature walks to strenuous day hikes. Most offer fabulous views across the rugged Kauai interior, when the clouds part. Pick up trail maps at the Kokee Natural History Museum.

- The short **Nature Trail** near the museum offers a quick stretch of the legs and a look at native plants.
- One of the most popular hikes in the park, the **Pihea Trail** *(3.5mi one way; allow 4 hours; trailhead located about 4mi past museum)*

Cabins for Rent

If you're looking for an economical place to stay, close to hiking trails and fabulous mountain scenery, check into the cabins for rent at **Kokee State Park**. The Lodge at Kokee operates 12 cabins, each sleeping up to six people. The older cabins feature one room with bunk beds, kitchen and bath.

Newer cabins have two bedrooms, a living area, kitchen and bath. All come equipped with bed linens and cooking utensils. You can rent the cabins year-round, but make sure you reserve months in advance *(contact the Lodge at Kokee, PO Box 367, Waimea, HI 96796; 808-355-6061; www.thelodgeatkokee.net).*

KAUAI

MUST SEE

Waimea Canyon

© Hawaii Tourism Authority (HTA) / Tor Johnson

traverses a high ridge between the Kalalau Valley and the Alakai Swamp, with sweeping views of valley cliffs dropping to the ocean.

+ If you're up for a challenge (and don't mind getting muddy and wet), try the **Alakai Swamp Trail**. The mossy 3.5-mile path cuts through thick rain forests and swampy bogs before reaching Kilohana Lookout.

Waimea Canyon State Park★★

11mi north of Kekaha on Hwy. 550 (Kokee Rd.). 808-274-3444. www.hawaiistateparks.org. Open year-round daily dawn–dusk.
Mark Twain called it the "Grand Canyon of the Pacific." Although it measures some 10 miles long, 1 mile wide, and some 2,700 feet deep, it's not only the size that's impressive about Waimea Canyon (the largest in the Pacific)—it's

Touring Tip

Pick up the island hiking map at the **Forestry and Wildlife Office** in Lihue at 3060 Eiwa Street, Room 306. The two-sided topo trail map costs $5 and is worth having if you plan to hike some of Kauai's trails, including those in Waimea Canyon State Park and Kokee State Park.

also the colors. The deeply scarred canyon walls, carved from rivers that pour down from Mt. Waialeale's wet summit, shimmer and shine in the sunlight like a palette of deep-hued jewels. Emerald-green folds and rugged, dark cliffs plunge into the rust-colored rivers below. On clear days (mornings are the best times), you may see waterfalls and rainbows against the eons-old volcanic rock.

Don't Feed the Birds

If you're hungry, the lodge next door to the **Kokee Natural History Museum** *(see p 86)* serves breakfast and lunch. Just don't feed the local jungle fowl that often congregate in the area. They may look like chickens but they're actually moa, brought over to the islands by early Polynesians. Today, moa live only on Kauai, the only island free of the mongoose, which loves to eat moa eggs for breakfast.

Bird watchers flock to the **Kilauea Point National Wildlife Refuge**, off Kuhio Highway *(Hwy. 56)* on the north shore of Kauai *(see p100)*. The refuge, overlooking rugged sea cliffs and Kilauea Bay, is home to nesting red-footed boobies (Feb–Aug), laysan albatrosses (Nov–Jun), wedge-tailed shearwaters (Apr–Oct), and red-tailed tropicbirds (Mar–Sept). Look for great frigate birds that come here to feed, and for the endangered nene goose *(see p 62)*. You'll also have fine views of the northern coastline from the refuge.

© Hawaii Tourism Authority (HTA) / Tor Johnson

Kilauea Point National Wildlife Refuge and Kilauea Lighthouse

There are several lookout points along the **Waimea Canyon Drive★★** *(see p89)*, and the canyon is accessible for hiking, camping and fishing. Check in with the staff at **Kokee State Park★★** headquarters *(see p 86)*, which also administers Waimea Canyon State Park, for information on recreational activities in and around the canyon.

Fern Grotto★

Off Hwy. 56 in Wailua Marina State Park. Boat rentals and guided excursions are available at the marina.

It's too bad you can't have this pretty place to yourself: a lava-rock cave heavily draped in tropical ferns, set along the historic Wailua River. Alas, misty Fern Grotto

is one of Kauai's most popular attractions and, some say, a bit too commercialized.

Rental boats, kayaks, pleasure boats and guided pontoons ply the Wailua River on their way to the grotto. It's a popular spot for weddings, too. On a guided trip, you'll see historic sites, tropical gardens and waterfalls. Several outfitters rent boats and offer guided trips of the grotto.

◆ **Kauai Kayak** – *866-482-9775; www.kauai-kayak.com.*

◆ **Wailua Kayak** – *808-822-3388. www.kayakwailua.com.*

◆ **Smith's Tropical Paradise** – *808-821-6895. www.smithskauai.com.*

MUST SEE KAUAI

SCENIC DRIVES

Almost everywhere you go in Kauai is a scenic drive, with views of waterfalls, misty mountains, pretty coves and sandy beaches.

Waimea Canyon Drive★★

*Map p81. **Begin in Waimea, on Hwy. 50, on the southwest coast of Kauai.***
Waimea Canyon is one of Hawaii's most dramatic sights. The 10-mile-long, 1-mile-wide, **2,700-foot-deep** canyon, the largest in the Pacific, offers majestic views akin to Arizona's Grand Canyon. Schedule a half-day for this excursion, more if you plan on doing one of the hikes in **Kokee State Park★★**.

Head west on Highway 50 to the town of **Waimea**, a good place to stop for picnic makings to take with you on the drive past the canyon. You'll pass the small **Captain Cook Monument** (the British explorer landed in Waimea Bay in 1778), before reaching Kokee Road (Highway 550) heading up to the canyon. As the narrow road climbs through wild sugar-cane fields, look back toward the southeast for glimpses of the blue ocean with its streaks of frothy, white surf.

Lookouts – Stop at **Waimea Canyon Lookout** for sweeping views of the plunging 2,700-foot-high walls and a kaleidoscope of multihued ridges.

Below, the Waimea River shimmers, snaking through the lush valley, and waterfalls tumble down the canyon like shiny silver ribbons. Continue on to **Puu Hinahina Lookout**, where, on clear days, you can look out to the ocean and the island of Niihau, 17 miles southwest of Kauai. There's also another fine view of the canyon from here. Follow Highway 550 to the **Kokee Natural History Museum** and park headquarters *(see p86)*, and stop to pick up information about the canyon, local flora and fauna, and hiking trails in **Kokee State Park★★** *(see p86)*. You'll be tempted to turn around here, but don't. Continue to the end of the road and you'll discover two more fine views of the rugged sea cliffs of the **Na Pali Coast★★★** *(see p85)* along the

View from Kalalau Lookout in Waimea Canyon State Park

©Photo75/iStockphoto.com

A favorite stop along Highway 50 on Kauai's western shore is the tiny **Shrimp Shack** in Waimea *(south side of Hwy. 50, in town center)*. Order a heaping plate of fresh coconut-battered Kauai shrimp, with hand-cut spicy fries and cold lemonade to go. Or, stop by **West Kauai Craft Fair** *(south side of Hwy. 50, in the center of Waimea)*, where a local vendor serves classic Hawaiian-style plate lunches of barbecue chicken, marinated pork or salmon, with sides of rice and cabbage *(Sat–Sun noon–5pm)*. Browse the open-air stands of locally made jewelry, art and wood products.

way at the **Kalalau** and **Puu O Kila lookouts**.

As you head back on your return trip, look for Makaha Ridge Road. You'll find it between mile markers 13 and 14 along Highway 550, near the Puu Hinahina Lookout. This is a great alternative return route. The road drops a dramatic 2,000 feet to the Pacific Ocean, with forest and valley views along the way. Makaha Ridge Road ends at the Pacific Tracking Station, part of the Pacific Range Facility owned by the US army. You'll find a nice oceanfront picnic area nearby.

North Shore★★★

Begin in the town of Kapaa on Kauai's east coast and take the Kuhio Hwy. (Hwy. 56) north.

Verdant taro fields, cloud-shrouded mountains, cascading waterfalls, postcard-perfect tropical beaches, rain forests, rivers and rugged sea cliffs await visitors who travel the narrow, winding roads and one-lane bridges of Kauai's pristine north shore.

Save some time to explore **Kapaa**, a pleasant 19C plantation town. There's plenty of shopping in town, including the open-air **Coconut Marketplace** *(see p101)*.

If you have time, you may also want to take a walking tour of the town, led by the **Kauai Historical Society**. The 90-minute tours highlight the town's history and unique architecture. If the wind is blowing and the waves are up, consider a walk on **Kapaa Beach**, a

Nounou mountain range between Wailua and Kapaa

© Hawaii Tourism Authority (HTA) / Tor Johnson

MUST SEE KAUAI

Touring Tip

The friendly town of **Hanalei** is a good place to stop for replenishment. There's a small shopping center with a cluster of craft and souvenir shops, and a handful of good restaurants. **Java Kai** *(5-5183C Kuhio Hwy.; 808-823-6887)* serves up breakfast and a great cup of coffee. Or you might want to hit the **Aloha Juice Bar** for fresh smoothies *(this mobile juice bar is parked in the lot of Old Ching Young Shopping Center, 5-5190 Kuhio Hwy, 808-826-6990).*

popular hangout with local surfers. Before heading north, take a side trip to view pretty **Opaekaa Falls** on the north branch of Wailua River. From Kuhio Highway, take Kuamoo Road (next to Coco Palms Resort) for 2 miles. You'll find a turnout on the right and a scenic overlook for the falls. Now, head north on the Kuhio Highway. If you've timed it right, stop by the 240-acre **Na Aina Kai Botanical Gardens** in Kilauea *(4101 Waiiapa Rd., 808-828-0525; www.naainakai.org)*. The gardens, including 12 theme gardens, a hardwood plantation, a moss-and-fern draped canyon and a sandy beach along the ocean, are open by guided tour only *(Tue, Wed, & Thu at 9am, 9:30am & 1pm)*. There's also a fun-filled Children's Garden, where kids can roam through a gecko-shaped maze of bushes and plants, and climb a treehouse. Farther up the road is the **Kilauea Point National Wildlife Refuge★★** *(see p100)*. Located on the northernmost point of the Hawaiian Islands, the oceanside preserve features a 1913 lighthouse, overlooking the crashing surf. This is a favorite spot for birdwatchers (look for soaring frigates and red-footed boobies). Back on the highway, you'll pass the ultra-luxe St. Regis Princeville Resort *(see Hotels)*, before reaching the beautiful Hanalei Lookout. Be sure to stop here for views of the luxuriant, ancient taro fields that spread across the valley. It's one of the finest views on Kauai and one of the island's most photographed vistas.

As you continue westward, you'll have good views of flat pasturelands (and a few grazing horses), bumping up against the folded mountain range.

Heading west out of town, there are pretty views of **Hanalei Bay★★★** and its crescent-shaped beaches *(see p82)*, as the road

Touring Tip

Keep your eyes peeled for the yellow and red **Lappert's Ice Cream** sign, and pull over fast when you see it *(1-3555 Kaumualii Hwy., Hanapepe; 808-335-6121; www.lappertshawaii.com)*. Lappert's super-rich Kauai-made ice cream (it contains 16-18 percent butterfat) is flavored with fresh island ingredients. Try Kauai pie, a decadent mixture of Kona coffee ice cream, chunky macadamia nuts, coconut and chocolate fudge, piled into a large waffle cone; or go for guava cheesecake, mango, Poha berry, banana fudge.

SCENIC DRIVES

Lumahai Beach

© Hawaii Tourism Authority (HTA) / Robert Coello

slices through mountains laced with waterfalls on one side and the turquoise-hued ocean on the other. There are a number of pullouts and overlooks along the way, including **Lumahai Beach★**, made famous by actress Mitzi Gaynor in the movie *South Pacific*. The pretty, white-sand beach, flanked by lava rocks, is fine for a stroll, but don't try swimming here. There are very strong currents and riptides that make it unsafe most of the time.

Next you'll pass **Tunnels Beach**, where deep, offshore caverns and a large reef make it a prime spot for diving and snorkeling, and **Haena Beach Park**, popular with locals and campers.

You'll reach pretty **Kee Beach★** *(see p84)* and the start of the **Na Pali Coast★★★** *(see p85)* at the end of the road. Take a refreshing swim in the balmy, gentle waters here; it's also a good place for snorkeling, around the reef toward the right side of the cove.

The backdrop is postcard-perfect, with sea cliffs and tropical forests. To your left as you approach the shoreline rises the impressive sea cliff, named Bali Hai in the movie *South Pacific*.

Still have energy and time? Consider a short jaunt on the **Kalalau Trail★★** *(see p97)*, which begins here. Even a short walk on this spectacular trail will reward you with sweeping views of the rugged **Na Pali Coast★★★** *(see p85)*.

Island-style Souvenirs

When touring the island, be on the lookout for local galleries, shops and roadside markets, where you're likely to find the best souvenirs and unique reminders of your visit to the islands. Look for body products made with local ingredients (lavender oils, kukui nut oil), or for these made-in-Hawaii souvenirs:

- Aloha shirts and surf shorts
- Lau hala placemats
- Woodcrafts (frames, ukuleles)
- CDs by local island musicians.
- Island-grown coffee (that doesn't say "Kona blend").

MUST SEE KAUAI

GARDENS

Look around: there are lush gardens and tropical forests everywhere, including some of the top formal botanical gardens in the country.

Limahuli Garden★★

Next to the entrance of Haena State Park, off Hwy. 560, Haena. 808-826-1053. www.ntbg.org. Open year-round Tue–Sat 9:30am–4pm. $15 self-guided tour, $30 guided tour, Tue–Sat 10am. Children under 12 free.

Located on the dramatic north shore of Kauai, Limahuli is considered one of the top botanical gardens in the US. A short loop takes you along ancient taro terraces and aside pretty Limahuli Stream, to a stunning overlook of cliffs and ocean views.

The garden specializes in native Hawaiian culture and plants, encompassing more than 1,000 acres, including a 17-acre public garden.

McBryde and Allerton Botanical Gardens★★

On Lawaii Beach Rd., across from the Spouting Horn, Poipu. 808-742-2623. www.ntbg.org. Open year-round daily 9am–4pm. Closed major holidays. McBryde: $20 adults, $10 ages 6–12. Allerton: guided tour only $45 adults, $20 ages 10–12. Minimum age on Allerton tour is 10 years old.

These two side-by-side gardens feature impressive displays of rare and endangered tropical plants, showcased against a backdrop of shimmering pools and garden sculpture. Self-guided and guided tours are offered at the McBryde Garden. Only guided walks are available at the Allerton Gardens, where you'll see the wavy roots of the Moreton Bay fig tree, featured in the movie *Jurassic Park*.

Irrigated terrace with taro, Limahuli Gardens

GARDENS

HISTORIC SITES

Legends and folklore surround the historic sites, including swinging bridges, ancient fish ponds and sugar-cane plantations.

Grove Farm Homestead★

Nawiliwili Rd., off Waapa Rd. near Lihue. 808-245-3202; www.grovefarm.net.
Visit by 2-hour guided tour only, year-round Mon, Wed, & Thu 10am & 1pm (reservations required). Closed major holidays. $20 suggested donation.

For a good look at life on an early sugar plantation, sign up for the two-hour tour of this historic homestead. Grove Farm, nestled in the pastures above Lihue, was founded in 1864 by George N. Wilcox, the son of Hanalei missionaries. The 80-acre farm, with gardens and orchards, preserves the lifestyle of the sugar plantation from the period 1864 to 1978, and includes the restored Wilcox family home, plantation office, and workers' houses.

MUSEUMS

The Garden Isle has little to offer traditional museum-hoppers, but the tiny Kauai Museum in Lihue provides a fine overview of island history.

Kauai Museum★

4428 Rice St., Lihue. 808-245-6931; www.kauaimuseum.org.
Open year-round Mon–Sat 10am–5pm. $10.

Kauai Museum
© Hawaii Tourism Authority (HTA) / Tor Johnson

You'll find all things Hawaiian at this small, but top-notch, museum in Lihue. The museum traces the island's history from its volcanic beginnings, through sugar-cane farming and missionary work. It houses an impressive collection of Hawaiian paintings and artifacts, including more than 1,000 stone implements, feather work, weapons, drums and other artifacts; 5,000 photographs dating from the 1890s, old plantation records and postcards; and a textile collection with 50 Hawaiian-made quilts. Don't miss the permanent collection of Hawaiian works from well-known artists, including 30 framed oil paintings by Alfred Gurrey.

Pick up Hawaiian-made artwork and handicrafts at the museum shop *(see p101).*

FOR FUN

Lofty helicopter rides, as well as hiking, golf, movie tours, underwater adventures and river kayaking offer non-stop fun.

Take a Helicopter Ride

For those unable or unwilling to hike and tour Kauai on their own, a helicopter tour provides a scenic, though hasty, overview of the island.

More than 90 percent of the island's diverse and spectacular landscape is inaccessible. Most tours fly out of Lihue, heading toward the sunny south shores of **Poipu★★★**, with its long stretches of sandy beaches and turquoise bays. You'll chopper up over the dramatic cliff of **Waimea Canyon★★**. If you're lucky, it will have just rained and you'll see countless, minutes-old waterfalls tumbling down the canyon walls. Heading north, the spectacular **Na Pali Coast★★★** comes into view, with its lush cliffs, plunging 3,000 to 4,000 feet to the sea. Inaccessible by roads, this remote coastline, with its rugged cliffs and verdant valleys, was once home to thousands of ancient Hawaiians. Its jungly, primeval landscape has been seen in several movies, including *Jurassic Park*.

A helicopter view of a waterfall in Waimea Canyon

© Hawaii Tourism Authority (HTA) / Tor Johnson

The flight continues up the coast, passing sparkling **Hanalei Bay★★★** and a smattering of pretty beaches. If weather permits, the pilot may take you into the middle of the island's crater, once a burial ground for kings, then over Mt. Waialeale, the center of the island and one of the rainiest spots on earth.

Do You Believe in Menehunes?

Hawaii folklore tells of mischievous "little people" named menehunes, who roamed the forests at night. The shy creatures, it's said, were great engineers and master builders, capable of completing major construction projects in one night. The creation of **Menehune Fishpond** and **Waimea Ditch** on Kauai is credited to the menehunes. Not just workers, these jolly folks also enjoyed singing and dancing, and have been known to use magic arrows to pierce hearts and ignite feelings of love. Some people believe that menehune still hide out in the forests of Kauai.

Join a Hawaii Movie Tour

*Basic tours run at about $90 per
person and include lunch and
pick-up and return from most resort
properties. For more information,
contact Hawaii Movie Tours:
800-628-8432; www.hawaii
movietour.com.*

Even if you're not a movie buff,
you'll enjoy the incredible scenery
on this fun-filled tour of famous
movie scenes and locations shot
on Kauai. The island has long been
a favorite of location scouts and
filmmakers, who've shot more
than six dozen movies on the
Garden Isle.

On this guided tour, you'll see a
variety of famous movie scenes on
the bus (shown on digital video
with surround sound), as you tour
the actual sites.

Along the way, you'll be treated
to in-depth commentary, behind-
the-scenes gossip, and a good
amount of hilarity.

The tour visits a number of
well-known public sites, like the
waterfall shown in the opening
scene of the TV show *Fantasy
Island*, and the beach where Mitzi
Gaynor vowed to "wash that man
right outta my hair" in the movie
South Pacific. But you'll also visit
private locales and hidden, off-the-
tourist-track spots.

On the four-wheel-drive tour,
you'll travel into the Wailua rain
forest, bumping over streams and
crossing rivers, to see remnants of
the giant gates in *Jurassic Park* and
scene locations from movies like
Dragonfly and *Flight of the Intruder*.

Hike the Na Pali Coast

*Kalalau trailhead begins at Kee
Beach at the end of Hwy. 560.
Permits are required on Kalalau
Trail beyond Hanakapiai Beach.
Camping along the Kalalau
trail costs $20 per person per
day for non-residents. Contact
the Division of State Parks (PO Box
621, Honolulu, HI 96809; 808-587-
0300; www.hawaiistateparks.org).*

Kalalau Hiking Trail★★★

If you're a hiker, or even a quasi
outdoor adventurer, you'll love
this well-known trail that hugs
the remote and rugged Na Pali

coastline. It's arguably one of the best short-distance hikes in the world. It's not easy. The 11-mile, one-way trek includes some 5,000 feet of elevation gain and loss, often across a narrow, steep, muddy, and slippery ridgeline. But you'll be rewarded with spectacular views.

On the first leg of the trip—the relatively easy one, though it gets slippery when wet—you'll walk through a tropical forest of dewy ferns, musty pandanus and mango trees, with sweeping ocean vistas, before descending onto sugar-white **Hanakapiai Beach**. Here, a freshwater stream bubbles into the ocean, and wet and dry caves line the shoreline. ☺*Swimmers should approach this beach with great caution—unwary visitors have been swept away*.

Back on the Kalalau Trail, you'll climb up and down into **Hoolulu Valley**, then **Hanakoa Valley**, rich with tropical plants, mango and guava trees.

The final leg takes you into breathtaking **Kalalau Valley★★**, rippled with streams and waterfalls. There's camping on the beach at Kalalau.

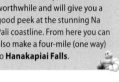

Touring Tip

If you can't carve out time to do the entire trail, the first two miles to Hanakapiai Beach are worthwhile and will give you a good peek at the stunning Na Pali coastline. From here you can also make a four-mile (one way) to **Hanakapiai Falls**.

Camp on Kauai

You'll find some of the best camping in Hawaii on Kauai, including three state parks and several county beach parks.

Cabins are available at **Kokee State Park★★** *(15mi north of Kekaha on Hwy. 550; see p 86)*, and backcountry permits are offered for sites in the **Waimea Canyon★★** *(11mi north of Kekaha on Hwy. 550)* and adjoining **Kokee State Park★★**.

For the best beach camping, consider **Polihale State Park** *(at the end of a 5mi-long dirt road from Mana Village, off Hwy. 50)*, with its lofty sand dunes, miles of secluded beach, picnic areas and fresh water. And you can pull your vehicle right up onto the beach here.

Kalalau Hiking Trail

©Lori Spiker/Fotolia.com

FOR FUN

Poipu Bay Golf Course

Courtesy of Grand Hyatt Kauai Resort and Spa

Touring Tip

Camping fees on Kauai are $5 per campsite per night; $10 per person per night on the Na Pali Coast. To purchase permits, contact the Division of State Parks *(PO Box 621, Honolulu, HI 96809; 808-587-0300; www.hawaii stateparks.org)*. For county park permits, contact the Kauai Dept. of Parks and Recreation *(4444 Rice St., Lihue; HI 96766; 808-241-4463; www.kauai.gov)*. The north and northeast sides receive almost daily showers, whereas around Polihale, it virtually never rains. If you're camping at Kokee, expect frequent rain showers. Be sure to have adequate rain gear.

Golf on Kauai

Golfers can hardly go wrong on the island of Kauai, home to several dramatic, award-winning resort courses. Here are three:

Kauai Lagoons – *3351 Hoolaulea Way, Lihue. 808-241-6000 or 800-634-6400; www.kauailagoons golf.com.* Kauai Lagoons boasts two Jack Nicklaus-designed courses on the southeast corner of the island, including the top-ranked Kiele course across 40 acres of tropical lagoons and oceanfront.

Poipu Bay – *At the Grand Hyatt Kauai Resort, 2250 Ainako St., Koloa. 800-858-6300; www. poipubaygolf.com (see Hotels).* A Robert Trent Jones Jr design, the course at Poipu Bay features rolling

Sunset Viewing on Kauai

It's tough not to slow down, stop, and gawk at the legendary sunsets on Kauai. There are plenty of prime sunset viewing spots, but for the very best, head to Polihale Beach. The three-mile stretch of mostly secluded white sand on Kauai's western coast gets bathed in sherbet-colored hues as the sun slips down past the horizon. Stick around for fabulous stargazing, too. Once a month, on the Saturday nearest the full moon, locals and visitors head to the Barking Sands Observatory near Polihale Beach to enjoy the brilliant night skies.

© Hawaii Tourism Authority (HTA) / Tor Johnson

terrain, sweeping ocean views, and a choice of four sets of tees at each hole. The PGA Grand Slam was held here from 1994 to 2006.

St Regis Princeville Resort – *5520 Ka Haku Rd., Princeville. 808-826-2250; www.stregisprinceville.com (see Hotels).* Robert Trent Jones Jr designed both of the resort's courses. Set against a backdrop of open ocean, the 18 holes of the **Prince Course** are named for Prince Albert, the only son of King Kamehameha IV; the **Makai Course**, among the top 100 resort courses in the country, features three sets of nines that skirt the ocean and wind their way through tropical forest.

Kayak a Sacred River

Take a guided kayak trip up the sacred **Wailua River**. The 20-mile-long river on Kauai's east coast (only three miles are navigable) is shrouded in mystery and mystique. Legend has it that the spirits of the dead would travel up the river to the cliffs of Haeleele, where they would jump to the next life.

The kayak-hike excursion, offered by **Kayak Kauai** *(800-437-3507 off island or 808-826-9844 on Kauai;*

Touring Tip

If you're a golfer, or you have duffers on your gift list, you'll want to check out **The Golf Shop at Poipu Bay Golf Course**, rated as one of the finest in America. PGA Grand Slam and Kauai Resort logo wear fly off the shelves here.

www.kayakkauai.com) begins with a 2.5-mile paddle upstream. The river is fairly gentle, and easy enough for families with young children.

After about a 45-minute paddle you'll reach a landing and the trailhead to **Secret Falls**. The gentle one-mile trail travels through overgrown forests of mango, ginger, and tall albizia trees, before reaching the picturesque 120-foot falls. There's a small swimming hole and perfect perches for a picnic lunch.

If you prefer coastal, sea-swept views, Kayak Kauai and other local outfitters offer sea-kayaking excursions, some combining stops at prime snorkeling spots.

© Hawaii Tourism Authority (HTA) / Tor Johnson

Kayaking on the Wailua River

FOR FUN

FOR KIDS

You'll find outdoor activities and non-stop adventure on laid-back and casual Kauai, arguably the family-friendliest of the Hawaiian Islands.

Go Snorkeling★★

A pair of rubber flippers and a snorkel mask (don't forget the sunscreen) is all you'll need to catch Kauai's amazing underwater show. The best family-friendly snorkeling beaches on the island are **Poipu Beach Park★★★** *(see p83)*, Anini and Salt Pond Beach on the south shore, and **Kee Beach★** on the north shore *(see p 84)*. Check out **Lydgate Park Beach** *(off Hwy. 56 between Kapaa and Lihue; take Leho Rd. past the Holiday Inn Sunspree)*, too, for great swimming, tide pooling, and snorkeling. Lydgate also has an awesome playground with a maze of caves, slides, and tunnels that will keep the little ones occupied for hours.

Red-footed booby

©Michael Stubblefield/iStockphoto.com

Kilauea Point National Wildlife Refuge★★

On the north shore, off Hwy. 56; take Kilauea Rd. to the end. 808-828-1413. www.fws.gov/kilaueapoint.

Take a hike on the wild side. Red-footed booby birds, soaring frigates, spouting humpback whales, basking monk seals and frolicking spinner dolphins are just some of the wildlife your family may see at the Kilauea Point National Wildlife Refuge, perched on a cliff overlooking the Pacific Ocean. Take a walk out to the 1913 lighthouse, stop by the visitor center for information and maps, then join a guided walk through the trails that crisscross the 203-acre preserve. Located on the northernmost tip of the Hawaiian Islands, Kilauea Point is one of the few Hawaiian refuges open to the public.

Head for the Backcountry★

Don a miner's helmet and bring your sense of adventure on a zip-line tour of the backcountry. Kauai Backcountry Adventures *(3-4131 Kuhio Highway. Hanamaulu, 888-270-0555 or 808-245-2506; www.kauaibackcountry.com)* takes small groups to a former 17,000-acre plantation, via a four-wheel-drive vehicle, and then the real fun begins!

Let 'er rip on a series of seven ziplines that descend and traverse an overgrown mountainside, above rain forests, streams, bamboo groves and waterfalls. Ride a tube down old irrigation canals and tunnels. Along the way, you'll learn about island history, flora and fauna. For kids 12 years old and up.

SHOPPING

The best shopping is clustered in a few marketplaces. For fresh produce and local goods, check out the island's Sunshine Markets.

Coconut Marketplace

4-484 Kuhio Hwy. (Hwy. 56), Kapaa. 808-822-3641. www.coconutmarketplace.com. Open year-round Mon–Sat 9am–9pm, Sun 10am–6pm.
This open-air marketplace, with more than 40 shops, is the largest on Kauai. If you're looking for one-stop shopping, this is it. You'll find fine specialty stores next to inexpensive gift shops, tacky souvenirs with pricey Tahitian pearls. The Tuesday Farmers' Market *(9am–noon)* is a highlight.

© Brigitta L. House/Michelin

Kauai Museum Shop

4428 Rice St., Lihue. 808-245-6931. www.kauaimuseum.org. Open year-round Mon–Sat 10am–5pm. Closed Thanksgiving Day & Dec 25.
This is the place where the locals go to shop for special gifts. It's also the best place for top-quality, one-of-a-kind, island-made arts and crafts. An impressive selection of items awaits you at this tiny museum shop, including fish-hook necklaces, hand-woven purses,

Lauhala hats, wooden koa and kava bowls, and authentic and rare Niihau shell necklaces ranging from $75 to $15,000.

Farmers' Markets★

Pick up fresh, locally grown produce at one of Kauai's farmers' markets. *www.kauai.gov or www.kauaigrown.org.*
Monday – noon at Koloa Ballpark *(Maluhia Rd., Koloa).*
Tuesday – 3pm at **Kalaheo Neighborhood Center** *(on Papalina Rd., off Kaumualii Rd., Kalaheo).*
Wednesday – 3pm at **Kapaa New Town Park** *(at the intersection of Kahau & Olehena Rds., Kapaa).*
Thursday – 4:30pm at **Kilauea Neighborhood Center** *(on Keneke Rd., off Lighthouse Rd., Kilauea);* and 3pm at Hanapepe Town Park *(behind the fire station in Hanapepe).*
Friday – 3pm at **Vidinha Stadium** in Lihue *(on Hoolako St., off Queen Kapuli Rd.).*
Saturday – 9am at Kekaha Neighborhood Center *(on Elepaio Rd., Kekaha).*

Kauai Made

Want to be sure your souvenir was made on Kauai? Look for the **Kauai Made label**. The award-winning county program focuses on promoting the island's small businesses, which sell products made on Kauai or with Kauai materials. For a brochure, list, and map of vendors, visit *www.kauaimade.net.*

SHOPPING

NIGHTLIFE

Kauai is not particularly known for its rollicking après-sun scene (moonlit walks on the beach and sunset toasts are more its style), but there are a handful of hot night spots you won't want to miss.

Keoki's Paradise
2360 Kiahuna Plantation Dr., at the Poipu Shopping Center, Koloa. 808-742-7534. www.keokisparadise.com.
This casual, lively Polynesian-themed restaurant, decked out with waterfalls, thatched roofs and plenty of plants, is a hangout for young party-goers on Friday and Saturday evenings when local bands perform in the bustling Bamboo Bar. A bar menu of pupus, salads and light fare is available until 11:30pm.

Bar Acuda
5-5161 Kuhio Hwy., Hanalei. 808-826-7081. www.restaurant baracuda.com.
This upscale eatery and watering hole in Hanalei is known for its creative tapas dishes by award-winning chef-owner Jim Moffat. It's also known for his hand-picked wine list, which includes 50 or so selections of estate bottles from small producers.
The indoor-outdoor, cool-vibe bar has warm woods and lush fabrics. It's a great place for an easy-going night in a beachfront setting. Consider a chilled glass of the house-made limoncello to enjoy as you watch the stars twinkle above the mountains.

🌺 Tahiti Nui
25-5134 Kuhio Hwy., Hanalei, 808-826-6277. www.thenui.com.
If you're going to party only one night on Kauai, make it at the

> **Moonbows**
> The best nightly performance on Kauai is often courtesy of Mother Nature. The Garden Isle is one of the few places in the world to see moonbows. Look for these ghostly light streaks when the moon is full, just after sunset. On the highway between Lihue and Waimea is a good place to spot them.

Tahiti Nui—or, as the locals call it "da nui." This long-standing North Shore watering hole and casual, family-owned restaurant has let the good times roll for more than five decades. Live music, just-right mai tais, and anything goes, friendly atmosphere draw locals, visitors, and celebrities alike to this beloved gathering spot. The Tiki Bar features a different theme every night from hula to Karaoke.

St. Regis Bar
Princeville Resort, 5520 Ka Haku Rd. 808-826-9244. www.stregisprinceville.com.
The bar at Kauai's most elegant resort is exactly as you'd expect, an elegant, dark-paneled retreat with leather lounging chairs and an expansive view over Hanalei Bay. Even better, the hotel's Sunday Jazz evenings bring in some of Hawaii's best musicians for an intimate performance event that matches its surroundings.

SPAS

You'll find a handful of day spas, popular with locals, but the most opulent and cutting-edge spas are located at the large resorts.

Anara Spa

Grand Hyatt Kauai, 1571 Poipu Rd., Koloa. 808-742-1234.
www.anaraspa.com.
This blissful and beautiful full-service spa, set on the lush grounds of the Grand Hyatt Kauai resort *(see Hotels)*, is considered one of the top-ranked spas in the country. It's also the largest on Kauai. From the moment you walk through the doors, you'll feel pampered in the luxurious indoor and outdoor facilities and by the spa's unique, therapeutic offerings. Popular treatments include the seaweed and mineral body masks, botanical baths, papaya pineapple polishes, and pohaku (hot stone) and lomilomi massages *(see box, below)*.
The outdoor shower and thatched-roof *hales* (huts) are special treats.

Anara Spa

Courtesy of Grand Hyatt Kauai Resort and Spa

Massage in Paradise

"Touching with loving hands" is the literal translation of lomilomi massage. The massage technique has been passed down by Hawaiian elders and is now offered in spas throughout the islands. Therapists use both gentle and vigorous kneading strokes and incorporate elbow and forearm work for a deep, all-over body massage. It's a bit firmer and faster than a Swedish massage, though less intense than mainland-style sports and therapeutic massage, leaving you de-stressed and as relaxed as a wet noodle.

Halelea Spa

St Regis Princeville at Hanalei, 5-4280 Kuhio Hwy. 808-826-9644.
www.stregisprinceville.com.
Ocean and garden views greet guests at this full-service spa located in the upscale St Regis Princeville at Hanalei resort. Relax in the steam and sauna rooms; take a swim in the five-lane pool, and then enjoy one of the Hawaiian-inspired treatments.
Lomilomi massages are popular, as well as the Limu (seaweed) body wrap, and the Hawaiian Salt Glow, guaranteed to leave your sun-dried body baby soft.

OAHU★★★

Aptly nicknamed "The Gathering Place," Oahu ranks as the most bustling and developed of all the islands. Tourists flood the area for its abundance of lodging, dining and shopping venues, and for its waterfront activities. Oahu is also home to the state's most popular tourist attraction, Pearl Harbor's USS Arizona Memorial, and to Iolani Palace, the only royal palace in the US. *Visitor information: 877-525-6248; www.gohawaii.com/oahu.*

Most of the island's activity is concentrated in the urban areas of **Honolulu** and **Waikiki**, resting on the south shore. But venture north along Oahu's 125 miles of coastline and you'll find impossibly blue bays, surf-slapped beaches and verdant valleys.

Across the **Koolau Range** from Honolulu extends the lush windward coast of the island, with its suburban communities of **Kailua** and **Kaneohe**. West of Pearl Harbor is the drier **Waianae** coast and the big-wave beaches of **Makaha**. A route through the agricultural center of Oahu leads to the north shore, fabled for its country living and renowned surfing venues. Oahu is the second-oldest of the islands. Populated before AD 1000, it was added to the island kingdom in 1795. By 1850, the

Fast Facts

♦ At 608 square miles, Oahu is the third-largest of the Hawaiian Islands. The island measures 44 miles long and 30 miles wide at its widest point.

♦ Three-fourths of Hawaii's population—more than 980,000 people—live on Oahu.

♦ Oahu claims the state capital, Honolulu, which also ranks as the state's largest city and the financial center of the Pacific.

♦ Oahu is the most visited of the Hawaiian Islands.

Hawaiian Royal Court had moved permanently to **Honolulu**, making it the center of government and commerce for the islands.

Today, Oahu, with its 21C vibe and wide cultural diversity, continues to beat as the heart of Hawaii.

Aloha Tower Marketplace, Downtown Honolulu

© Hawaii Tourism Authority (HTA) / Chuck Painter

MUST SEE OAHU

CITIES

From world-class Honolulu to quaint and artsy Haleiwa on the North Shore, Oahu's cities boast rich cultural diversity and must-see sites.

Downtown Honolulu

© Brigitta L. House/Michelin

Honolulu★★

Map inside back cover. Sprawling across the southeast quadrant of Oahu, the world's largest Polynesian city boasts a bustling modern **downtown** with traffic and skyscrapers, extending from Waikiki's surf-washed beaches to the 3,000-foot crest of the jungle-swathed Koolau Range *(from Honolulu Harbor to Vineyard Blvd., between Ward Ave. & River St.).* Here the first missionaries gathered their Hawaiian congregations, and the only royal palace in the US was erected in 1882. Like most big

cities, Honolulu can be congested, noisy and difficult to get around, so it's best to avoid driving during morning and evening rush hours.

Honolulu Museum of Art★★ – *900 S. Beretania St., at Ward Ave. See p120.*

Iolani Palace★★★ – *S. King & Richard Sts. See p124.*

Kawaiahao Church★ – *957 Punchbowl St. 808-469-3000. www.kawaiahao.org.*
King Kamehameha IV married Queen Emma in this venerable house of worship, made from 14,000 blocks of coral cut from the

---

Aloha Tower★★

Pier 9, downtown Honolulu. 808-566-2337. www.alohatower.com. Observation deck open year-round daily 9:30am–5pm. Free. There's no missing this long-time beacon in downtown Honolulu. For nearly eight decades, the ten-story Aloha Tower—named for the greeting etched above its four clock faces (one on each side of the square column)—has greeted cruise-ship passengers and other visitors. Progress may have stripped the 1926 tower's claim to fame as Hawaii's tallest building, but it still offers some of the best views in town from its outdoor **observation deck** and some of the liveliest entertainment and shopping in the city The **Aloha Tower Marketplace★**, surrounds the base of the tower *(see p140).*

CITIES

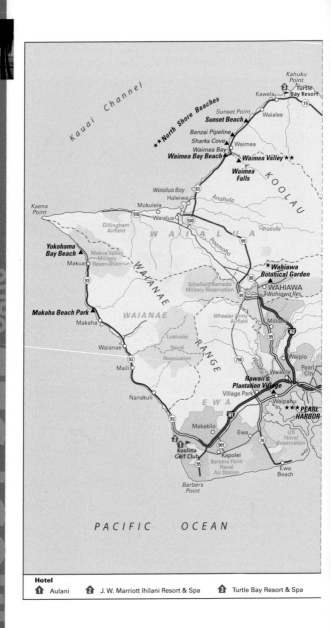

North Shore Beaches ★★
Sunset Point
Sunset Beach ▲
Banzai Pipeline
Sharks Cove
Waimea Bay
Waimea Bay Beach ▲
Waimea Valley ★★
Waimea Falls

KOOLAU

Kauai Channel

Kahuku Point
Kawela
Turtle Bay Resort
Waialee
19

Waimea
Anahula
Opaeula

Waialua Bay
Haleiwa
Mokuleia
83
Waialua
930
530
99

Kaena Point
Dillingham Airfield

W A I A L U A

Yokohama Bay Beach ▲
Makua Valley Military Reservation
Makua
93

Poamoho

Wahiawa Botanical Garden ★
80
WAHIAWA
Wahiawa Res.

W A I A N A E
R A N G E

Schofield Barracks Military Reservation
99

Wheeler Army Airfield

Makaha Beach Park ▲
Makaha

WAIANAE

Mililani
95
112

750

Waianae

Lualualei Naval Reservation

Waipio
Pearl City

Maili
93

Waikele
Waipahu

Hawaii's Plantation Village ★
Village Park

PEARL HARBOR ★★★

Nanakuli

E W A

H1

Makakilo

Koolina Golf Club

901
Kapolei
Ewa

Barbers Point Naval Air Station

Waipahu

US Naval Reservation

76

95

Barbers Point

Ewa Beach

PACIFIC   OCEAN

Hotel
🏠 Aulani   2️⃣ J. W. Marriott Ihilani Resort & Spa   🏠 Turtle Bay Resort & Spa

MUST SEE OAHU

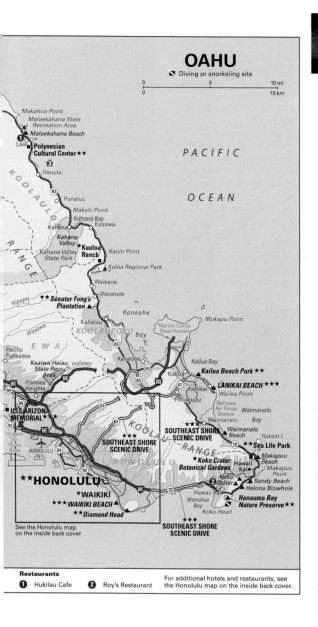

OAHU

◥ Diving or snorkeling site

0   5   10 mi

0   15 km

Makahoa Point

Malaekahana State Recreation Area

Malaekahana Beach

Laie

Polynesian Cultural Center ★★

Hauula

PACIFIC

OCEAN

83

Punaluu

Makalii Point

Kahana Bay

Kahana   Kaaawa

KOOLAULOA

Kahana Valley

Kahana Valley State Park

Kualoa Ranch

Kaoio Point

Kuloa Regional Park

Waikane

Waiahole

Kipapa

★★ Senator Fong's Plantation ▲

Kaneohe

Waiawa

Kahaluu

KOOLAUPOKO   Bay

Mokapu Point

Marine Corps Base Hawaii

Pacific Palisades

E W A

Keaiwa Heiau State Recr. Area

Halawa

Kaneohe

83

Kailua Bay

Kailua Beach Park ★★

Halawa Heights

99

USS ARIZONA MEMORIAL ★★★

92

Hickam Air Force Base

HONOLULU INTL.

H1

64

61

Kailua

Lanikai

Pohakupu

LĀNIKAI BEACH ★★★

Wailea Point

Bellows Air Force Station

Waimanalo

SOUTHEAST SHORE SCENIC DRIVE ★★★

Waimanalo Bay

★★HONOLULU

92

★★★ SOUTHEAST SHORE SCENIC DRIVE

HONOLULU

72

Waimanalo Beach

Rabbit I.

★★ Sea Life Park

★ Koko Crater Botanical Gardens

Hawaii Kai

Makapuu Beach

Makapuu Point

★WAIKIKI

★★★ WAIKIKI BEACH ▲

★★Diamond Head

Hawaii Kai

Manalua Bay

Koko Crater

▲ Sandy Beach

Halona Blowhole

Hanauma Bay Nature Preserve ★★

Koko Head

See the Honolulu map on the inside back cover.

★★★ SOUTHEAST SHORE SCENIC DRIVE

Restaurants

❶ Hukilau Cafe   ❷ Roy's Restaurant

For additional hotels and restaurants, see the Honolulu map on the inside back cover.

CITIES

107

offshore reefs. It took five years and a thousand men to complete the church, which was dedicated in 1842. Today the "Westminster Abbey of Hawaii" offers Sunday services in Hawaiian and English.

Mission Houses Museum★★ – *553 S. King St., at Kawaiahao St. See p122.*

Hawaii State Capitol★ – *S. Beretania St., between Richards & Punchbowl Sts. 808-274-3141.* Completed in 1969 to replace the capitol at Iolani Palace, this modern structure rises out of a shallow pool to represent volcanoes emerging from the sea.

Waikiki★

Once a lounging place for Hawaiian royalty, the suburb of Waikiki is recognized by the forest of towers created by its hotels, its bustling tourist atmosphere, and its nonstop activities.

Stretching 1.5 miles from Ala Wai Canal to Diamond Head, **Waikiki Beach** *(see p109)* remains one of

Statue of Duke Paoa Kahanamoku, Waikiki Beach

© Brigitta L. House/Michelin

the best places in the world to learn surfing, a sport invented here hundreds of years ago. At Waikiki Beach Center stands a statue of **Duke Kahanamoku** *(Kalakaua Ave. near Kaiulani Ave.)*, Hawaii's three-time Olympic swimming champion (1912–1920), who introduced surfing to California and Australia. Non-surfers may ride the waves in an outrigger canoe or take a cruise on a sailboat that casts off right from the shoreline.

Kapiolani Park – Located at the east end of Waikiki, 140-acre Kapiolani Park encompasses the **Honolulu Zoo** *(see p135)* and **Waikiki Shell**, an outdoor, beachfront venue for open-air concerts and exhibitions.

Ala Moana Beach Park

Virtually all Waikiki visitors pass by this park *(just northwest of Waikiki)* on their way to the main resort district, without realizing that it contains paths, picnic areas, gardens and old banyan trees. A beach called Magic Island lagoon at the outer eastern corner is protected by a breakwater. That's where Honolulu residents take their kids to learn to swim, a serene alternative to Waikiki beach strip.

Waikiki Beach

© Brigitta L. House/Michelin

BEACHES

Waikiki, Waimea and Lanikai beaches are well-known hot spots, but you'll also find secluded gems along the island's 112 miles of coastline.

Lanikai Beach

© Brigitta L. House/Michelin

Lanikai Beach★★★

Map p197. In Lanikai, on the east shore. Access via public walkways off Mokulua Dr.

It's no wonder this sun-drenched oasis on Oahu's east shore is a magnet for photographers—and ranks as one of the top beaches in the US. Picture paradise: a white, sandy beach fringed with palm trees and fragrant tropical plants, licked by crystal-clear, aqua-blue surf. That's Lanikai Beach. This nearly mile-long jewel has the added bonus of calm waters, making it perfect for swimming, too. If you're feeling energetic, you can kayak to the nearby islands of

Mokumanu and Mokulua. Bring your binoculars; both islands are great for bird-watching. For a special treat, arrive at Lanikai at dawn for the best view of the rising sun you're likely to see anywhere.

Waikiki Beach★★★

On Oahu's south shore, from the Outrigger Canoe Club at 2909 Kalakaua Ave. to Kahanamoku Lagoon at 2005 Kalia Rd.

This 1.5-mile stretch of sand, flanked by high-rise hotels and warm, turquoise waters, is one of the best big-city beaches in the world. It's also one of the most famous, drawing 4 million visitors a year to its high-energy, people-packed shoreline.

Running from the dramatic Diamond Head crater to the Ala Wai Yacht Harbor, the beach was once swampland, referred to by ancient Hawaiians as *Waikiki*, or "spouting water." Today it's a hotbed of activity; if you like to be in the center of the action, this is it. Waikiki Beach offers something

Touring Tip

A residential neighborhood development sits in front of Lanikai Beach, but you'll find several beach-access walkways off **Mokulua Drive**. Snag an on-street parking spot where you can.

Waikiki Beach with Diamond Head in the background.

© Brigitta L. House/Michelin

for everyone: gentle waters for bathers; big, offshore breaks for surfers; and 80-degree waters for swimming. You can snag a warm patch of soft sand, slather yourself with lotion, and spend the day relaxing in the sun.

Or pick your pleasure: rent an outrigger canoe, take a surfing lesson (on-the-beach outfitters offer instruction for all ages), snorkel, play beach volleyball—the list is nearly endless. Stop for a brain-freezing but delicious shave ice on busy **Kalakaua Avenue**, and take in the sights, sounds and smells of this famous outdoor playground—surprisingly user-friendly despite all the many thousands who congregate here.

Kailua Beach Park★★
East shore, at the end of Kailua Rd.
You'll find this beachy gem on the windward side of the island, just around the corner from Lanikai Beach *(see p109)*. Wide, sloping sands and calm waters make this a perfect place for sunbathing and swimming. Plentiful parking, concessions, lifeguards, picnic areas, restrooms and showers on-site are other benefits, adding to the overall comfort level. Kailua's fine, soft sand stretches for a mile, and the swaying palms and offshore islands in the distance make a postcard-pretty backdrop. While the setting is serene, there's likely to be a lot of action on the water. Kailua Beach is a world-class **windsurfing** locale, drawing some of the best in the sport. Pull up your beach chair and take a front-row seat. Or get in on the action yourself; shops in the nearby town of Kailua offer gear and lessons.

Touring Tip

Waikiki is actually a series of connecting beaches; each has its own name and each has something special to offer. For fabulous sunset viewing, head to the beach in front of the Outrigger Reef on the Beach. For sea-turtle watching, look offshore near the breakwater in front of the Moana Surfrider. Families will appreciate the calm waters in front of the Royal Hawaiian Hotel. For picnics, consider lovely Kapiolani Park *(see p108)* at the foot of Diamond Head.

North Shore Beaches★★

During the winter months, the seven-mile string of beaches ringing Oahu's northern waters is most famous for its hugely popular surfing venues. **Sunset Beach Park** is a lovely stretch of white sand and clear waters; though often calm in the summer, there's raging surf in the winter. The point is a good spot for tidepooling.

Waimea Bay Beach Park is said to have the wildest, most dangerous surf in the world. Spectators line the beach during the winter months when the surf can reach 30 feet or more. **Ehukai Beach Park** is best known for the **Banzai Pipeline**, a legendary tubed surfing break. **Note:** When visiting any of the North Shore beaches, remember to read the posted warnings, ask lifeguards about swimming conditions, and adhere to Hawaii's common sense law: If in doubt, stay out.

Sharks – If you're lucky, you might be able to spot the fins of white-tipped reef sharks at **Sharks Cove**, on Oahu's north shore.

Giant wave, Waimea Bay
© Hawaii Tourism Authority (HTA) / Kirk Lee Aeder

Giovanni's Shrimp

Beach boys, hungry locals and savvy visitors know fresh shrimp when they taste it. That's why Giovanni's is the favorite nosh on the north shore. You'll find this battered lunch truck parked along Highway 83, between Turtle Bay and Kahuku. Order a heaping, half-pound plate of farm-raised, steamed Oahu shrimp, then top it with garlic or hot chili sauce. Numerous other shrimp trucks and small cafes line the north and east shore highways on Oahu.

But for virtually guaranteed shark spotting, **Hawaii Shark Encounters** (*808-351-9373; www.hawaiisharkencounters.com; departures are weather dependent; $105 adults, under 12 years $75; no under 5s*) offers shark encounters from the safety of a plexi-glass cage three miles offshore. It's not uncommon to have 10 sharks circling around the cage! Tours include conservation information about sharks and their importance to the ocean's overall health.

🐾 "From Here to Eternity" Beach

Located below the Halona Blowhole parking lot.

Put on your best walking shoes and climb down the steep hill to this secluded beach, protected by the surrounding sea cliffs and crags. Most people are turned off by the trek down and back, but it's a good place for swimming. A long, sloping sandy bottom calms the open-ocean surf. Look for sea turtles that hang out in the cove.

BEACHES

Touring Tip

Hawaii's beaches, including hotel beaches, are open to the public. Of course, you'll pay for using cabanas and ordering beverages. Most hotel beaches have lifeguards and loads of facilities; at public beach parks, facilities vary; some have restrooms, most do not have lifeguards. Heed the warning signs and flags for swimming conditions: red flag indicates severe hazard, usually dangerous waves or currents; yellow indicates caution, for waves or currents; blue or purple flags, waterborne hazards such as jellyfish, though rarely seen (visitors should exercise caution at all times); green indicate safe conditions.

Yokohama Bay Beach

Map p106. Take H-1 West until it connects to Farrington Hwy. The beach is located at the end of Farrington Hwy.

This is the perfect place to spend a day. Pack a picnic basket, take bottled water and a fishing pole if you like to dangle a line. This isolated, hidden beach on the Waianae coast is rarely crowded, and the waters are calm in summer. It's a great place for shell collecting and snorkeling. During the winter months, however, the surf can be treacherous: it's a lure for local surfers who tackle the 20-foot waves. Stick around for views of some amazing sunsets.

PARKS AND NATURAL SITES

Explore volcanic tuff cones and craters, underwater preserves, ancient ruins and sacred waterfalls.

Diamond Head★★

Diamond Head Rd., Waikiki Beach. 808-587-0300. www.hawaiistateparks.org.

Open year-round daily 6am–6pm. Note: Hikers must enter the trail by 4:30pm, as the gates are locked at 6pm (see box top p113).

Diamond Head seen from Kapiolani Park

You can't miss it: this 760-foot-high natural landmark is a dominating feature in Oahu. The volcanic tuff cone and crater, once the site of an ancient Hawaiian temple, has been extinct for more than 150,000 years. Legend has it that ancient Hawaiian kings worshipped at the site and that some of the last human sacrifices were performed here. In the 1800s, British sailors named the crater Diamond Head when they mistook calcite crystals for diamonds shining in the lava rock.

+ **Best reason to visit Diamond Head:** To walk the trail to the summit for incredible **views**—some of the best on Oahu.

Hanauma Bay Nature Preserve★★

Off Hwy. 72 in Hanauma Bay (10mi east of Waikiki). 808-396-4229. www.gohawaii.com/oahu. Open Jun–Aug Wed–Mon 6am–7pm. Rest of the year Wed–Mon 6am–6pm. $7.50 (free for children ages 12 & under).

This stunningly beautiful horseshoe-shaped reef, surrounded by coral sand and the sunken walls of an ancient volcano, ranks among America's top beaches and is one of the most popular in all of Hawaii. Up to 3,000 people visit

Hiking Diamond Head

Pack your sunscreen, sturdy boots and plenty of bottled water before heading to the base of Diamond Head for the short hike to the summit. The hike is a round-trip of less than two miles, but includes some steep sections, and more than 270 steps! It's worth every grunt and groan: you'll be rewarded with sweeping views of Oahu's stunning southeast coastline.

Hanauma Bay each day to swim in its warm emerald-green waters and snorkel among schools of brilliantly colored tropical fish. Technically, the reef is now designated a State Underwater Park and Conservation District and strict conservation efforts in recent years have begun to pay off. Feeding fish is now banned at the preserve, and all visitors must watch a mandatory conservation and safety video.
Tip: The park limits the number of guests; arrive early in the morning because once the parking lot is full, you'll be turned away.
Snorkeling – The reef is perfect for snorkeling year-round (masks, fins and snorkels are available for rent at the visitor center).
Here, more than 150 species of fish might flitter around your fins.

Under the Sea

The gentle, warm Pacific waters of Hawaii nurture colorful reefs that match any on earth—but you must don mask and snorkel to experience them. Hawaii's reefs are generally smaller and younger than others in the Pacific, but dynamic and colorful nonetheless. About 680 species of fish and 40 species of reef-building corals, including cauliflower coral, lobe coral and finger coral, grace the waters. Look for urchins, sea cucumbers, snails, damselfish, triggerfish, puffers, yellow tangs, snappers and spotted eagle rays. You may also see fish like the Hawaiian cleaner wrasse and the pebbled and milletseed butterfly fish, which are only found in Hawaii.

SCENIC DRIVES

Flip the car top down and take off through vibrant neighborhoods, amid lush valleys and along the 112-mile coastline.

Halona Blowhole
© Brigitta L. House/Michelin

Southeast Shore★★★

Map pp106-107. Begin at Waikiki and drive east on the H-1 Freeway to Hwy. 72.

This 30-mile loop drive along Oahu's southeast shore features the island's most spectacular scenery and some of its more popular sites. You can do this drive in a half-day,

but it's better to take your time and plan a day for the trip. It will be crowded, typically packed with tour buses and slow-driving visitors—all the more reason to relax and slow down. There are plenty of great stops for swimming and sightseeing along the way.

◗ *Head out of Waikiki on H-1 to Highway 72, and follow it east as it curves around the rugged coastline.*

Your first stop is pretty **Hanauma Bay★★** *(see p113)*. This protected marine reserve features some of the island's best snorkeling. As you leave the bay and circle around the Koko Head area, the coastline becomes much more rugged, and you'll have fine views of waves crashing against rocky outcrops. About two miles past the bay is the turn-off for the **Halona Blowhole**, where the water gushes and spouts through underwater lava tubes and tunnels.

Aerial view of Hanauma Bay
© Hawaii Tourism Authority (HTA) / Heather Titus

OAHU

MUST SEE

View from Pali Lookout

© Hawaii Tourism Authority (HTA) / Tor Johnson

A short distance to the northeast you'll find **Sandy Beach**, popular with boogieboarders, bodysurfers and kite-flyers *(see box p136)*. Across the road lies **Koko Crater**. Inside the crater are the **Koko Crater Botanical Gardens**★ *(see p117)*, a nice place to stretch your legs and take in top-of-the-crater views. As Highway 72 winds around Makapuu Point, up the east coast of Oahu, sweeping views open up to the sea and Koolau Range that hugs the coastline.

Ready to get out of the car again? Take the short half-hour trail to the summit of Makapuu Point for views of Rabbit Island and beautiful **Makapuu Beach** *(trailhead is 1.5mi north of Sandy Beach; park and walk along the service road to the lighthouse)*.

Continue north and you'll pass **Sea Life Park**★★ *(see p134)* and **Waimanalo Beach**, a good place to stop for a swim.

Take the coastal route and you'll end up in the bustling town of Kailua. From here, take Pali Road *(Route 61)*, back to Honolulu, leading across the jagged Koolau Range. A final must-stop along the way is the **Pali Lookout**, affording awesome mountain views.

Touring Tip

For a short drive that feels worlds away from the bustle of Honolulu, take scenic **Tantalus Drive** *(map inside back cover)*. The two-hour excursion takes you through a tropical preserve and the rolling foothills of the Koolau Range. *Take the Wilder St. exit off H-1 and follow Wilder to Makiki St. Turn right on Makiki St. and then left on Round Top Dr.; Round Top becomes Tantalus Dr. Continue around to Makiki Heights Rd., and loop back to Makiki St.* You'll climb to about 2,000 feet and have expansive views of Honolulu, Diamond Head, Waikiki and Pearl Harbor. Hikes, through rain forests and thick bamboo stands off Tantalus Drive, range from one hour to a full day. *For trail information, visit the Division of Forestry and Wildlife's www.hawaiitrails.org.*

SCENIC DRIVES

GARDENS

Oahu's botanical gardens and nature preserves—some of the finest in the country— boast an impressive array of exotic and rare plants.

Foster Botanical Garden

© Brigitta L. House/Michelin

Foster Botanical Garden★

Map inside back cover. 180 N. Vineyard Blvd., Honolulu. 808-522-7060. www.honolulu.gov/parks. Open year-round daily 9am–4pm. Closed Jan 1 & Dec 25. $5.

Garden enthusiasts won't want to miss this 14-acre botanical gem on the north side of Honolulu's Chinatown, a flowery, exotic oasis smack-dab in the middle of the city. Where else can you see the nearly extinct wild East African *Gigasiphon macrosiphon*, with its evening-opening white flowers? Or the double coconut palm that can drop 50-pound nuts? The unusual and rare specimens here are neatly organized by plant groups. The more than 150-year-old garden began when German botanist and physician William Hillebrand leased a tract of land from Queen Kalama. Some of the original trees Hillebrand planted are still standing.

Let Me Lei it on You!

You'll find some of the best displays of leis at the stands in **Chinatown**. Familiar favorites are still made with plumeria, ginger, orchid, ilima and carnation flowers, but you'll see more permanent varieties, too, made with nuts, herbs, seashells and dried leaves.

The ancient Hawaiians presented leis to their gods during religious ceremonies to ensure their blessings. Today, as in the past, leis are given and worn to mark memorable moments in life, special occasions and celebrations. Want to string your own necklace of flowers? Complimentary lei-making lessons are offered at many hotels and resorts throughout Hawaii.

© Hawaii Tourism Authority (HTA) / Tor Johnson

Koko Crater Botanical Gardens

🌵 Koko Crater Botanical Gardens★

Map p107. Off Kealahou St. from Hwy. 72, on Koko Head. 808-522-7066. www.honolulu.gov/parks. Open year-round daily dawn to dusk. Closed Jan 1 & Dec 25. 1 hr. self-guided walk. $5.

Best part about this place? Even if you're not a gardening aficionado, you'll appreciate the dramatic crater setting. Koko Crater is a volcanic tuff cone, created some 10,000 years ago. The 60-acre basin is home to a newly developing hot and dry garden of desert-loving plants. Take the 2-mile self-guided walk through the garden, then head over to nearby Sandy Beach to cool off.

Lyon Arboretum★

Map inside back cover. 3860 Manoa Rd., Honolulu. 808-988-0456. www.hawaii.edu/lyonarboretum/. Open year-round Mon–Fri 8am–4pm, Sat 9am–3pm. Closed major holidays. Free. $10 for guided tours.

This 193-acre nature preserve showcases more than 5,000 exotic trees and plants found in, or introduced to, Hawaii. The woodsy oasis is crisscrossed with walking paths through stands of mountain apple, candlenut trees and taro, and along grand patches of ferns, bromeliads and magnolias.

Take the trail up to **Inspiration Point** for lovely valley views; along the way, stop at the bo tree, a descendant of the tree that

Lyon Arboretum

GARDENS

Touring Tip

Why not make a day of it? Stop at Wahiawa Botanical Garden on your way to the north shore, where you can take in the surfing scene at **Waimea Bay**, and take the kids to **Waimea Valley**★★ (see p129).

Gautama Buddha sat under for enlightenment.

Just beyond the arboretum, you'll find the hiking trail to 100-foot **Manoa Falls**.

Senator Fong's Plantation★★

Map p107. 47-285 Pulama Rd., off Hwy. 83, Kaneohe. 808-239-6775. www.fonggarden.net. Open year-round daily 10am–2:30pm. Closed Jan 1 & Dec 25. $14.50, including 1 hour guided tour.

An open-air tram ride takes you through the gardens that feature more than 70 edible varieties of fruits and nuts, 80 different types of palms, slopes of pili grass (once used to make thatch houses), a collection of early Polynesian plants, and 100 rare sandalwood trees. An easy one-mile guided walking tour is also offered.

Red, White and Pink

Some 5,000 varieties of hibiscus grow in Hawaii, including plants brought by the original Hawaiians like the hau tree with flowers that change from yellow to orange, and the native sweet-smelling *kokio keokeo*, which can reach up to 60 feet.

The gardens embrace 700 acres, rising from 80 feet to 2,600 feet above sea level.

Once owned by Hiram L. Fong, the first Asian American elected to the US Senate, the plantation is divided into five areas, each named after presidents Fong served with during his 17 years in the US Senate. When you're not taking in the sights and scents of the flora, peek at the Koolau Range and the vast ocean views.

Wahiawa Botanical Garden★

Map p106. 1396 California Ave., Wahiawa. 802-522-7060. www.honolulu.gov/parks. Open year-round daily 9am–4pm. Closed Jan 1 & Dec 25.

Take a deep breath, stop, and smell the spices! This 27-acre rain-forest garden overflows with West Indies spice trees (allspice, nutmeg, ginger), palms and pom poms—all tropical plants that require a cool, moist environment.

Pick up a map *(free)* at the information desk, then walk the terraced paths down into a shady, humid ravine. Bring your raincoat—the area gets 52 to 80 inches of rainfall each year.

Tree Ferns – The garden has a large collection of tree ferns, both the Hawaiian variety and tree ferns from other tropical places, such as Australia and Tasmania. The seeds of large, leafy Hawaiian tree ferns (*Cibotium glaucum*) most likely came to the islands on the wind, millions of years ago. These ancient plants still form the understory of many of the state's forests.

MUSEUMS

Had enough fun in the sun? No problem; cosmopolitan Oahu has first-rate art, cultural, and history museums.

Hawaiian Hall, Bishop Museum

© Bishop Museum

Bishop Museum and Planetarium★★★

Map inside back cover. 1525 Bernice St., Honolulu. 808-847-3511. www.bishopmuseum. org. Open year-round Wed–Mon 9am–5pm. Closed Dec 25. $19.95 adults, $14.95 children (ages 4–12). If you have time to see only one museum on Oahu, make it this one. Considered perhaps Hawaii's finest museum, the sprawling repository of natural and cultural history is the state's largest museum; its collection of Hawaiian and Pacific artifacts is regarded as the best in the world, including more than 1.3 million artifacts, documents and photographs relating to Hawaii and other Pacific island cultures, and a grand total of 24 million items relating to the Pacific Hemisphere.

What's What at the Bishop?

Hawaiian Hall★★★ – The three-story Victorian-style gallery houses objects of Hawaiian culture from the Stone Age to the 21C. You can't miss the 55-foot sperm whale suspended from the ceiling (a tribute to Hawaii's whaling past) or the magnificent ceremonial robes made from the feathers of thousands of birds.
Pacific Hall★★ – Two floors of artifacts from Pacific cultures

---

Beyond the Exhibits: Guided Tours at Bishop Museum

For a great introduction to the Bishop Museum, catch one of the free 15- or 20-minute guided tours, offered in Hawaiian Hall. Several tours and demonstrations are scheduled throughout the day. Are you interested in native plants and traditional gardening? Show up for the 25-minute tour of the museum's gardens. In addition, live music and dance performances and storytelling sessions are held daily and free lei-making and hula lessons are offered at the museum's Learning Activity area.

Pacific Hall exhibit, Bishop Museum
© Bishop Museum

across Polynesia, Micronesia and Melanesia and exhibits explaining the spread of Polynesians across earth's largest ocean.

Kahili Room★ – This small gallery displays an impressive collection of *kahili*, the feather staffs traditionally used at royal ceremonies.

Mamiya Science Center★ – Interactive exhibits here introduce visitors to the scientific endeavors in which Hawaii is a world leader, including oceanography, astronomy, biodiversity and volcanology.

Planetarium★ – Find out what's different about the sky over Hawaii

at changing shows, included in the museum admission *(daily at 11:30am, 1:30pm & 3:30pm).*

Sports Hall of Fame – from Duke Kahanomoku to modern athletes, Hawaiian standouts reflect the islands' diverse peoples.

Honolulu Museum of Art★★

Map inside back cover. 900 S. Beretania St., Honolulu. 808-532-8700. www.honolulumuseum.org. Open year-round Tue–Sat 10am–4:30pm, Sun 1pm–5pm. Closed major holidays. $10 (includes entry to Spalding House p123).

This world-class museum holds more than 50,000 works of art and is internationally recognized for its extensive Asian collection, considered one of the finest in the country. Housed in a Mediterranean-style building, the collections are equally divided between Western and Asian works. More than 30 galleries surround six landscaped courtyards, including the Henry R. Luce Pavilion, home to the museum's permanent collection of traditional Hawaiian art. Here's an overview:

Asian Art★★ – The collection consists of 23,000 objects from China, Japan, Korea and Southeast Asia. You'll see some 300 Japanese paintings from the 12C to the 20C. Also of note: Buddhist cave sculpture dating from the 4C to the 10C; the collection of *Scenes of Kyoto*, painted by well-known Japanese artist Kano Motohide; and author James Michener's collection of woodblock prints.

Western Art★★ – There are more than 18,000 works from European and American artists here, including paintings, sculptures, crafts,

Feather cape of King Kamehameha
© Hawaii Tourism Japan (HTJ)

Honolulu Museum of Art

© Honolulu Museum of Art

Under the Monkey Pod Tree

Bet you worked up an appetite roaming the more than 30 galleries of the Honolulu Museum of Art. No problem. Head to the **Museum Café**, popular with locals, and non-museum visitors, too. The open-air eatery serves up fresh-made soups, salads and sandwiches against a backdrop of ferns and palms, swirling fans and teak furniture. Tables overlook gardens, waterfalls, and ceramic sculptures by Jun Kaneko. Pull up a seat under the shade of the 70-year-old monkey pod tree. *The cafe is open Tue–Sat 11:30am–1:30pm; call 808-532-8734 for reservations.*

Shangri La★

Map inside back cover. Tours depart from the Honolulu Museum of Art, 900 S. Beretania St., Honolulu. 808-532-3853. www.honolulumuseum. org. Visit by 2¹/₂-hour guided tour only, Nov–Aug Wed–Sat 8:30am–1:30pm. Closed Sept, Jan 1, Jul 4, Thanksgiving Day & Dec 25. $25.

Imagine an Islamic palace in Hawaii and you have Shangri La, the private estate of Doris Duke, the wealthy, only child of American tobacco baron James Duke. Built in 1937, Shangri La features Duke's furniture, textiles and graphic works. Paintings by Paul Cézanne, Vincent Van Gogh, Claude Monet, Henri Matisse and others can be found in the European gallery. **Hawaiian Art★** – This gallery displays indigenous and traditional Hawaiian art and artifacts, from 18C works to contemporary sculpture, paintings and photographs.

©David Franzen/Doris Duke Foundation for Islamic Art

Turkish Room, Shangri La

MUSEUMS

eclectic collection of Islamic art, which she amassed over a span of almost 60 years.

More than 3,500 objects are displayed throughout the home's exterior and interior spaces, which are exquisitely decorated with painted and gilded wood ceilings, intricate mosaic panels and textiles.

Mission Houses Museum★★

Map inside back cover.
553 S. King St., at Kawaiahao St., Honolulu. 808-447-3910. www.missionhouses.org. Open year-round Tue–Sat 10am–4pm. Closed major holidays. $10.

The pieces of Hawaii's oldest Western-style structure were shipped around Cape Horn from New England and assembled here in 1821 by the first American Calvinist missionaries, with the help of the Hawaiian people.

With the coming of the missionaries, Hawaii's culture changed forever. You'll learn how by taking a self-guided, or guided, tour of these three historic houses, which date from 1821 to 1841.

Polynesian Cultural Center★★

Map p107. 55–370 Kamehameha Hwy. (Rte. 83), Laie. 808-293-3333 or 800-367-7060. www.polynesia. com. Open year-round Mon–Sat 11:45am–6pm. Closed Thanks- giving Day & Dec 25. $39.95 adults for general admission,$23.95 children (ages 3–11).

Operated by the Mormon Church, this cultural theme park is Hawaii's number-one paid attraction. Located on the north shore of Oahu, about 25 miles from downtown Honolulu, the

Touring Tip

Your visit to the **Polynesian Cultural Center** can also include a canoe tour, the interactive cinematic presentation of *Hawaiian Journey*, the Rainbows of Paradise water show, and the high-energy evening extravaganza, **Ha: Breath of Life,** featuring a cast of some 100 islanders performing traditional Polynesian songs and dances. Several packages including general admission, luaus, shows and activities are offered.

Polynesian Cultural Center features the islands of Hawaii, Samoa, Aotearoa (Maori, New Zealand), Fiji, Tahiti and Tonga, spread out across a 42-acre setting. You could spend all afternoon here, wandering the villages, touring island dwellings and learning about traditional skills. Go Native activities, interactive demonstrations and presentations are held throughout the day. For example, in Hawaii,

Hawaiian Journey Theater

© Polynesian Cultural Center

Hawaiian canoe paddling, Polynesian Cultural Center

you can discover the heritage of the hula, learn to play the ukulele, and see how taro is harvested and cooked into poi. In Tonga, there are drumming presentations, or try your hand at *tolo* (spear throwing). The Halau Waa, or canoe house of learning, houses Iosepa, a traditional voyaging canoe, and exhibits showcasing Polynesian voyaging techniques.

Spalding House★

Map inside back cover. 2411 Makiki Heights Dr., Honolulu. 808-526-1322. www.honolulumuseum. org. Open year-round Tue–Sat 10am–4pm, Sun noon–4pm. Closed major holidays. $10 (includes admission to Honolulu Museum of Art, p120).

Part of the Honolulu Museum of Art, this small museum is set on 5 acres of sculpture and meditation gardens overlooking Diamond Head. Interactive exhibits related to school subjects—literature, math—feature works from the museum's permanent collection.

On permanent view is David Hockney's installation *L'Enfant et les sortileges,* his design for the Ravel opera. The cafe is a favorite of art-scene insiders.

Hawaii's Plantation Village

Map p106. 94-695 Waipahu St., Waipahu Cultural Garden Park, Waipahu.808-677-0110. www. hawaiiplantationvillage.org. Open year-round Mon–Sat 10am–2pm. $13 adults, $5 children (ages 4–11).

This living history museum re-creates life on a Hawaiian sugar plantation, spanning 100 years, from 1850 to 1950. Through those years, more than 400,000 workers, from Japan, Portugal, Korea and elsewhere, worked the fields and lived here in camp houses. One-and-a-half-hour tours are given on the hour, as docents tell stories about plantation life and the people who worked here.

The plantation has several restored buildings and replicas of original plantation structures, including more than 30 houses of various ethnic groups, community buildings such as the plantation store, the infirmary, the community bathhouse, and the camp office.

MUSEUMS

HISTORIC SITES

The top tourist attraction in the state (Pearl Harbor) and the only royal palace in the country are highlights of Oahu's must-see sights.

Iolani Palace

© Brigitta L. House/Michelin

Iolani Palace★★★

Map inside back cover. S. King & Richards Sts., Honolulu. 808-522-0832. www.iolanipalace.org. Open year-round Mon–Sat 9am–5pm. Self-guided audio tour $14.75; guided tour $21.75.

This rococo structure, a dominant feature in downtown Honolulu, is the only royal palace in the United States. If you're intrigued by kings and queens, and the compelling story of the Hawaiian kingdom, join the 90-minute docent-led tour on three floors of the four-story palace, with plenty of history provided. You can also roam the galleries on your own for a peek at rare treasures and crown jewels, including the king's crown, studded with 521 diamonds, 54 pearls, 20 opals, 8 emeralds and 8 rubies, as well as other artifacts such as a temple drum carved from a coconut tree and decorated with human teeth.

King David Kalakaua, back from travels in Europe, erected the palace in 1882; its last royal occupant was **Queen Lili'uokalani,** whose government was overthrown in 1893. A modern statue of her graces the other side of the palace facing the capitol. Across King Street stands a statue of **Kamehameha the Great**.

Palace Highlights

Throne Room – Dripping with crimson and gold, the Throne Room hosted many a royal ball and reception over the years. It was a meeting place for the House of Representatives from 1893 to 1968, when the Palace served as the Territorial and, later, the State capitol.

Statue of Lili'uokalani

© Brigitta L. House/Michelin

MUST SEE OAHU

State Dining Room – With its ornate, carved sliding doors and three massive sideboards, the dining room was used for State dinners. The Senate Chamber was housed in this room before the new state capitol was completed in 1969.

Coronation Pavilion – Built in 1883 for the coronation of King Kalakaua and Queen Kapiolani, the pavilion stands in the corner of the grounds *(near King and Richards Sts.)*. In more recent times, several of Hawaii's governors were inaugurated here.

Pearl Harbor★★★

Map pp106-107. 6mi west of downtown Honolulu via H-1 Freeway & Kamehameha Hwy. (Rte. 90). 2-day pass covering all the area's sights is $65 at www. pearlharborhistoricsites.org.
The infamous bay, site of the attack that hurled the United States into World War II, is Hawaii's most popular tourist attraction, drawing nearly 1.5 million visitors each year. Here on December 7, 1941, more than 2,300 servicemen were killed in a surprise early-morning Japanese air attack on the US naval fleet anchored in the bay. Eighteen ships, including six battleships and

---

Queen Emma Summer Palace

See map inside back cover. 2913 Pali Hwy. 808-595-6291. www. daughtersofhawaii.org. $10.
For a peek at royal life, visit the palace where **Emma**, wife of King Kamehameha IV, spent her summers. Emma was of Hawaiian-British heritage and thus was an early symbol of cosmopolitanism in the isles. Royal Hawaiian and personal artifacts are displayed in her Victorian-era Nuuanu Valley retreat.

---

three destroyers, sank in America's greatest military disaster. President Franklin Roosevelt declared it "a date which will live in infamy" as America plunged into World War II. The harbor is still surrounded by active military bases, but it also includes three must-see visitor sites.

USS Arizona Memorial★★★

1 Arizona Memorial Dr., Honolulu. 808-423-7300. www.nps.gov/valr. Open year-round daily 7am–5pm. Boat trips 8am–3pm. Closed Jan 1, Thanksgiving Day & Dec 25. Note: waiting time in line can be 1hr-plus.
Perhaps no war memorial is more poignant than the USS *Arizona*. Floating over the hulk of the sunken battleship, the concave,

---

Visiting the USS Arizona Memorial

Though summer is the busiest, expect crowds year-round. Boat-launch tickets can run out by noon, and waits at the launch can be as long as 2hrs. Tickets are first-come, first-served and must be picked up in person. Reserve tickets online beforehand ($1.50 fee) at www. nps.gov/valr. Otherwise, show up when the visitor center opens at 7am *(lines begin as early as 6am)* to pick up boat-launch tickets, then browse the exhibits and museum gift shop while you wait for the launch.

© National Park Service

History doesn't have to be boring. Have your kids pick up a free Junior Ranger booklet at the front desk of the USS Arizona Memorial Visitor Center. The fun-filled book, best for ages 7 to 12, guides kids through the events of the infamous attack on Pearl Harbor, with colorful photos, sketches and activities. Added bonus: kids get a Junior Ranger badge when they complete the book.

USS Arizona Memorial

©Andre Nantel/iStockphoto.com

Closed Jan 1, Thanksgiving Day & Dec 25. Submarine & museum tour $10 adults, $4 children (ages 4–12). Museum only $5 adults, $3 children. Children under age 4 are not permitted on the submarine, but may visit the museum and mini-theater at no charge. Tickets and trolley shuttles to the Battleship Missouri Memorial (see below) are available here.

A walk through the Bowfin, credited with sinking 44 Japanese ships, helps define the claustrophobia of submarine missions. Visitors are given cassette players narrating their tour through the cramped spaces. The additional 10,000-square-foot on-site **museum** showcases submarine life with a collection of artifacts, weapons, missiles and memorabilia.

Waterfront Memorial – This memorial honors the more than 3,500 submariners and 52 American submarines lost during World War II.

184-foot white-concrete bridge marks the permanent tomb of 1,177 sailors killed in the Pearl Harbor attack. Each victim's name is inscribed in white marble on one wall. The macabre outline of the ship's hull is visible below. Launches depart on a first-come, first-served basis from a newly-renovated shoreline visitor center, where historical exhibits and a 25-minute documentary film are presented.

USS Bowfin Submarine Museum & Park★

11 Arizona Memorial Dr., Honolulu. 808-423-1341. www.bowfin.org. Open year-round daily 7am–5pm (last tour of submarine at 4:30pm).

Battleship Missouri Memorial★

11 Arizona Memorial Dr., Honolulu. Access only by shuttle bus from USS Bowfin Submarine Museum & Park; tickets and trolley shuttles available there. 808-455-1600. www.ussmissouri.com. Open Jun–Aug daily 8am–5pm (rest of year until 4pm). Ticket window closes 4pm. Closed Jan 1, Thanksgiving Day & Dec 25. Guided tour $25 adults, $12 children (ages 10-12). This historic battleship, docked near the remains of the USS Arizona, features the site of the September 2, 1945, surrender that ended World War II. The six-deck ship is chock-full of models, maps, photographs and other exhibits.

MUST SEE OAHU

© Hawaii Tourism Authority (HTA) / Tor Johnson

Pali Lookout

Map inside back cover. This cloud-shrouded perch, only five miles from Honolulu, is one of Oahu's most historic sites, where the famous 1795 Nuuanu Pali battle took place, uniting Oahu under King Kamehameha's rule. Thousands plunged to their death off the 1,000-foot cliffs. The view from the lookout, across the lush Windward Coast, is stunning.

You can meander through the rooms, including the gunfire-control station, mess deck, galley, bakery, ship's store and sleeping area, and browse the exhibits.

Tip: You'll get more out of the visit if you sign up for the **one-hour guided tour**. Tour guests also get to experience a flight simulation of the assault on Iwo Jima in 1943 aboard a plane that was launched from the deck of the *Missouri*.

National Memorial Cemetery of the Pacific★

Map inside back cover. 2177 Puowaina Dr., Honolulu. 808-532-3720. www.cem.va.gov/cems. Open Mar–Sept daily 8am–6:30pm. Oct–Apr daily 8am–5:30pm. Memorial Day 7am–7pm.

Occupying an extinct crater known simply as The Punchbowl, the "Arlington of the Pacific" is the final resting place for the more than 40,000 US military men and others whom the government has honored. Many come to visit the graves of World War II correspondent Ernie Pyle, and Hawaii's astronaut Ellison Onizuka, who died in the Challenger space-shuttle disaster of 1986.

The Punchbowl – The crater in which the cemetery rests was formed between 75,000 and 100,000 years ago. Ironically, the site's Hawaiian name, Puowaina, translates to "Hill of Sacrifice"; ancient islanders once offered human sacrifices to the gods here. During the reign of Kamehameha the Great, cannons were mounted at the rim of the crater to salute distinguished arrivals. Later, it was used as a rifle range.

© Battleship Missouri Memorial

Battleship Missouri Memorial

HISTORIC SITES

FOR FUN

Not surprisingly, entertainment centers on outdoor recreation like snorkeling, surfing and cruising at sunset.

Watch Expert Surfers

Surf's up! No trip to Oahu would be complete without watching the expert antics and athleticism of the island's top surfers.

Oahu is touted as the **surfing capital** of the world, renowned for its big-water beaches, high-profile championships, and famous surfing personalities. The waters off Oahu feature 600 different types of surf breaks, offering gentle breaks for beginners and formidable surf for the most experienced wave riders. For the best shows, head to Oahu's north shore.

Sunset Beach – *North of Waimea, on the north shore.* Here you'll find a pretty two-mile band of sand and some of the best surfers in the world. Throw your blanket down, take a seat, and watch the show. You're likely to see talented surfers riding powerful, 15-foot and higher waves. Technically, this entire stretch of sand is Sunset Beach, but surfers divide it up according to surf break, with names like Gas Chambers, Back Doors, Off-the-Wall, Cloud Break, Pele's Followers, and the renowned Banzai Pipeline. The sunsets here are awesome, too.

Waimea Bay – *South of Sunset Beach, on the north shore.*
The beach at Waimea boasts one of the longest rideable surf breaks in the world. Spectators crowd the sands during the winter months when the surf is at its highest. Ironically, during the summer the water is generally calm and the beach is a fine swimming spot—but if the surf is up, be careful!

Makaha Beach Park – *South of Makua, on the west shore.* On the leeward side of the island, Makaha is a longtime favorite with island surfers, especially during the winter months when the northerly swells bring in big waves.

Touring Tip

© Leslie Forsberg/Michelin

All that sun and surf pique your thirst? While you're on the north shore, head to **Matsumoto's** *(66–087 Kamehameha Hwy.; 808-637-4827; www.matsumoto shaveice.com)* near the town of Haleiwa for what's known as the best shave ice on the island. The Matsumoto family has been serving up shave ice here (sometimes more than 1,000 a day) since 1951. Try the local favorite: shave ice, ice cream and red beans.

MUST DO OAHU

Go Whale Watching

Follow a team of marine biologists to the untrammeled Leeward Coast. You'll board a catamaran and sail to the place where humpback whales breed and endangered spinner dolphins frolic. **Wild Side Specialty Tours** *(808-306-7273; www.sailhawaii.com)* takes small groups *(no more than six passengers per boat)* on its research trips to observe humpback whales. You'll watch as they (as many as 3,000 migrate to Hawaiian waters) hurl themselves out of the water and sing and chase each other as part of the mating ritual.

Then don a pair of fins and a mask to swim alongside spinner dolphins—the most acrobatic of all dolphins—sea turtles, and schools of tropical fish. Along the way, you'll learn about sea creatures, habitat, and conservation. Whale-watching season runs mid-December through April; snorkel trips are offered year-round. It's a 45-minute drive to the boat launch but the company will pick you up in Waikiki and shuttle you to and from the boat.

Take a Sunset Cruise

There are few things more romantic than a sunset cruise along the Oahu coast. You'll slip past world-famous Diamond Head *(see p112)* and along the sparkling Kohala Gold Coast, with the rolling Koolau mountains as a backdrop. Take your beloved out on the open deck, where you'll be caressed by balmy tropical winds and treated to a view of a purple-and-pink-streaked sky. Watch the twinkling lights of Waikiki Beach and Honolulu dot the landscape, as the sun seems to head for the other side of the

world. Contact the **Oahu Visitors Bureau** *(877-525-6248; www.gohawaii.com/oahu)* for a list of companies offering cruises. Most feature dinner and entertainment, and cost $75 up to $200.

Roam Waimea Valley

59-864 Kamehameha Hwy., Haleiwa. 808-638-7766. www.waimeavalley.net. Open year-round daily 9am–5pm. Closed Jan 1 & Dec 25 (park closes at noon on Thanksgiving Day & Dec 31). $15 adults, $7.50 children (ages 4–12). Pick up a map and pamphlet at the visitor center. Guided tours offered.

This tranquil 1,875-acre oasis, nestled in the lush Waimea Valley on Oahu's north shore, offers a peaceful escape from the concrete jungle and never-ending action of Honolulu and Waikiki Beach. It's also a great place to learn about ancient Hawaiian culture and natural history; there's a spiderweb of nature trails to meander on your own, some leading to archaeological sites.

Botanical Gardens – You could spend hours roaming the park's colorful gardens that include

Touring Tip

Has all that Waikiki hustle and bustle got you frazzled? Here's a quick cure: participate in a tea ceremony at the **Urasenke Tea House** in Waikiki *(245 Saratoga Rd.; 808-923-3059)*. The soothing, centuries-old ceremony offers a peek into the Japanese "Way of Tea." The ceremony, including an informative video presentation, is held on Wed and Fri from 10am to noon. Everyone is welcome *($3 donation suggested)*.

FOR FUN

Waimea Valley Botanical Gardens

© Reinhard Dirscherl / age fotostock

more than 5,000 species of plants spread across 36 themed areas and covering 150 acres. Plants from around the world include native Hawaiian collections and rare species, identified by small signs. Or sign up for one of the guided tours, including wildlife walks and native Hawaiian plant walks. There are arts and crafts demonstrations, too.

Waimea Falls – Be sure to save time for a walk to Waimea Falls, the spectacular centerpiece of the preserve. A 3.5-mile self-guided hike leads to the 40-foot-high falls. Stand back and take a good look: do you think the falls form the shape of a woman? Some locals think so and have thus nicknamed the waters "Wahine Falls" (*wahine* is the Hawaiian word for woman). Pack your bathing suit; swimming in the crystal-clear pools is allowed when the weather and winds cooperate (lifeguards are on duty).

Snorkel at Hanauma Bay

Off Hwy. 72, Hanauma Bay (10mi east of Wailkiki). 808-396-4229. www1.honolulu.gov/parks/facility/hanaumabay. Open Jun–Aug Wed–Mon 6am–7pm. Rest of the year Wed–Mon 6am–6pm. Closed Tue. $7.50 (free for children ages 12 and under).

Crystal-clear, turquoise-blue Hanauma Bay is one of the best places in the islands for snorkeling. The underwater treasure, now a designated marine conservation district, teems with some 400,000 tropical fish (more than 150 species) that swim around the impressive reef and coral formations.

Don your masks and fins (*rentals are available on-site*) and swim with colorful parrotfish, tangs, Moorish idols, butterfly fish, triggerfish and others. A snowy white beach ringing the half-mile horseshoe-

---

Luau, Anyone?

This outdoor feast—complete with a kalua pig roasted in an *imu* (underground oven)—may be the best way to hear traditional tunes and sample typical Island foods. Expect to be served poi (taro-root paste, offered fresh or fermented), *laulau* (steamed meat, fish and taro leaves wrapped in ti leaves), *lomi-lomi salmon* (salted salmon mixed with tomatoes and onions) and *haupia* (coconut pudding).

Snorkeling at Hanauma Bay

Touring Tip

Alas, **Hanauma Bay** is not an undiscovered gem. Located on the southeastern shore of Oahu, about a 30-minute drive from Honolulu, this place is hugely popular. The park now limits the number of people admitted each day; arrive early in the morning to snag a parking spot and admittance. Facilities at the beach park include restrooms, showers, concessions and equipment rentals.

shaped bay, and flanking volcanic cliffs are scenic bonuses.

Marine Education Center – When you need a break from snorkeling and swimming, check out the Marine Education Center at the park: it features programs and exhibits on the history of the bay and conservation efforts.

Camp on Oahu

Oahu has several state and county park campgrounds that sure beat the price of an upscale hotel. State park campgrounds include the 5,228-acre **Malaekahana Beach** *(off Hwy. 83)* and the 110-acre **Kahana Valley** *(52-222 Hwy. 83, Kahana)*, both with swimming, picnic areas and hiking trails. Near Honolulu, **Keaiwa Heiau State Recreation Area** *(end of Aiea Heights Dr., Aiea)* offers rustic camping, and **Sand Island State Recreation Area** *(end of Sand Island Access Rd., off Hwy. 92, Honolulu)* offers 14 acres of camping along the coast.

Golf Oahu

Oahu brims with top-notch golf courses. You can't go wrong with these highly rated links:

Ala Wai – *404 Kapahulu Ave., Honolulu. 808-733-7387. www. gohawaii.com/oahu.* This busy 18-hole municipal course near Waikiki has a pro shop, restaurant, driving range and views of Diamond Head.

Hawaii Kai – *8902 Kalanianaole Hwy., Honolulu. 808-395-2358. www.hawaiikaigolf.com.* Revel in splendid views of the Pacific Ocean and Makapuu Cliffs at this 6,614-yard, 18-hole championship course.

Koolau Golf Club – *45-550 Kionaole Rd., Kaneohe. 808-247-236-4653. www.koolaugolfclub. com.* The US Golf Association deems Koolau one of the toughest courses in the country.

FOR FUN

Camping is allowed at four state parks on Oahu: Ahupua'a Kahana State Park, Malaekahana State Recreation Area, Keaiwa Heiau State Recreation Area and Sand Island State Recreation Area. Fees start at $18 per campsite per night. Camping is allowed Friday through Wednesday nights, except at Sand Island, where camping is permitted Friday through Sunday only. Permits are required *(obtain permits from the Division of State Parks, Kalanimoku Building, 1151 Punchbowl St., Room 310, Honolulu; 808-587-0300; www.hawaiistateparks.org).*

Koolina Golf Course – *92-1220 Aliinui Dr., Kapolei. 808-676-5300. www.koolinagolf.com.* This 6,867-yard Ted Robinson design is ranked among the top courses on the island, and each year hosts an LPGA tournament.

Turtle Bay Resort – *57-049 Kuilina Dr., Kahuku. 808-293-8574. www.turtlebayresort.com.* Boasting 36 holes of championship golf, including an 18-hole course designed by Arnold Palmer and Ed Seay, Turtle Bay challenges all skill levels with five to six sets of tees on each hole.

Soar the Skies

For an unbeatable bird's-eye view, hop aboard a seaplane. **Island Seaplane Service** *(808-836-6273; www.islandseaplane. com; rates start at $179 for a 30min flight; $299 for 1hr flight),* the only seaplane service on the island, offers a sky-high tour from Hanauma Bay to the North Shore, with plenty of colorful commentary and anecdotes along the way. The plane departs from the same water runways used by the PanAm clipper ships, and flies across the same path the Japanese used to bomb Pearl Harbor. Passengers will be treated to overhead views of Diamond Head's crater and the USS *Arizona* Memorial, among other sights.

Made in Hawaii

Visiting Oahu in late August? You're in luck. The annual three-day Made in Hawaii Festival *($4)* showcases Hawaii-made items, created by more than 300 companies—all displayed under one roof at the Neal S. Blaisdell Center in Honolulu *(777 Ward Ave.).* There are cooking demos and live music, too. *For more information, call 808-533-1292 ext 3 or visit www.madein hawaiifestival.com.*

© Hawaii Tourism Authority (HTA) / Sri Maiava Rusden

How Did Surfing Begin?

Surfboarding, or wave riding, was an integral part of the ancient Hawaiian culture. By the time Captain Cook arrived on the islands in 1778, surf boarding was widespread, and an important aspect of sacred and religious ceremonies and practices. However, when the Europeans came to settle in the islands, Hawaiian culture, including surfing, was suppressed. At the end of the 19C, surfing had all but disappeared. It wasn't until Jack London visited Waikiki and wrote about the sport in 1907, and Alexander Hume Ford founded the Hawaiian Outrigger Canoe Club in 1908, that surfing began its modern-day resurgence. A few years later, **Duke Paoa Kahanamoku** put the sport of surfing on the map for good. Duke was a famous Olympic gold-medal swimmer—and avid surfer. Known as "the fastest swimmer alive," Duke used his fame to introduce the world to surfing. Today he's known as "the father of surfing," and you'll find tributes to him throughout the islands, including the famous Duke statue on Waikiki Beach and the popular Duke's Canoe Club bar and restaurant at the Outrigger Waikiki Hotel in Honolulu *(2335 Kalakaua Ave.; see Hotels)* and on the island of Kauai *(on Kalapaki Beach, in front of the Kauai Marriott Resort; 808-246-9599; www.dukeskauai.com)*.

© Hawaii Tourism Authority (HTA) / Joe Solem

Listen to the Royal Hawaiian Band

If you happen to be king and like music, what do you do? You create a band, by royal decree. That's what King Kamehameha III did in 1836, and the band plays on. Today the Royal Hawaiian Band is an agency of the city and county of Honolulu and the only full-time municipal band in the US.

For an earful of traditional island music (including conch-blowing), attend a free concert *(Fridays noon–1pm)* at the Coronation Pavilion at **Iolani Palace** *(S. King and Richard Sts.; see p124)*. The band also plays several times a week at various locations throughout the city.
For more information and a schedule of appearances, call 808-922-5331 or check online at www.rhb-music.com.

Take a Hike

Get out of the bustling city and into the jungle! Oahu has an extensive system of hiking trails through tropical forests, and to waterfalls and mountain summits. Several tour operators offer guided hikes *(visit hawaiitrails.ehawaii.gov)*.
Popular hikes include the:

♦ Pu'u Ohia trail, an easy trek through tropical forest
♦ Tantalus forest trails, leading to a 1,200-foot summit
♦ 9-mile Maunawili Trail
♦ Diamond Head trail
♦ Aiea Loop with views into Halawa Valley
♦ Manoa Falls through a bamboo rain forest to a 150-foot waterfall
♦ Maunawili Falls, a family-friendly, beginner's hike to a waterfall and swimming hole.

FOR FUN

133

FOR KIDS

With aquariums, a hands-on children's museum, a zoo and an authentic working ranch, it's easy to keep *keiki* **happy on Oahu.**

Dolphin show, Sea Life Park

© Tibor Bognar / age fotostock

Sea Life Park★★

Map p107. 41-202 Kalanianaole Hwy., Waimanalo. 802-259-2500. www.sealifeparkhawaii.com. Open year-round daily 10:30am–5pm. $29.99 adults, $19.99 children (ages 3–11).

At this popular attraction you'll get a close-up look at the rich life that thrives within Hawaii's waters. The oceanfront marine park sits on Makapuu Point, 20 miles outside Honolulu on the windward coast. Just inside the gates, an impressive 300,000-gallon aquarium is home to more than 2,000 species of marine life. Watch as huge schools of neon-colored tropical fish, sea turtles, eels and sharks swim by in the 18-foot-high **Hawaiian Reef Tank**. Stop by the sea lion feeding pool and the **sea turtle lagoon**, then make your way to the stingray exhibit, where you can watch rays slide through the water—and touch them, if you wish. The newest exhibit educates visitors about the key role **Hawaiian sharks** play in island waters. Entertaining dolphin and sea lion **shows** are presented throughout the day, and the park offers a number of special tours. Also offered daily *(extra fee)* are behind-the-scenes programs such as swimming with stingrays or working with dolphins. Though it's an entertainment venue, the park has played a

Oahu Sea Turtles

The sea turtle lagoon at the Sea Life Park on Oahu doubles as a breeding sanctuary for threatened Hawaiian green sea turtles. The program, the only one of its kind in the US, releases 200 to 800 hatchlings into the wild each year. The cold-blooded reptile gets its name from the color of its body fat, which turns green from the algae it eats. Once plentiful on the islands and heavily hunted by natives, the Hawaiian green sea turtle is now protected by law. More than 90 percent of the nesting of these island reptiles now occurs inside the National Wildlife Refuge at French Frigate Shoals.

134

MUST DO OAHU

key role in the restoration of the Hawaiian green sea turtle, and continues to raise turtles for release each year *(see box p134)*.

Honolulu Zoo★

Map inside back cover.
In Kapiolani Park, 151 Kapahulu Ave. (between Diamond Head & Waikiki), Honolulu. 808-971-7171. www.honoluluzoo.org. Open year-round daily 9am–4:30pm. Closed Dec 25. $14 adults, $6 children (ages 4–12).

Kids and animals—this is one combination where you can't go wrong. Make a beeline for the Diamond Head side of town to this small but sure-to-please zoo, home to more than 1,200 animals. The zoo stretches over 42 flat acres in Kapiolani Park; you can see the entire place in half a day—then go off to the beach.

Children and adults alike vote the **Kabuni Reserve** as their favorite area. This African Savannah habitat covers 12 acres, where you can walk along a path and peer at free-roaming zebra, rhinos, lions, hippos, giraffes, chimps and others. Don't miss the tropical forest, the Galapagos tortoises, and the reptile

Touring Tip

Why not combine a day at the beach with some kite-flying? **Sandy Beach** on Oahu's east shore is considered the kite-flying capital of the islands. Look up and you'll see blue skies, wispy clouds and a riot of colorful wings and tails. There's plenty of action in the water here, too. The wild shore break and big swells make it a favorite among body boarders and surfers. Bring a picnic and enjoy the show.

house. Chances are you haven't spotted Hawaii's state bird *(see p62)* in the wild, but you'll see the rare nene goose here.

Kualoa Ranch★

Map p107. 49-560 Kamehameha Hwy., Kaaawa. 808-237-7321. www.kualoa.com. Open year-round daily 7:30am–5:30pm. Closed Jan 1 & Dec 25. Ranch and movie set tour, $27 adults, $16 (ages 3-12); other tours offered; prices vary, depending on activity.

Play cowpoke for a day at this authentic working ranch, sitting on

© Kualoa Ranch

Horseback riding, Kualoa Ranch

FOR KIDS

4,000 acres on Oahu's north shore, about an hour north of Honolulu. The property is stunning, encompassing three mountains and two valleys, spreading from steep mountain cliffs to the seashore. Of course, your kids won't care much about the views, but they will enjoy **horseback riding** (*pony rides for ages 3–7*), ATV trail rides, catamaran trips to ancient fish ponds and ranch tours.

If the scenery looks familiar, it's because Kualoa Ranch has been used as a backdrop for several movies, including *Jurassic Park*, *Mighty Joe*, *Along Came Polly*, *Pearl Harbor* and *Windtalkers*.

Waikiki Aquarium★

Map inside back cover. In Queen Kapiolani Park, 2777 Kalakaua Ave., Honolulu. 808-923-9741. www.waikikiaquarium.org. Open year-round daily 9am–4:30pm. Closed Dec 25; limited hours Jan 1 & Thanksgiving Day. $12 adults, $5 youth (ages 13–17), $2 children (ages 5–12).

Dating back to 1904, the second-oldest public aquarium in the country showcases more than 2,500 underwater animals at its location on the Diamond Head end of Waikiki Beach. Here, you'll see moray eels, living corals, and giant, two-foot-long clams, the largest in the world. Kids love the **Hunters on the Reef** exhibit, with its reef sharks circling the tank. The tide-pool area and the outdoor tank, home to endangered and oh-so-cute monk seals, are also popular. Watch squid change colors and find a hiding octopus at the Jet Set Exhibit, then visit the Ocean Drifters Gallery to get up close to sea jellies.

🐾 Hawaii Children's Discovery Center

Map inside back cover. 111 Ohe St., Honolulu. 808-524-5437. www. discoverycenterhawaii.org. Open year-round Tue–Fri 9am–1pm, Sat–Sun 10am–3pm. Closed major holidays and 2 weeks after Labor Day. $10.

If you have little ones in tow and need to get out of the sun for a while, here you'll find four galleries of please-touch exhibits where youngsters can pretend to be firefighters, bankers or mechanics, make rainbows, and learn about other cultures.

Waikiki Aquarium

© Waikiki Aquarium

PERFORMING ARTS

The world-class city of Honolulu supports one of the most thriving cultural and musical arts scenes in the islands.

Production of Turandot with soprano Susan Foster, Hawaii Opera Theatre

© Cory Lum

Hawaii Opera Theatre

Map inside back cover. 999 S. King St., Honolulu. 800-836-7372. Box office: 808-596-7858. www. hawaiiopera.org. Season runs Jan–Mar. Ticket prices vary per performance. Free introductory tours offered 30min and 60min before the performance.

The Hawaii Opera Theatre—HOT for short—reflects the Hawaiian monarchy's fascination with all things European: Queen Emma supposedly sang in a production of *Il Trovatore*. Productions held at the 2,000-seat **Neil S. Blaisdell Concert Hall** range from Gilbert and Sullivan light opera to Puccini and Verdi.

Hawaii Theatre Center

Map inside back cover. 1130 Bethel St., Honolulu. Box office: 808-528-0506. www. hawaiitheatre.com. 1hr guided tours ($10) of the performance hall are offered every Tuesday at 11am (subject to change).

You'll find first-class music, theater, film and dance performances at

Honolulu's historic Hawaii Theatre Center. Built in 1922, the 1,400-seat hall, dubbed the "Pride of the Pacific," has been a landmark venue in downtown Honolulu for more than eight decades and is listed on both the State and National Register of Historic Places.

Diamond Head Theatre

Map inside back cover. 520 Makapuu Ave., Honolulu. 808-733-0274. www.diamond headtheatre.com. Ticket prices vary per performance.

Founded in 1915, this theater is the third-oldest continuously operating community theater in the US. It is located at the foot of Diamond Head and run by all volunteers, from the front office to the director and the performers. Beloved by locals, this intimate venue is home to several large-scale and ambitious productions. Performances have included *The King and I, Spamalot* and *Hairspray*.

Touring Tip

The best way to tap into local culture: time your visit to coincide with an **"Only in Hawaii"** event. Tops in this category include the annual Merrie Monarch Festival on the Big Island, the Ki Ho'alu Slack Key Guitar and Ukulele Concert series on Kauai, and the Friday concerts by the Royal Hawaiian Band on the grounds of Iolani Palace on Oahu. *See Calendar of Events (pp10–11) for other options.*

PERFORMING ARTS

SHOPPING

High-end fashion malls, designer boutiques, colorful open-air venues and giant flea markets will keep even serious shopaholics satiated.

Flower shop, Chinatown

© Hawaii Tourism Authority (HTA) / Tor Johnson

Chinatown★★

Map inside back cover. West of Nuuanu Ave., between Ala Moana & Vineyard Blvds., Honolulu. 808-521-4934. www.chinatownhi.com. Outside vendors open year-round daily 8:30am–5pm.

This fascinating 15-block historic enclave—one of the oldest Chinatowns in the country—is an eclectic place to roam, shop and eat. The ethnic neighborhood, dating back more than 120 years, buzzes with energy and brims with local color and culture. Browse the sidewalk markets that overflow with exotic fruits, flowers (this is *the* place to buy a lei), herbal medicine shops and foodstuffs. Visit the

Maunakea Market area, one of the more colorful spots in Chinatown, where locals gather to play mahjong and pick up groceries at the bustling, open-air markets. When hunger strikes, stop at one of the more than 30 ethnic eateries, like **Legend Seafood Restaurant** *(100 N. Beretania St.; 808-532-1868)* offering some of the best dim sum in the islands, or **Ruby Restaurant and Bakery** *(119 North Hotel St., 808-523-0801)*. Pause for a traditional afternoon tea at **TEA** *(1024 Nuuanu Ave., 808-521-9596, www.teaat1024.net)*.

The first Friday of every month, the neighborhood hosts an evening street festival, with live music and

---

Best Source for Aloha Wear

Established in 1963, **Hilo Hattie** *(800-233-8912; www.hilohattie.com)*, with stores scattered throughout the islands, remains one of the best places to buy Aloha wear and island-made fashions. For the widest selection and affordable prices, visit the Nimitz Flagship Store and manufacturing facility in Honolulu *(700 N. Nimitz Highway; 808-535-6500; www.hilohattie.com)*. It's open daily from 9am to 7:30pm.

MUST DO OAHU

The Waikiki Trolley is one of the best ways to get around Honolulu. The open-air trolleys travel from major hotels to top attractions and sites, as well as the big malls in Honolulu and Waikiki. For schedules and routes, contact **The Trolley Company** *(808-593-2822; www.waikikitrolley.com)*. A one-day all-city pass costs $34 and offers unlimited on-and-off boarding; a 4-day pass is $57. You can pick up a **Waikiki Trolley Map Guide** at the Royal Hawaiian and Ala Moana malls, as well as at many hotels.

entertainment. Art galleries and shops throw out their welcome mats, sponsoring special events and tastings.

Showcasing Chinese art and culture, the **Narcissus Festival** is the oldest ethnic festival in Hawaii. The celebration is held in Chinatown in conjunction with the Chinese lunar New Year.

Ala Moana Shopping Center★★

Map inside back cover. 1450 Ala Moana Blvd., Waikiki. 808-955-9517. www.alamoanacenter.com. Open year-round Mon–Sat 9:30am–9pm, Sun 10am–7pm. Closed Dec 25.

Dubbed the world's largest open-air shopping center, Ala Moana boasts more than 290 stores. Located in the heart of Waikiki, overlooking **Ala Moana Beach Park**, this shopping venue includes retail biggies like Macy's, Nordstrom and Neiman Marcus, as well as top-name designers— Escada, Chanel, Prada, Gucci and Hermès. Several stores specialize in Hawaiian-made products and island wear.

The outdoor space is opulently landscaped, and there are nearly 70 restaurants, from fast food to fine dining. A **farmers' market** is held *(Saturdays 9am–noon)* across the street; look here for

delights ranging from island-grown chocolate to fresh wasabi.

The Ala Moana Shopping Center **shuttle** runs from 12 locations in Waikiki to the shopping center.

Aloha Stadium Swap Meet★★

Map inside back cover. Aloha Stadium, 99-500 Salt Lake Blvd., Honolulu. 808-486-6704. www.alohastadiumswapmeet.net. Open year-round Wed, Sat & Sun 6am–3pm. Closed Dec 25, and at 1pm on days when University of Hawaii football games are held. $1 entry fee, children under 11 free.

If you're looking for a bargain and consider haggling a sport, this popular outdoor flea market held outside the University of Hawaii's Aloha football stadium is one of the largest flea markets in the islands, with more than 700 vendors. Hordes of people gather around the stalls of vendors, bargaining for arts and crafts, souvenirs, housewares, ethnic food items, fine art and knick-knacks. It's a great place to rub elbows with the locals.

Aloha Tower Marketplace★

Pier 9, downtown Honolulu. 808-566-2337. www.alohatower.com. Open year-round Mon–Sat 9am–9pm, Sun 9am–6pm.

SHOPPING

Aloha Tower

© Rolf Richardson / age fotostock

Special holiday hours apply on Thanksgiving Day & Dec 25.
You can't miss this entertainment, dining and shopping complex, wrapped around the imposing **Aloha Tower★★** *(see p105).*
And you can't beat the location, sitting on downtown Honolulu's oceanfront harbor. This is a popular place to hang out, pick up souvenirs and sundries, and grab a bite to eat. Some 38 stores run the gamut from gift and apparel shops to home furnishings and jewelry stores. With its array of casual restaurants and bars, the marketplace is a lively place both day and night.

Royal Hawaiian Shopping Center

Map inside back cover.
2201 Kalakaua Ave., Waikiki.
808-922-2299. www.royalhawaiian center.com. Open year-round daily 10am–10pm. Special holiday hours apply on Thanksgiving Day & Dec 25.
Located in the heart of Waikiki, this mall is one of Hawaii's largest: two blocks with more than 110 shops and restaurants. Upscale designer boutiques are scattered among souvenir shops, arts and crafts, sundries and convenience stores. Check out the free Hawaiian cultural and arts programs, including demonstrations and lessons on hula, ukulele, lei-making, Hawaiian quilting and lomilomi massage techniques. Torch-lighting ceremonies and free concerts are also regular occurrences.

NIGHTLIFE

Oahu heats up when the sun goes down, with the hottest nightlife of all the islands. You'll find extravagant luaus, live music, beach bars and nightclubs, especially in Waikiki Beach and downtown Honolulu.

🏖 Barefoot Bar at Duke's Waikiki

2335 Kalakauna Ave., Waikiki Beach. 808-922-2268. www.dukeswaikiki.com.

This classic beach bar, named in honor of surfing legend Duke Kahanamoku, is a longtime favorite with visitors and locals alike. It helps that the rollicking, open-air bar overlooks busy Waikiki Beach. The koa-wood-paneled room is chock-full of surfing memorabilia, including an outrigger canoe, antique surfboards and posters. Duke's features live entertainment most nights, and concerts on the beach every weekend.

House Without a Key

2199 Kalia Rd., Halekulani Hotel, Honolulu. 808-923-2311. www.halekulani.com/dining/house_without_a_key.

Even the most jaded local has to admit that this longtime indoor-outdoor venue is magical at sunset. Views of Diamond Head and the

Touring Tip

Begin your evening by watching the traditional torch-lighting ceremony at **Kuhio Beach Park** in Waikiki. The nightly event begins with the blowing of a conch shell, as the first torches are lit. A hula dancing performance follows. Torch-lighting ceremonies are also held throughout Waikiki, at most of the major hotels. Ceremonies usually begin around 6pm.

sherbet-colored dusk-lit skies are stunning. Add Hawaiian music and the hula, performed by talented locals, and you've got the perfect place to begin the evening. The sunset entertainment is held nightly from 5:30pm–8:30pm.

Kani Ka Pila Grille

2169 Kalia Rd. (Outrigger Reef on the Beach), Honolulu. 808-

House Without a Key

© Tor Johnson/Photo Resource Hawaii / Alamy

NIGHTLIFE

Free-for-all happenings in Honolulu

- The Royal Hawaiian Band plays at Iolani Palace, Friday noon–1pm and at Kapiolani Park, Sunday 2pm–3pm.
- Fireworks are held Friday night on the beach in front of the Hilton Hawaiian Village Resort.
- Sunset on the Beach, held weekends at Queen's Beach in Waikiki, features free outdoor movies, food vendors and local entertainment, too.

924-4990. www.outriggerreef-onthebeach.com.
Locals flock here to the Outrigger resort's restaurant-bar, the "secret" home of Hawaiian slack-key guitar music in Waikiki. After all, the bar's name means "to make music." One may expect to see luminaries of distinctive island music styles such as Cyril Pahinui or Kawika Kahiapo in an intimate setting poolside; music begins most nights at 6pm.

Luaus and Extravaganzas

For a Waikiki beachfront luau, head to the Ahaaina Luau held at the **Royal Hawaiian** resort (see p185). *808-931-8383; www.royal-hawaiian.com*. Unlike many other such shows, this one is strictly Hawaiian—no fire-dancing here.

Other luaus include local favorite **Germaine's Luau** (*808-949-6626; www.germainesluau.com*), the **Paradise Cove Luau** (*808-842-5911; www.paradisecovehawaii.com*) held on a beach on the west of the island, and the **Alii Luau** held at the Polynesian Cultural

Center (*808-293-3333; www.polynesia.com*).
The Magic of Polynesia dinner show, at the **Waikiki Beachcomber Resort** (*2300 Kalakaua Ave.; 808-971-4321*), combines illusions from John Hirokawa with an extravagant dinner, Polynesian dance performance and music.

Mai Tai Bar

1450 Ala Moana Blvd., in the Ala Moana Shopping Center, Honolulu. 808-947-2900. www.maitaibar.com.
You'll find plenty of action at this popular bar, perched over the Ala Moana Shopping Center. It's been voted Best Happy Hour Bar, Best Outdoor Bar, Best Singles Bar, and Best Place to listen to Live Music in Hawaii. It's a great place to hear live music, and locals cram the airy, tropical bar during late afternoon Happy Hour—one of the best deals on the island.
Sink into a comfy couch and sip one of their signature *mai tais*—made with three types of rum and fresh-squeezed fruit juices—as you listen to island rhythms.

Ahaaina Luau, Royal Hawaiian

© Starwood Hotels & Resorts Worldwide, Inc

SPAS

Oahu boasts some of the most lavish spas in the country. Many are located in the island's upscale, luxury resorts and hotels, with lush, tropical gardens, waterfalls and the Pacific Ocean as their backdrops.

Ihilani Spa

JW Marriott Ihilani Resort at Ko Olina, 92-1001 Olani St., Kapolei. 808-679-3321 or 808-679-0079. www.ihilanispa.com.

Ihilani means "heavenly splendor," an apt name for this 35,000-square-foot sanctuary on Oahu's sunny western shore. Spend a few hours here getting a Maui ginger sugar body scrub, an Hawaiian Ti leaf detoxifying wrap or a pure collagen face mask, followed by a lomilomi or hot stone massage. The spa is known for its authentic thalassotherapy, a seawater-jet massage, coupled with pure colored light and essential oils, designed to de-stress body and mind. You can relax in a steam room or sauna, take a lap in the pool, or a plunge into a Roman bath (bathing suit optional).

🌿 Laniwai

Aulani Resort, 92-1185 Aliinui Dr., Kapolei. 808-674-6200. resorts.disney.go.com.

More than 150 different treatments are on hand at this Disney complex on the West Shore. An outdoor water circuit, innumerable uses of island products ranging from volcanic mud to mango, and family *(ohana)* treatments distinguish the spa menu. As appropriate for a Disney facility, there is a separate spa for kids—including teens, with signature treatments just for those between 12 and 18, such as faux Hawaiian tattoos for boys.

Na Hoola Spa

Hyatt Regency Waikiki, 2424 Kalakaua Ave., Honolulu. 808-923-1234. www.waikiki.hyatt.com.

This two-story, 10,000-square-foot spa, the largest on Waikiki, offers an oasis from the bustling beach scene below. You'll find 16 treatment rooms as well as a sauna, steam showers, and a couple's massage room. Feeling a bit jet-lagged? Take a signature Hawaiian sea-salt jet bath. If your skin's feeling parched from the tropical sun, consider the spa's Polynesian body scrub, done with Hawaiian sea salt and kukui-nut oil, followed by the Lomi Pahaku massage using warm lava stones.

Plantation Spa

Waikiki Outrigger on the Beach Hotel, 2335 Kalakaua Ave.,

© Hyatt Regency Waikiki Beach Resort and Spa

Na Hoola Spa

SpaHalekulani

© Hotels & Resorts of Halekulani

Honolulu. 808-926-2880.
www.waikikiplantationspa.com.
Take your time and savor the views
from this lofty spa, occupying the
penthouse level of the Waikiki
Outrigger on the Beach. The
rooftop terrace, in a simple Zen-
garden setting, offers bird's eye
views of the Honolulu skyline
and Pacific Ocean.

For a sun-dried body, try the
Papaala polish; after a lavender
spritz, you'll be drenched with
cooling aloe vera and cucumber
gels, or the Plantation Wrap, which
uses ocean minerals and seaweed.
The aromatherapy facials include
a lava stone massage and volcanic
mud mask.

🌺 SpaHalekulani

Halekulani Hotel, 2199 Kalia Rd.,
Honolulu. 844-288-8022.
www.halekulani.com.
This small but tranquil spa, located
at the plush Halekulani Hotel,
combines treatments from a variety
of South Pacific islands. Each room
has a private terrace, fronting the
ocean and a sandy beach.

You may begin with the pre-
treatment foot kneading. Next
choose from a menu of exotic
treatments, like the Polynesian
Nonu massage (using warm stones
and medium pressure with oil of

noni), or the four-handed massage
with two therapists.

Spa Luana

Turtle Bay Resort, 57-091
Kamehameha Hwy., Kahuku.
808-293-6000. www.turtlebay
resort.com.
Hawaiians have long believed in
the healing powers of sea water.
This spa will make a believer out of
you, too. Outdoor treatment rooms
overlook the rugged East Shore
coast. Book a makai massage and
have the therapist throw open the
cabana's oceanfront flap.

Spa Suites

Kahala Resort, 5000 Kahala Ave.,
Honolulu. 808-739-8938.
www.kahalaresort.com/spa.
The soothing, private ambience
at this spa contrasts with bustling
Waikiki, 10 minutes away. You'll
be escorted through gardens to
your private room, with changing
area, infinity-edged bath, shower,
and a small, private garden terrace
(to relax in before and after your
treatments). Most services begin
with a traditional foot ritual.
Treatments include the Kua Lani
back, face and scalp massage,
a detoxifying body wrap with
warmed Hawaiian algae, and the
volcanic mud envelopment.

LANAI ★

Billing itself as the "most enticing" island, tiny Lanai is central in the chain, with Molokai to the north, Maui on the east, and Kahoolawe to the southeast. A ferry serves Lanai from Lahaina on Maui's west coast. Flights to Lanai's small airport are offered from Honolulu and Maui. *Visitor information: 800-947-4774; www.gohawaii.com/lanai.*

Formed by a single volcano, Lanai boasts stretches of white sandy beaches, pristine bays and pine-shrouded mountaintops. A series of gulches snakes down the island's east side. To the west, sea cliffs—some 1,000-feet tall—rise from remote Kaumalapau Harbor. Long after the other islands had been populated, small settlements of Native Hawaiians occupied the island until it was settled by American ranchers in the late 19C. Lanai was once the world's largest **pineapple plantation**; Lanai City was built in 1924 by the Hawaiian Pineapple Company, later named Dole Food Company. The Hawaiian corporation of Castle & Cooke then bought the plantation, retaining Dole's name. When market demand for Lanai pineapples plummeted in the 1990s, the company turned to high-end tourism, plowing under thousands of acres of the former plantation and developing the land with two posh hotels and two premier golf courses. Most of the island was purchased in 2012 by California software billionaire Larry Ellison, who has vowed to make Lanai a model of sustainability with wind and solar power, and is entertaining the idea of restoring pineapple production.

Fast Facts

- 18 miles long and 13 miles wide, Lanai is Hawaii's second-smallest populated island.
- Only about 3,200 people live on Lanai.
- Pineapple king James Dole purchased Lanai in 1922 for $1.1 million.
- Today about 96 percent of the island is privately owned by software magnate Larry Ellison.
- There are no traffic lights here.

Lanai cliffs

© Leslie Forsberg/Michelin

LANAI

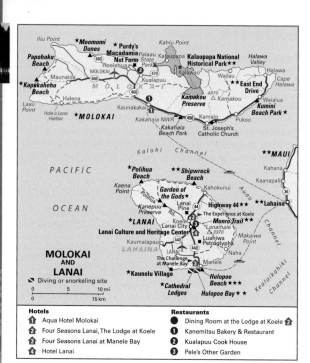

Hotels

🏨 Aqua Hotel Molokai

🏨 Four Seasons Lanai, The Lodge at Koele

🏨 Four Seasons Lanai at Manele Bay

🏨 Hotel Lanai

Restaurants

🍽 Dining Room at the Lodge at Koele

1 Kanemitsu Bakery & Restaurant

2 Kualapuu Cook House

3 Pele's Other Garden

Watch out for demons!

According to legend, Lanai was once an undesirable place, overrun by evil spirits. It was not until the demons were driven out by Kaululaau, the exiled son of a West Maui king, that people finally came to live on Lanai.

Lanai City, nestled on a 1,620-foot mountain plateau, is home to the majority of the island's 3,200 residents. It's laid-back and quaint. Lanai lures two types of travelers: adventure seekers and luxury lovers. The shallow waters and offshore reefs surrounding the island offer some of the best

snorkeling and **diving** in Hawaii, including the legendary **Cathedral Ledges**. With only 30 paved roads, many rugged, remote sites are accessible only by four-wheel drive vehicles. More than 400 unpaved roads on Lanai cross the island's undeveloped 80,000 acres of sere deserts and tropical jungles. A popular four-wheel drive outing (or arduous hike) is the trek up the **Munro Trail** to 3,370-foot Lanaihale, the island's highest peak. Two upscale resorts, the **Lodge at Koele** and the Four Seasons at **Manele Bay** *(see Hotels)* pamper guests and please golfers. Those in search of adventure, seclusion and upscale pleasures will find it all on Lanai.

BEACHES

Many of Lanai's prettiest beaches are secluded, rugged, and treacherous. Hulopoe and Puu Pehe are the best for swimming.

Hulopoe Beach★★★
Follow Manele Rd./Hwy. 440 south to the coast.

Considered one of the top beaches in the US, this popular stretch of white sand on Lanai's south shore, fronting the Four Seasons Resort Lanai at Manele Bay, draws crowds of swimmers, sunbathers and snorkelers. *(Daily excursion boats from Maui land here.)* The crystal-clear waters and shallow offshore reefs make it a great place to snorkel *(see p153)*. To the left of the beach is **Puu Pehe Rock**, also known as Sweetheart Rock. *(see box, left)*. Facilities include restrooms, showers and a picnic area with grills. 😊 *Visitors are advised to stay well away from the spinner dolphins that circle the bay during the day—it is a violation of federal law to swim with or harass the marine mammals in any way.*

Sweetheart Rock
This lovely spot has a tragic history, according to Hawaiian lore. Long ago, a Lanai warrior kidnapped a young, beautiful Maui girl and hid her on this rock. While the warrior was away, a storm blew in and washed the girl into the roiling surf, where she drowned. Heartbroken, the warrior flung himself from the cliff into his own watery grave.

Shipwreck Beach★★
At the end of Keomuku Rd. (Rte. 44), 8mi northeast of Lanai City.

You'll need a four-wheel drive vehicle to get to this remote beach, located about a half-hour north of Lanai City. Be sure to get local directions. This beach is a great place to walk, search for shells and driftwood, take in the salt air, and listen to the rhythmic hiss of the surf. The beach lines the island's northeast shore, stretching from Kahokunui at the end of Highway 44 to Polihua Beach to

Puu Pehe Rock, Hulopoe Beach

© Hawaii Tourism Authority (HTA) / Tor Johnson

Rock Art

While you're in the area of **Shipwreck Beach**, be sure to go see the petroglyphs, or rock carvings, at the end of Highway 44 *(when the paved road ends, take the north branch sand road all the way to the end)*. Follow the trail, marked with white paint on the rocks, to a cluster of stones—many of which are etched with ancient drawings. You'll see lots of primitive images of men, women and children engaged in a variety of activities, such as surfing, fishing and hunting. Dogs, brought to the islands by the first Polynesians, and deer, brought from India in the mid-1800s, are also depicted.

© Hawaii Tourism Japan (HTJ)

the northwest. Ancient Hawaiians called this eight-mile span of beach Kaiolohia, or "choppy seas." Today it's the site of a number of shipwrecks, beginning with American and British ships in the early 19C. You'll still see remnants of the rusting hulk of a World War II vessel, forever grounded on the reef offshore. The water isn't great for swimming—it's too muddy and rough—but nature-lovers will enjoy the wild, pristine surroundings.

Polihua Beach★

On the northwest coast, at the end of dirt Polihua Rd., beyond the Garden of the Gods (for directions and touring tip, see p151); four-wheel vehicle access only.

Polihua, meaning "eggs nest" or "bay of eggs," was named for the large numbers of sea turtles that once nested on this two-mile stretch of beach, across the channel from Molokai. After nearly becoming extinct, the sea turtles are starting to return—if you do see them, please remember to keep your distance.

Forget about swimming here—the waters are too dangerous—but the wild, rugged character of the beach, with its crashing surf and solitude, is worth the drive.

Polihua Beach with Maui in background

© Ron Dahlquist / age fotostock

NATURAL SITES

With only one town, and just 30 miles of paved roads, much of Lanai's stunning landscape remains pristine, a boon for visitors.

Petroglyph Sites

Without a written language, ancient Hawaiians used rock carvings— known as **petroglyphs**—to record their experiences. Tiny Lanai is home to three ancient petroglyph sites. *For driving directions to these sites, ask your local concierge or contact the Hawaii Tourism Authority* (*800-525-6284 or www.gohawaii. com/lanai*).

♦ At the end of a dirt road on the northwestern tip of the island, you'll find **Kaena Point**, Lanai's largest *heiau* (ancient place of worship).

♦ On the island's south shore, west of **Hulopoe Beach** (*see p147*), are the ruins of **Kaunolu Village★**, an ancient Hawaiian fishing village abandoned in the mid-19C. Here you can see the remains of Halulu Heiau, and a variety of petroglyphs on the surrounding boulders and rock walls.

♦ On a hillside above the Palawai Basin, **Luahiwa petroglyphs**, Lanai's largest concentration of ancient rock drawings, or *kaha kii*, are carved on large boulders scattered in the field (*off Hwy. 440, south of Lanai City*).

MUSEUMS

Although Lanai's dominance in pineapple production is long gone, the island treasures its past—and wants visitors to understand it.

Lanai Culture and Heritage Center

730 Lanai Ave., Lanai City. 808-565-7177. www.lanaichc.org. Open year-round Mon–Fri 8:30am– 3:30pm, Sat 9am–1pm. Free. Housed in the former Dole Pineapple administration building, this center introduces the island's history using photographs and pineapple-growing artifacts to honor the island's past pre-eminence in the industry. Learn how a largely arid island gets its water from a single mist-shrouded mountain. Local demonstrations of weaving and other traditional native arts are often given.

Rent a Jeep

A sturdy four-wheel drive vehicle is the best and often only way to explore the backroads of Lanai; the access to the remote sites and scenery is worth the expense. **Dollar Rent-A-Car** (*1036 Lanai Ave.; 808-565-7227, ext. 23 or 800-533-7808; www.dollarlanai.com*) is the only full-service option on the island.

© Hawaii Tourism Authority (HTA) / Dana Edmunds

GARDENS

Undeveloped Lanai has no formal public gardens, but it does have an extraordinary natural landscape to explore.

Keahiakawelo★

225 B3 Polihua Rd., 6mi northwest of Lanai City. (Polihua Rd. starts just beyond The Lodge at Koele; a four-wheel drive vehicle is necessary for access.) 800-525-6284. www.gohawaii.com/lanai. Open year-round daily 24hrs.

Keahiakawelo

© Hawaii Tourism Japan (HTJ)

Touring Tip

Polihua Road on the way to Keahiakawelo is a rutted dirt trail; you'll need a four-wheel-drive vehicle to navigate it. Call before you go; if there's been a recent rain, the road may be closed. To reach it takes about 45 minutes from Lanai City. Also, allow at least an hour for your visit, and make sure you have plenty of gas before setting out—there are no facilities along this route.

Dubbed the **Garden of the Gods**, this rugged, lunar-like landscape of randomly scattered volcanic boulders is indeed eerily stunning. Visit at sunrise or sunset, when the gold-tinged sky seems to illuminate the rocks from within.

HISTORIC SITES

Petroglyphs, ancient villages, former temples, shipwrecks and sacred sites dot the landscape, many in remote and rugged areas.

Kaunolu Village★

On the southwest coast. From Lanai City, take Hwy. 440 toward Kaumalapau; turn left onto Kaupili Rd. and go south to Kaunolu Trail. Ready for an adventure? Put on your walking shoes and rent a hefty four-wheel-drive vehicle for this trek to an old **fishing village** on Lanai's southwest coast. The area is said to contain one of the best collections of ancient Hawaiian ruins in the islands, and if you look hard enough, you'll find crumbled house foundations and parts of

buildings, as well as ruins of the Halulu Heiau temple.

You won't have any problem spotting the impressive 1,000-foot-high sea cliffs. Look for **Kahekili's Jump** at the top of the stone wall, where early Hawaiian warriors would amuse the chief by jumping off the 60-foot-high ledge. Today it's the site of cliff-diving competitions.

Note: *Kaunolu Village is registered as a National Historical Landmark, and visitors should not touch the excavated finds.*

SCENIC DRIVES

Highway 44★★

Map p146. Begin in Lanai City, and take Hwy. 44 north.

This eight-mile drive, along Lanai's northeast coast, packs a lot of splendid scenery into its short distance. Also called Keomuku Road, the paved, two-lane byway, one of only two paved highways on Lanai, heads north out of Lanai City, past the Lodge at Keole. You'll enter a neon-green rain forest, backed by misty mountains. Along the way, there are turn-offs for the **Munro Trail** *(see below)* and the **Garden of the Gods** *(see opposite)*.

The road makes a final descent toward scenic **Shipwreck Beach** *(see p147)*. This is a great spot to get out and explore; you'll find remnants of old shipwrecks and fabulous coastal scenery here.

Munro Trail★★

Map p146. Off Hwy. 44, near The Lodge at Koele.

If you've rented a four-wheel-drive vehicle (and you should), don't miss driving this bumpy dirt road to Lanai's highest point.

The Munro Trail, located off Highway 44, is one of Lanai's most popular driving excursions, with exceptional views from its 3,370-foot summit.

The trail is named after George Munro, who planted the tall Cook Pines in the early 1900s along the ridge of the mountains. The trees were planted to draw water from the clouds, releasing it into the underground aqueducts, thus providing fresh water for the island. The seven-mile trail zigzags up Lanaihale Mountain, then back down to the Palawai Basin, with lots of lookouts along the way. Chances are, it will be drizzling in the cloud-shrouded mountains, an occurrence that only adds to the ambience of the place.

Touring Tip

Be sure to check the condition of the unpaved roads of Munro Trail and to the Garden of the Gods *(see p150)* before driving on them. When you're driving on Munro Trail, stay on the main road; it's easy to get lost on the spider web of trails and dirt roads leading off the beaten path.

A Language as Beautiful as its Home

Having trouble keeping Waimea straight from Wailoa and Waikoloa? It isn't you—there are only 12 letters in the Hawaiian alphabet (5 vowels and 7 consonants). The vowels are a, e, i, o, u; the consonants are h, k, l, m, n, p, and w. Most of the time, you must pronounce all of the vowels. Once you get the hang of it, melodious words like "Waianapanapa" and "Haleakala" will roll off your tongue naturally. It is now becoming more common to hear Hawaiian spoken in casual conversation, and the language is widely reflected in place names, street names, and in often-used words like "keiki" (children) and "mahalo" (thank you).

When in Hawaii

Do as the Hawaiians do. Ancient Hawaiians revered nature, and respect for the land still holds a strong place in the lives of the Islanders. Treat all property with care while visiting, especially sacred sites and natural areas. Don't touch anything, take anything or leave litter behind. Other local customs include removing shoes before entering a private home, and obeying the speed limit. Don't pat children on the head, as the head is considered to be a sacred part of the body. Is it okay to say "aloha" if you're not Hawaiian? Sure, everybody does (*aloha* works for both "hello" and "goodbye"). *Mahalo* ("thank you") is handy, too, and *kapu* means forbidden.

The Backroads

If you really want to see the best of Lanai's scenery, you'll have to brave its bumpy backroads. Stay on the road more traveled and you'll miss the heart of this tiny island. In fact, only 30 miles of Lanai's 141 square miles are paved; the rest are open for the adventurous to explore. Lanai has about 400miles of unpaved, rough roads to travel, with spectacular views and remote vistas. Four-wheel-drive rental vehicles and road maps are available at Dollar Rent A Car in Lanai City *(see box p149)*.

Don't miss a trip through the **Kanepuu Preserve**, about five miles northwest of **Lanai City**
(Polihua Road, the dirt route leading to the preserve, is just beyond The Lodge at Koele). The 590-acre preserve boasts a large collection of native Hawaiian plants. Continue about a mile on the Polihua Road to the **Garden of the Gods** *(see p150)*, a bizarre stand of nature-sculpted rock formations. From here, strap on those seat belts and follow the dusty, dirty, rock-strewn road across the island to windswept **Polihua Beach★** *(see p148)*, a favorite sea turtle nesting ground on the north shore. You won't be disappointed: the beach here is wild, rugged and hauntingly beautiful.

Backroads of Lanai

© Quincy Dein / age fotostock

FOR FUN

Adventurous travelers love Lanai for its top-notch snorkeling, diving, and remote and rugged four-wheel driving.

Snorkel at Hulopoe Bay

Hulopoe Bay is located next to the Four Seasons Resort Lanai at Manele Bay off Manele Rd./Hwy. 440 (7mi south of Lanai City). The adjacent beach park has restrooms and showers.

Ultra-clear waters and abundant fish make **Hulopoe Bay★★** on Lanai's south shore one of the best snorkeling spots. The protected marine conservation area features a shallow reef just offshore and tide pools, creating some great marine animal-watching opportunities. Head to the rocky sides of the beach for the best snorkeling; here, you'll find neon-colored coral and reef fish. If you arrive at Hulopoe early in the morning, you may see spinner dolphins offshore. Do not attempt to swim with the dolphins; it's against the law.

Scuba Dive at Cathedral Ledges

Off the western edge of Hulopoe Bay, off Hwy. 440 (7mi south of Lanai City).

You might spot green sea turtles, white-tipped reef sharks, spinner

Snorkeling, Hulopoe Bay
© Leslie Forsberg / Michelin

dolphins, octopi, eagle rays and rare tropical fish in the waters surrounding Lanai. Divers flock here to explore the underwater ledges known as **Cathedral Ledges★**, arches, caves and lava tubes, neon-colored fish and reef corals. A popular place to dive is the **Cathedrals**, a large underwater amphitheater 60 feet below the water's surface, just outside the western edge of Hulopoe Bay. Light shines through the openings of this massive lava formation, creating the effect of a cathedral. Bright colors streak the lava walls and eels hide in the crevices.

Cliff Diving

Legend has it that Kahekili, chief of Lanai during the 18C, challenged his followers by leaping 60 feet off the sacred cliffs at Kaunolu into the waters of the Pacific Ocean. For decades, **lele kawa** (cliff diving) was an honored Hawaiian tradition, a way for ancient island warriors to prove their courage and loyalty, and to honor the gods. Today, Lanai, considered the birthplace of cliff diving, is sometimes a stop along the **Red Bull World Cliff-Diving Championship Tour**, where the best cliff divers compete for the international title on Kaunolu Point on the island's south shore.

Golf Lanai

Lanai's two resort courses, The Experience at Koele and The Challenge at Manele Bay, have both received oodles of accolades and are consistently ranked as two of the top resort courses in the country, if not the world.

The Challenge at Manele Bay – *Four Seasons Resort Lanai at Manele Bay, 7mi south of Lanai City on Manele Rd./Hwy. 440. 808-565-2000. www.fourseasons. com/manelebay/golf.* Take the Challenge at this Jack Nicklaus-designed course, across gorges and ravines with sweeping ocean vistas from every hole. The rugged 7,039-yard, Par 72 course rolls over ancient lava fields, with jaw-dropping coastline views. Three holes perch on the cliffs of Hulopoe Bay, using the Pacific Ocean as a water hazard!

The Experience at Koele – *Four Seasons Resort Lanai The Lodge at Koele, .5mi north of Lanai City on Hwy. 430. 808-565-4000. www.fourseasons.com/koele/golf.* Greg Norman and renowned golf course architect, Ted Robinson, laid out this 163-acre course, which meanders through a highland landscape of woodsy ravines, amid large stands of koa, eucalyptus and distinctive Cook pines. There are views of Maui and Molokai from the 2,000-foot plateau. Along the course you'll find seven lakes, cascading streams, waterfalls and enjoy views of the mountains and ocean.

Pull. Aim. Fire!

If you're looking for a unique experience (or just want to practice your rifle shooting), check out the **Lanai Pine Sporting Clays** *(Hwy. 44, North Central Lanai, just past mile marker 1; 808-559-4600; www.fourseasons.com/koele/ sporting_clays/).* Located on the picturesque plains of Mahana, on the north side of the island, this 14-station clay-shooting course welcomes both first-timers and experienced shooters. If you've never tried clay shooting, this is the place. There's also a 12-station archery range and a six-station air rifle range.

The Challenge at Manele Bay

© Hawaii Tourism Japan (HTJ)

FOR KIDS

Forget formal museums, amusement parks and entertainment centers; outdoor recreation reigns on Lanai's giant natural playground.

Outdoor Adventures

Lanai's 140 square miles of sandy shoreline, secluded bays, green valleys, lofty plateaus and dense forests make for some great recreation—perfect for outdoor enthusiasts and adventurous families.

♦ **Take a hike** through the forest and valleys of the island's pretty uplands for views of sheer valley walls and open vistas, with the islands of Maui and Molokai on the horizon. Maps are available at **The Lodge at Koele** *(.5mi north of Lanai City on Hwy. 430; see Hotels)*. Other activities, like arts and crafts, lei making and hula lessons are also offered.

♦ Sign up for a **guided horseback ride** through the countryside. Equestrians young and old will enjoy this excursion; even the little tykes can hop in the saddle for a gentle ride around the corral. Carriage rides are also offered. *Call the stables at The Lodge at Koele for more information and reservations: 808-565-4000.*

Adventure Lanai EcoCentre

Door-to-door pickup. 808-565-7373; www.adventurelanai.com. The owners and outfitters at this company love showing off their favorite island and introducing you to some wild adventure. They offer guided 4x4 treks, kayaking and snorkeling adventures, surfing lessons, and other fun activities. The 4-hour kayak eco excursion includes instruction, equipment, and a paddle to a favorite snorkeling spot to view sea turtles, dolphins, whales, and other critters.

Morning surfing safari – Ready to ride the waves? This 5-hour morning surfing safari takes beginners of all ages to a secluded beach to learn how to surf. Or, you can try your hand at kayak surfing.

Prefer 4x4? – Private 4x4 adventure tours of the island—perfect for families—include Cook pines along the Munro Trail, Garden of the Gods, and Shipwreck Beach.

Outdoor Kids'-only Programs – The EcoCentre offers snorkeling, swimming, kayaking, body boarding, and surfing for children only.

Rental – If your family would rather go it alone, the EcoCentre has a variety of sports equipment and 4x4 vehicles for rental. The company will transport you to and from all activities and deliver the equipment to your door.

SPAS

There are not a lot of spas to choose from on Lanai, but those that are here are definitely worthwhile.

The Spa at Manele Bay

At the Four Seasons Lanai at Manele Bay (7mi south of Lanai City on Manele Rd./Hwy. 440). 808-565-2000. www.fourseasons.com/manelebay.

Reserve one of the open-air cabanas at the ultra-luxe spa at the Four Seasons for your personal massage. The private outdoor rooms are perched on a slope above the open seas, where you can listen to the sound of the surf while the therapist kneads your tired muscles (no piped-in nature CDs needed, here!). If you prefer, there's also the Garden Hale outdoor room, set amidst lush greenery, exotic flowers and

© Four Seasons / Don Riddle

Open-air cabanas, The Spa at Manele Bay

cascading waterfalls. There are 11 treatment rooms with dry saunas, eucalyptus steam rooms and rain-forest showers.

From Poi to Pineapple: Eating Hawaiian-style

© Hawaii Tourism Japan (HTJ)

Many Hawaiian food treats incorporate a dollop of several cultures and a dash of island ingredients. One example: Spam musubi, which consists of sticky rice topped by Spam and wrapped in dried seaweed. Introduced to Hawaii by the military during World War II, good old Spam (spiced ham in a can) remains a favorite here. The ubiquitous plate lunch, a local favorite at roadside stands, consists of white rice, pasta salad, and an entrée—perhaps Chinese-style chicken in soy sauce, Japanese teriyaki, curry stew, fried fish, barbecued pork or even an American hamburger. **Poi** is uniquely Hawaiian. Made out of pounded taro root, this purplish, pasty stuff is said to have special healing properties. If you're not tempted by poi, you may well want to sample **shave ice**, an old-fashioned treat from the days when islanders would shave ice into powder and flavor it with fruit juice. (Remember, it's shave ice, not shaved ice.) Of course, the fresh pineapples widely available in the islands (especially Maui) are superb, several steps above those you'll find in mainland stores. Vendors will often prepare them for you—and explain the right and wrong ways to do so. Another popular island treat is the apple banana, a smallish, delicate fruit that does indeed bear a hint of green-apple flavor.

LANAI

MUST DO

MOLOKAI★

Nontouristy. Relaxed. Authentically Hawaiian. That's Molokai! These are the words that Molokai residents use when describing their island. Local sentiment helped close down the one major hotel resort on the island, whose former golf course is now gathering dust.
Visitor information: 808-525-6284; www.gohawaii.com/molokai.

This long island was once the province of *kahuna* (priests) whose religious practices might have included human sacrifice. The island was considered sacred then. Now a grove of kukui trees (which are sacred themselves) marks the burial site of Lani Kauli, one of the most powerful *kahunas*.

Molokai was also the home of Father Damien, the Belgian Roman Catholic priest who devoted his life to caring for the victims of Hansen's Disease (aka leprosy). His place of exile is now the site of **Kalaupapa National Historical Park★★** (*see p160*), reachable by foot, small plane, or mule.

In more recent years, the island was a sleepy community of ranches and pineapple plantations. Since the Del Monte® plantation closed in the early 1980s, tourism has become an economic necessity, but it's extremely low-key. Downtown **Kaunakakai** is a mere two blocks long. You can still buy a burger for five bucks at the Molokai Drive-In. This island is all about wide-open spaces, where mountains meet ocean. The downside to Molokai (or the upside, depending

Sunset at Molokai

© Hawaii Tourism Authority (HTA) / Ron Dahlquist

Touring Tip

Kayak, snorkel and reef dive trips are offered by **Molokai Fish and Dive** *(808-553-5926; molokaifishanddive.com)* and **Molokai Outdoors** *(808-553-4477; www.molokai-outdoors.com)*.

on your point of view) is that there's not much in the way of posh restaurants, boutiques or nightclubs. A popular T-shirt here reads, "Molokai Night Life." Pictured below the heading: nothing!

Fast Facts

- Molokai measures 38 miles long and 10 miles wide.
- Some of the world's tallest ocean cliffs rise above Molokai's north shore.
- Molokai has 8,100 residents and the state's highest percentage of native Hawaiians (62 percent). Its Filipino community composes 30 percent.
- Site of a leper colony from 1866 to 1969, the island was long shunned by most visitors.

BEACHES

Papohaku Beach hosts dancers and musicians from all over the state for the Ka Hula Piko Festival (first weekend in May).

Kumini Beach Park★

Map p146. Mile marker 20, Kamehameha Hwy. (Rte. 450), in eastern Molokai. Parking on the south side of the highway, just beyond mile marker. No restrooms or showers on-site.

Also known as **Murphy's Beach** and 20 Mile Beach, this beach is truly an excellent snorkeling spot, thanks to the barrier reef that runs alongside it. Enjoy great views of Maui and Lanai from a choice spot on the tawny sand. Just beyond the beach is a fish pond.

The beach makes a great stop if you're driving **East End Drive** (Kamehameha V Highway), especially if you halted for snacks along the way (there are no cafes here). Heading east, stop at **Mana'e Goods** and **Grindz** for cold drinks, sandwiches and interesting bagged snacks such as dried shrimp and spicy cuttlefish.

Papohaku Beach

Map p146. Kaluakoi Rd., 5mi northwest of Maunaloa, western Molokai. The beach has three access points from Kaluakoi Rd., all marked with signs.

Nearly three miles long and 100 yards wide, Papohaku has more surface area than any other beach in the islands. It also has great views of Oahu across the channel. This broad, gorgeous stretch of beige-colored sand is backed by dunes and lapped by turquoise waters—great for sunbathing but not good for swimming, since riptides and rogue surf often threaten. The beach has restrooms, picnic tables and campsites.

Kapukahehu Beach★

Map p146. Off Kaluakoi Rd., northwest of Maunaloa, western Molokai. Take Kaluakoi Rd. to Papokahu Rd.; 5mi past Papohuku Beach Pk, turn right.

Also known as **Dixie Maru Beach**, this fine scoop of bronze sand is the only truly swimmable beach on Molokai. There are no facilities, just water and sand, bordered by lava rock and a fringe of trees. It takes some driving to get here—most beachgoers get no farther than Papokahu Beach—so it never gets crowded, but then, what does on Molokai?

Hula, Anyone?

According to ancient legend, the goddess Laka first danced the hula on a hill in Molokai, thus making the island the birthplace of the hula. This explanation certainly seems plausible in May, when the **Ka Hula Piko Festival** brings scores of hula groups and musicians from the other islands. Held on the shores of Papohaku Beach Park, the festival, whose name translates to "center of the dance," celebrates the different forms of traditional hula, accompanied by arts and crafts exhibits, Hawaiian games, and music. *For schedules and information, call 808-552-2800 or check online at www.molokaievents.com.*

NATURAL SITES

Mo'omomi is one of the last strongholds of native coastal plants and animals in Hawaii. It's an important nesting site of the endangered green sea turtle and home to four rare plant species.

Mo'omomi Dunes★

Hwy. 480, 3mi past Hoolehua town. 808-553-5236. www.nature.org.

Set on the northwest coast of the island, this wild landscape is managed by the Nature Conservancy of Hawaii. The 921-acre property is a haven for wildlife-watchers looking for shorebirds like sanderlings and golden plovers.

Hawaiian monk seals are often spotted on the golden sands. It is also the last stand for 22 native Hawaiian plants, most severely endangered on other islands. The conservancy runs monthly **guided hikes** here *(Mar–Oct)* and you can contact the office *(808-553-5236)* for information before you go, to be sure the area is open.

SCENIC DRIVES

The southeast shore has stunning views. And, Molokaians point out, you can watch the sun rise and set from the same spot!

East End Drive (Kamehameha V Highway)★★

Map p146. Hwy. 450, along the southeastern and eastern shoreline, from Kaunakakai east to Halawa. 27mi one way (allow a half-day for round-trip).

This spectacular drive skirts Molokai's mountains on one side (including 4970ft Kamakou mountain, the island's highest peak) and the Pacific Ocean on the other. Heading east from Kaunakakai, you'll quickly reach **Kakahaia Beach Park**, a wildlife refuge that's a haven for local birds. At mile marker 10, look for St. Joseph's Catholic Church, built by Father Damien in 1876 and marked by a statue of the famous priest.

Big tumbles of black lava rock are scattered along the winding, one-lane road, which gets really gorgeous after mile marker 20

Halawa Valley

© Hawaii Tourism Authority (HTA) / Ron Dahlquist

or so. If you have yet to see the endangered nene (Hawaiian goose, see p 62), you're likely to see them crossing the road here, near mile marker 23. The road heads inland, and you'll pass through a stand of long-needled Australian pines. After a series of wild twists and hill climbs, the road emerges at **Halawa Valley**, Molokai's most breathtaking spot, set off by velvety green hillsides and sparkling waterfalls.

159

HISTORIC SITES

About 8,000 visitors each year arrive at one of the country's most poignant but beautiful spots, the former leper colony of Kalaupapa.

Kalaupapa National Historical Park★★

Map p146. Access by Molokai Air Shuttle (800-428-1231; $249 from Molokai), foot, or mule ride (808-567-7550; www.muleride.com; $199/person; includes park tour and lunch). A steep 2.9mi trail with 26 switchbacks begins at Palaau State Park (Rte. 470, 10mi north of Kaunakakai). No road access between Kalaupapa and the rest of Molokai. 808-567-6802. www.nps.gov/kala. Park open Mon–Sat by tour only (Damien Tours 808-567-6171; $60; no tours Sun or 16th of the month). Ages 16 and up. **Note: whether you are on foot or mule, this trail is not for those with a substantial fear of heights.**

This unique site encompasses a 13.6-square-mile peninsula separated from the rest of Molokai by a 1,700-foot cliff. Victims of Hansen's Disease (leprosy) were relocated to this beautiful windswept promontory in 1866. In 1873 Father Damien de Veuster, a

Belgian priest, arrived to live and work (and die, in 1889) among the infected. His original St. Philomena's Church stands above the ruins of the village of Kalawao. A few very elderly leprosy patients, who pose no health threat to adult visitors, continue to live here.

Halawa Valley Falls & Cultural Hike

Contact Molokai Fish & Dive, 808-553-5926. www.molokaifishanddive.com. Tours last 4 hours; hiking distance is 4.5mi. Wear good hiking shoes and a swimsuit under your clothes. Bring water, lunch and insect repellent. $75.

The site of the first Hawaiian settlement on Molokai, the Halawa Valley is steeped in history. With native guide Pilipo Solatorio, you'll hike past ancient loʻi (taro patches), taste wild apples, see ancient temple ruins, and view two grand waterfalls, Moolua and Hipuapua. Swimming in the cool, deep pools of 250ft Mooula Falls is refreshing, indeed.

Aerial view of Kalaupapa

© Hawaii Tourism Authority (HTA) / Ron Garnett

FOR FUN

Having a good time on Molokai isn't about visiting tourist attractions:
it's all about soaking up the raw scenic beauty and laid-back vibe.

Na Kupuna

© Hawaii Tourism Authority (HTA) / Dana Edmunds

Purdy's Natural Macadamia Nut Farm★

Map p146. Lihi Pali Ave., Kualapuu. 808-567-6001. http://molokai-aloha.com/macnuts. Open year-round Tue–Fri 9:30am–3:30pm, Sat 10am–2pm, weather permitting.
You may stop simply to buy a bag of home-roasted macadamia nuts, but you'll find yourself admiring the five-acre orchard, and end up with a hammer in your hand, cracking nuts with a member of the Purdy family.

Aloha Friday Na Kupuna

Aqua Hotel Molokai, Kamehameha V Hwy., Kaunakakai. 808-553-5347. www.hotelmolokai.com.
It'll take you just a few minutes to make new friends at the open-air hotel, but if it's Friday night, you won't have much time to chat. Once the tiki torches are lit, the band sets up, the music begins and the sunset celebration has officially begun. This is the place for nightlife on Molokai.

Molokai Hoe Canoe Race

Considered Molokai's biggest annual social and athletic event, the 41-mile race across the treacherous waters of the Kaiwi Channel to Oahu ranks as the world championship of long-distance outrigger-canoe racing. The contest, held in October, starts at the rocky harbor of Hale o Lono, on the southwest coast of Molokai, and ends at Duke Kahanamoku Beach in Waikiki. What began as an inter-island race with three teams in 1952 has mushroomed into a popular event that lures as many as 100 teams of racers from around the world each year.
For information, call 808-676-4272 or visit www.molokaihoe.com.

© Hawaii Tourism Authority (HTA) / Tor Johnson

FOR FUN

Hike Kamakou Preserve

In east central Molokai. Maps and directions are available from the Nature Conservancy office at 23 Pueo Pl. (off Hwy. 460, 3mi west of Kaunakakai). 808-553-5236. www.nature.org/hawaii. Open year-round Mon–Fri 7:30am–3pm. Best months to visit are Aug–Sept.

The jewel of Molokai is the 2,774-acre Kamakou Preserve, home to more than 200 species of Hawaiian plants, at least 219 of which are found no place else in the world. The peak of the preserve, about 5,000 feet above sea level, is the highest point on the island. The Nature Conservancy runs monthly **guided hikes** *(Mar–Oct; call or check online for schedule; limited number of spots)* through the rain forest, providing transportation to trailheads from their office. If you do it yourself, you'll need a four-wheel-drive vehicle just to reach the preserve, and then you'll park and walk from the entrance to **Waikolu Lookout**. August and September, the driest months, are the best time

Kamakou Preserve

© Grady Timmons/TNC

Touring Tip

Want to ferry from Maui to Molokai? The **Molokai Princess** *(877-500-6284; www.molokaiferry.com)* offers service (90min) between Lahaina and Kaunakakai Harbor, departing from Lahaina Harbor on Maui *(7:15am and 6pm Mon–Sat)*. The crossing is sometimes a bit rough, but it's a good vantage for whale watching in winter. Spend the day exploring Molokai and return to Maui in late afternoon—in time for dinner at the oceanfront **Hula Grill**, north of Lahaina in Kaanapali *(see Restaurants)*.

to visit, since it's notoriously easy to get stuck in the mud around here. Waikolu means "three waters" in Hawaiian, and you'll quickly figure out why: waterfalls are everywhere. The elevation at the lookout is 3,700 feet, although rain and clouds often affect visibility. Check in with the Nature Conservancy before you go, so you'll be updated on trail conditions; routes are well marked with some boardwalks. The main trail in the preserve is Pepeopae Trail, from where you'll end up at **Pelekunu Valley Overlook**.

Snorkel or Dive Molokai

Trips available from Molokai Fish & Dive in downtown Kauakakai, 808-553-5926. www.molokaifish anddive.com. Dive/snorkel catamaran trip to two sites, $69 and up.

Some of Molokai's best scenery is underwater—the island's south shore is home to Hawaii's largest fringing reef (28mi long), and access from shore can be difficult.

KAHOOLAWE AND NIIHAU

**Kahoolawe is off-limits to visitors without specific authorization.
A portion of privately owned Niihau is reachable via helicopter tour.**
See map on inside front cover.

Kahoolawe

Historically home to a small population of Native Hawaiians, the smallest of Hawaii's eight major islands is part of Maui County. Its extreme aridity and lack of food limited settlement. Following European contact it may have served briefly as a penal colony and then a ranch, before it became a base for US army military exercises. After the attack on Pearl Harbor in 1941, the US navy took over, and began using it for bombing practice. Nearly every non-nuclear instrument of war used by the US military and its allies since World War II has bombarded this island, where unexploded munitions still remain. In 2003 the island was returned to Hawaii, with much fanfare and conch-shell blowing. A $400-million clean-up plan was launched, and some of the island is now deemed safe for controlled visits, but access to Kahoolawe, and the two miles of ocean surrounding it, is strictly limited. The only people on the island are archaeologists, volunteers restoring native habitat, and Hawaiians engaged in spiritual practices. *For more information, access kahoolawe.hawaii.gov.*

Niihau

Hawaii's so-called "Forbidden Island," Niihau (pronounced Nee-ee-how) lies 17 miles off the west coast of Kauai. This unspoiled, 72-square-mile island has been owned by the same family since 1864, when Elizabeth Sinclair bought it from

Touring Tip

Half-day tours ($385) and hunting safaris are available, but no overnight trips. Contact the **Niihau Helicopters** office *(877-441-3500; www.niihau.us).*

King Kamehameha V for $10,000. Niihau has remained virtually the same since then. The 160 or so inhabitants are mostly native islanders and descendants of Elizabeth Sinclair, and they practice a traditional Hawaiian lifestyle. Residents speak a Hawaiian dialect not heard anywhere else. The island is also an important habitat for endangered Hawaiian **monk seals**. Niihau is home to the largest colony in the main islands, and a primary nursery for seal pups. Niihau was once a ranching outpost. Now this arid island stays afloat financially by serving as a base for support services for NASA and the US navy, and by operating **helicopter tours** that reveal a small portion of the island to visitors.

A Wealth of Shells

Niihau is famous for its beautiful, intricate shell leis. Local **kahelelani shells** are fashioned into exquisite pieces that sell for thousands of dollars. A Niihau shell lei is displayed in the British Museum in London as a memento of Captain Cook's first visit to the Hawaiian Islands.

Hawaiian Culture

About 9.2 percent of Hawaii's people call themselves Native Hawaiian, although the number with pure Hawaiian blood may be far less than that—many Hawaiians died in the 19C from diseases introduced by European settlers. Over the past 150 years, native islanders intermarried readily, especially with Caucasians (*haoles* in Hawaiian) and Chinese. But the natives' influence on local culture goes far beyond their

© Hawaii Tourism Authority (HTA) / Tor Johnson

numbers: some of the best-known aspects of Hawaiian culture—music, dance, food and the welcoming aloha attitude—have been absorbed by all those who live in Hawaii. For more than 1,000 years, Polynesian Hawaiians lived alone in the islands. They came in large double-hulled canoes, first from the Marquesas Islands between AD 300 and 750, later from Tahiti about 1100, navigating by the stars and following seabirds. On the islands, they built houses of stone, timber and thatched grass. Their lives revolved around fishing, cultivating sweet potatoes and taro, gathering fruit and raising pigs. With their knowledge of astronomy, they calculated the effect of seasons on farming. They imbued animals and inanimate objects with spiritual powers; things that were sacred were called *kapu*, or forbidden. As centuries passed, stories of their former lands became songs and lore.

Language: Hawaiians retained the basic spoken Polynesian language, adapting it to their own needs. After 1820, American missionaries transliterated Hawaiian to make it a written language, reducing the number of consonants to just seven—h, k, l, m, n, p, and w.
The Hawaiian language today is undergoing a major renaissance: children attend immersion schools, and younger generations greet the 21C by restoring daily use of their native tongue. Other islanders are also learning Hawaiian and incorporating it into daily life. Many resorts, such as Disney's Aulani on West Oahu, have programs dedicated to introducing visitors to one of the world's most beautiful languages.

Music: Other cultural aspects were incorporated after contact with the West. From Spanish-speaking cowboys (*paniolo*) on the Big Island, Hawaiians learned guitar; they loosened the strings to change the tuning and invented the "slack-key" style. To mimic island breezes, they developed the **steel guitar**, later adopted by country-western musicians. When the Portuguese arrived in the late 19C, Hawaiians learned to play the four-stringed braga, renaming it the **ukulele**, which is a very popular instrument today. Along with a drum, the ukulele accompanied the **hula**. Originally performed only by men as part of an ancient religious ritual, hula evolved into a graceful dance for women. Grass skirts were a 20C import from Micronesia; dancers were traditionally clad in ti leaves.

RESTAURANTS

The venues listed below were selected for their ambience, location and/or value for money. Rates indicate the average cost of an appetizer, an entrée and a dessert for one person (not including tax, gratuity or beverages). Most restaurants are open daily for lunch and dinner (except where noted) and accept major credit cards. Call for information regarding reservations, dress code and opening hours.

| *Luxury* | **$$$$** Over $75 | *Moderate* | **$$** $25–$50 |
| *Expensive* | **$$$** $50–$75 | *Budget* | **$** Under $25 |

Big Island

Expensive

Huggo's
$$$ **Seafood**
75-5828 Kahakai Rd., Kailua-Kona.
808-329-1493. www.huggos.com.
Dinner only.
This place is a local institution, complete with views of multi-hued sunsets and technicolor cocktails that reflect the food—dishes such as seared ahi, pasta with vegetables and mushrooms, and guava-braised babyback ribs. The thatched bar, **Huggo's on the Rocks**, is an island hot spot for noshing on pupu (appetizers) and dancing at the water's edge.

Merriman's
$$$ **Hawaiian Regional**
65-1227 Opelo Rd., Kamuela.
808-885-6822. www.merrimans hawaii.com.
Owner Peter Merriman is one of Hawaii's superstar chefs, and a founder of Hawaiian regional cuisine. Lamb comes from nearby Kahua Ranch, and local beef, pork and seafood round out the menu. Wok-charred ahi is a signature dish, as is macadamia-crusted monchong. Coconut crème brûlée, lilikoi mousse and macadamia brioche anchor the dessert menu.

Moderate

Bamboo
$$ **Hawaiian Regional**
55-3415 Akoni Pule Hwy., Hawi.
808-889-5555. bamboo restaurant.info. Closed Mon.
It's definitely worth a drive to Hawi to discover Bamboo. Set in an old plantation house filled with wicker furniture and local art, this restaurant is a fun place to kick back with a lili-tini and contemplate tasty starters like kalua pork quesadillas and sesame-nori crusted shrimp. Many of the menu items have a Thai twist, like the green papaya salad (with spicy chili-lime vinaigrette) and coconut prawns. Fish of the day may come coconut-crusted or grilled and finished with liliokoi mustard, served atop a bed of organic greens with goat cheese polenta.

Fish in Thai style, Bamboo

Hilo Bay Cafe
$$ **American**
123 Lihiwai St., Hilo. 808-935-4939.
www.hilobaycafe.com.
Recently moved to a location with
a view, this restaurant wins fans
with vibrantly flavored dishes that
often incorporate local ingredients.
Local grass-fed steak, grilled
eggplant and hamakua mushroom
curry pot pies exemplify the
eclectic menu. Service is casual
and friendly. (**Tip:** Go for lunch,
when the menu is basically the
same, but prices are lower.)

Kilauea Lodge Restaurant
$$ **Continental**
Old Volcano Rd., Volcano Village.
808-967-7366. www.kilauea
lodge.com.
Cozy, rustic Kilauea Lodge is an
inviting stop on a cool night in
Volcano, especially when there
are logs crackling in the fireplace.
The lodge is the fine-dining option
near the Kilauea volcano, with
classic entrées featuring game
(perhaps antelope schnitzel)
and hasenpfeffer (rabbit braised
in wine), along with vegetarian
offerings and great soups.
Though exotic, to say the least,
the European-style menu is an
intriguing contrast to the island's
ubiquitous Hawaiian cuisine.

Kona Pub & Brewery
$$ **Pizza/Pub Food**
75–5629 Kuakini Hwy.,
Kailua-Kona. 808-334-2739.
konabrewingco.com. Brewery
tours daily 10:30am and 3pm.
Sometimes you crave a pizza and
a beer, or after a day of hiking
a volcano, you simply want to
unlace your boots and unwind.
Kona Brewing Company's pub

is the place. A large lanai draws
diners outdoors to nosh on pizza,
pupus and sandwiches, washed
down with a Black Sand porter.
The imu pork and pineapple
pizza with smoked mozzarella is a
worthy choice, as are the shrimp
tacos. Creative use of reclaimed
materials, like the giant mahogany
log on the bar (washed ashore in
Kailua Bay) and the tin roof of the
lanai (from an old ti root distillery)
distinguish the building.

Budget

Big Jake's Island BBQ
$ **Barbecue**
83-5308 Mamalahoa Hwy. (mile
marker 106), Captain Cook.
808-328-1227. Closed Mon.
Barbecue takes a unique form
on the islands—wood-grilled
meats (usually cooked over *kiawe*,
the omnipresent mesquite) are
added to the "plate lunch" repast,
so you might find beef brisket
with macaroni salad and, as here
at Jake's, lilikoi bread pudding.
Chicken and brisket are best
here. Big Jake's is a perfect lunch
spot between Kona and Hawaii
Volcanoes National Park.

Island Lava Java
$ **American**
75-5799 Alii Dr., Alii Sunset Plaza,
Kailua-Kona. 808-327-2161.
www.islandlavajavakona.com.
This little waterfront bistro is a
real find. It's open for breakfast
as well as lunch and dinner. The
menu features grass-fed beef,
local organic goat cheese and
house-baked breads and desserts.
Nice touch: plates are garnished
with purple orchids. For breakfast,
you can't go wrong with banana-

mac-nut pancakes with coconut syrup, and it's always a good time for kalua pork tacos with garlic mashed potatoes and island beef fillet with Hamakua mushrooms.

Ken's House of Pancakes
$ Hawaiian
1730 Kamehameha Ave., Hilo. 808-935-8711. www.kenshouse ofpancakes.com. Breakfast served daily 24hrs.
"K-Hop," as the locals call it, is an old-fashioned coffee shop—with a massive side order of local color. Favorites include shredded kalua pig on a hoagie, French toast made with sweet Portuguese bread, and coconut custard pie. Several versions of loco moco spice the menu, including a corned beef hash moco that makes a very hearty breakfast. Specials are available certain days of the week.

What's Shakin'
$ Health Food
27-999 Old Mamalahoa Hwy., Pepeekeo. 808-964-3080. No dinner.
Set along scenic Onomea Drive *(see p38)*, this unassuming wooden house is *the* place for a fresh-fruit smoothie. Among the best you'll ever taste, they consist of delectable blends of fruits from the owner's farm. No dairy products, just fresh fruit (or nuts, if you go for the Peanut Brudda, a creamy-cool version of a peanut butter cup.) The Papaya Paradise is a "Best of Hawaii" medley featuring pineapple, papaya, banana and coconut. Tasty organic lunch options include What's Shakin's fabulous fish wrap, tasty tuna burger, and blue-corn tamale with homemade salsa.

Maui

Expensive

Lahaina Grill
$$$ New American
127 Lahainaluna Rd., Lahaina. 808-667-5117 www.lahaina grill.com. Dinner only.
Helmed by owner-chef Jurg Munch, this bright little bistro has been a Maui favorite (and perennial "Best Of...." winner in city magazines) for years. It's not the place for a quiet conversation since the tables are closely packed, but no matter—the food is the draw here, and the menu has a determinedly mainland slant. Kona coffee-roasted rack of lamb, or salmon, mainland veal and beef, are shaped into dishes such as meatballs, osso buco and even escargot for meals that are memorable in all the right ways.

🐟 Mama's Fish House
$$$ Seafood
799 Poho Pl., 1.5mi east of Paia. 808-579-8488. www.mamasfish house.com.
Mama's is acknowledged universally as the best seafood restaurant on Maui. The breezy, converted beach house overlooks an ivory-sand beach lined with palm trees. Tables are adorned in tapas-print cloths, a lively backdrop for fresh fish dishes that look like art on a plate—and taste equally fine. Stand-out dishes include Tahitian poisson cru, an appetizer of ono (a local fish) marinated in lime and coconut milk, and a fillet of mahi mahi, stuffed with a scrumptious mixture of crab and lobster. Selections of fresh island fish always include at least four different preparations.

Macadamia Nut Ono,
Mama's Fish House

Mama's Fish House

For dessert, ask for the chocolate mousse "pearl," presented in a tuille cookie shell. Guests of the **Inn at Mama's Fish House** *(see Hotels)* get a discount on meals here.

Monkeypod Kitchen
$$$ Hawaiian
10 Wailea Gateway Pl., Unit B-201, Kihei. 808-891-2322. www.monkey podkitchen.com. Another location on Oahu island.

The focus here, at uber-chef Peter Merriman's newest bistro, is on locally-sourced, sustainably caught food, exquisitely prepared. Keahole lobster, fish and coconut stew, Merriman's kiawe-grilled Ahi tuna, and even the humble pizzas cooked in a kiawe wood-burning oven, are superbly conceived and executed. Dine in or outside, at communal tables, where live music adds to the festive scene. For a finale, fresh fruit pies are a grace note: the Kula strawberry is a hands-down favorite.

Moderate

Hula Grill
$$ Hawaiian Regional
Whalers Village, 2435 Kaanapali Pkwy., Kaanapali. 808-667-6636. www.hulagrill.com.

Waves lapping the beach nearby, a Mai Tai in your hand, the smell of good food wafting from the kitchen. Hula Grill is a huge favorite for many reasons, including the sensational food. Fresh fish is grilled on wood or paired with a choice of sauces and salsas, and some of the smallest dishes, like crab-macadamia-nut wontons, make the biggest splash. Coconut-seafood chowder is chef Peter Merriman's admirable take on an island bisque. The tasting menu is worth a try if you're dining early *(4:45pm–5:45pm)*; three mini-courses will set you back $24.95. This is one of the few places where you can try *ulu* (breadfruit), melded with coconut and macadamia nuts into pono pie.

Budget

Anthony's Coffee Company
$ American
90 Hana Hwy., Paia. 808-579-8340 or 800-882-6509. www.anthonys coffee.com. No dinner.

Breakfast and lunch are the way to go here. Anthony's roasts its own coffee, and sells it by the pound and by the cup, including pure Kona and their own special blends. For a hearty way to start your day, try Kalua Pork Benedict or the breakfast wrap (eggs, tomato, cheese, rice bacon); you'll want to go lighter if you can't resist a pineapple-coconut muffin. Anthony's makes an fantastic picnic lunch too, with hefty sandwiches and wraps and a side salad, if you choose. Coolers are available for rent to those who want to take their picnic to the beach for a day.

Beach Bums Bar & Grill
$ Barbecue
300 Maalaea Rd., Maalaea, in the lower part of the mini-mall. 808-243-2286. beachbumsshawaii.com.
This joint near the Maui Ocean Center serves breakfast, lunch and dinner daily. Its low-brow name belies what is actually an excellent Texas-style barbecue purveyor. Though the menu spans everything from loco moco and crab cakes benedict at breakfast to fish tacos, the highlights are the kiawe- and guava-smoked ribs, turkey and, best of all, brisket. Onion rings, sweet potato fries and fried zucchini prove worthy sides.

Jawz Fish Tacos
$ Mexican
Across the street from Makena Beach, Makena. 808-874-8226. www.jawzfishtacos.com.
The original Jawz was, and still is, a wood-shingled taco truck, parked across from Makena Beach, where tasty fish tacos and delicious smoothies issue forth. **Jawz Fish Tacos Restaurant** *(1279 S. Kihei Rd., in the Azeka Mauka Shopping Center, Kihei; 808-874-8226)* offers the same great tacos, burritos and salads, plus Maui's largest salsa bar, in a space simply furnished with tables and chairs. Top your taco with roasted habanero-pepper salsa, made with pineapple and carrots.

Kihei Caffe
$ American
1945 S. Kihei Rd., Kihei. 808-879-2230. www.kiheicaffe.net. Open 5am–3pm. No dinner. Cash only.
Locals love this place—where breakfast is served all day, in portions large enough to share.

You order at the counter, and then grab one of the umbrella-shaded outdoor tables. Somehow, they match you up with your big ole' order of banana-macadamia nut pancakes (with coconut syrup), biscuits with sausage gravy, loco moco, pork-fried rice and scrambled eggs, huevos rancheros, or fresh fruit and granola. Fresh shakes are irresistible (try a mash-up of banana, peanut butter, and mac-nut syrup). Work off your meal with a swim or snorkel, post-breakfast: the beach is right across the street.

Leoda's Kitchen and Pie Shop
$ American
820 Olowalu Village Rd., Lahaina. 808-662-3600. www.leodas.com.
Much more than handmade pies are offered here: breakfast, lunch and dinner are served 7 days a week. But pies still rule the day in this very popular cafe along the main road south of Lahaina. Macadamia nuts, chocolate, lime, lilikoi, coconut, banana, pineapple and other island fruits are melded into various sizes and combinations, including mini-pies perfect for a one-person dessert after a meal, or at breakfast, or whenever. Superb salads and hearty sandwiches on home-baked bread are worthy precursors to the pies. Pot pies as well as burgers and hot dogs can be ordered.

Star Noodle
$ Asian
286 Kupuohi St., Lahaina. 808-667-5400. www.starnoodle.com.
Crowds line up out to the street for tables at this Asian-fusion bistro; reservations are highly recommended for larger parties.

Noodles range from thick to thin to crepes, rice to wheat, Japanese to Indonesian. Plates, bowls, seafood, meats, heaps of vegetables and a wide array of spices create a vast menu; a signature dish is kim chee Brussels sprouts.

Kauai

Luxury

Kauai Grill
$$$$ French-Asian
5520 Ka Haku Rd., Princeville, St. Regis Princeville Resort. 808-826-2250. www.kauaigrill.com. Dinner only.
One of the more elegant places to dine on Kauai, this sleek and sophisticated restaurant features signature dishes from world renowned chef Jean-Georges Vongerichten. The dining area, located in the St. Regis Princeville Resort overlooking Hanalei Bay, has warm zebra woods and cocoa brown hues, punctuated with black leather. The billowy fabric ceiling and giant fiber optic and ruby glass hibiscus chandelier are focal points. The menu changes seasonally but includes dishes like glazed pork with crispy grits and onaga with shiitake and asparagus.

Expensive

Beach House Restaurant
$$$ Pacific Rim
5022 Lawai Rd., Koloa. 808-742-1424. www.the-beach-house.com.
This restaurant on the south shore not only boasts some of the best sunset views on Kauai, it's also won a slew of awards for its cuisine. The emphasis here is on local seafood. Their version of poke is seared

Beach House
© The Beach House Restaurant

ahi; the daily fresh catch can be sauteed with crab or wasabi, or grilled with furikake, a Japanese dry condiment. The Hawaiian carrot cake, filled with macadamia nuts and pineapple and topped with cream-cheese icing, is a great way to end a Beach House meal.

Eastside
$$$ Pacific Rim
4-1330 Kuhio Hwy., Kapaa. 808-823-9500. Closed Sun & Mon.
Locals voted this lively, come-as-you-are restaurant as the best on Kauai in 2009. The atmosphere is casual and the food is fresh. Start with the ahi tuna poke or shrimp and scallop spring rolls, followed with the sesame seared ono with green soba noodles. The huli huli chicken with key lime, coconut and cabbage slaw is a fine rendition of a traditional island dish.

Red Salt
$$$ Pacific Rim
2251 Poipu Rd., Koloa. 808-828-8888. www.koakea.com.
Set in the sexy Koa Kea boutique hotel on Poipu Beach, this classy and modern eatery features creative and freshly-prepared dishes with oceanfront views to boot. Breakfast is a real treat, with

MUST EAT

Banana Joe's

What's on offer at this venerable local institution is simple—fresh-fruit "frosties" made by pulverizing frozen papayas, pineapples, bananas and other fruit into a delicious, chilled ultra-healthful concoction. You'll also find banana bread, local fruit—up to five kinds of bananas, naturally—and other oddments. It's a long-treasured snack stop on the road to Hanalei and the Na Pali coast. *5-2719 Kuhio Hwy., Kilauea. 808-828-1092. www.bananajoekauai.com.*

just-right eggs benedict and nap-inducing pineapple pancake souffles. For dinner, try the signature red salt ahi poke or the Kauai shrimp fettucine, with a side of Maui onion and king crab home fries. Prime rib and lamb are popular choices among meat lovers.

Roy's Poipu Bar & Grill

$$$ Hawaiian
2360 Kiahuna Plantation Dr., Koala. 808-742-5000. www.roysrestaurant.com. Dinner only.
Renowned Chef Roy Yamaguchi brings his signature Hawaiian fusion cuisine to this sleek dining room in the Poipu Shopping Center. Start with Roy's Canoe Appetizer, with shrimp sticks, Szechuan baby back ribs, island ahi poke, pork and shrimp lumpia, and crisped seafood potstickers. You'll find all his favorite entrées here, too, like the pesto-steamed monchong, blackened ahi with spicy mustard butter, sesame-crusted shrimp and honey-mustard short ribs. Despite the proliferation of Roy's restaurants across the country, this place still draws crowds and raves.

Tidepools

$$$ Hawaiian
1571 Poipu Bay Rd., Grand Hyatt Kauai, Koloa. 808-240-6456. www.kauai.hyatt.com. Dinner only. Reservations recommended.
Love is in the air at this open-air, thatched-roof dining room, suspended over exotic koi ponds and cascading waterfalls. Gas-lit lanterns twinkle in the surrounding tropical gardens and candles flicker as diners feast on appetizers like ahi, lobster and tako poke, or grilled Kauai shrimp. Follow up with entrées such as grilled paniolo ribeye with shishito peppers.

Budget

Ono Family Restaurant

$ American-Hawaiian
4-1292 Kuhio Hwy., Kapaa. 808-822-1710. No dinner.
What's not to like about a place that serves meatloaf and eggs for breakfast? This family-owned, longtime island favorite is a great place for casual eats. You'll find more than 15 omelette choices as well as a variety of special egg dishes on the menu, along with hotcakes (try the macadamia nut) and specialty coffees and fruit smoothies. For lunch, there's a massive lineup of sandwiches and burgers, plus stir-frys, pancakes with Portuguese sausage, and fish and chips—all at prices that won't bust the budget.

Oahu

Luxury

Chef Mavro
$$$$ **French/Hawaiian**
1969 S. King St., Honolulu. 808-944-4714. www.chefmavro.com. Dinner only.
One of the finest restaurants on Oahu, Chef Mavro serves up unique fusion dishes, combining French haute cuisine with fresh Hawaiian ingredients. Owner-chef George Mavrothalassitis, a native of southern France, has won acclaim for his tasting menus that pair each item with suggested wines. The catch of the day seared with Provencale raito sauce, and lobster with island avocado and sweet corn are some of the exquisite dishes you may find on the ever-changing menu.

La Mer
$$$$ **French**
2199 Kalia Rd., Halekulani Hotel, Honolulu. 808-923-2311. www.halekulani.com. Dinner only.
This formal, top-drawer restaurant offers the best in haute cuisine—and is one of the few Hawaiian restaurants with a dress code. The food, combining French techniques with fresh Hawaiian

La Mer
© Hotels & Resorts of Halekulani

ingredients, matches the spectacular setting overlooking Waikiki beach. Chef Yves Garnier offers up creative twists on classics, like the crispy skin onaga fillet with baby vegetables in clam broth, and the foie gras casserole with Asian vegetables.

Expensive

Alan Wong's Restaurant
$$$ **Hawaiian Regional**
1857 S. King St., 3rd floor, Honolulu. 808-949-2526. www.alanwongs.com. Dinner only.
Arguably the best restaurant in Honolulu despite lack of ocean views from its third-floor perch in an office building, Alan Wong's continues to rack up well-deserved accolades. The dining room's design is clean, crisp and inviting, with neutral walls, white tablecloths and an open kitchen. Start with appetizers like wrapped tempura ahi or seafood cakes. For entrées, try the ginger crusted onaga or the grilled Maui rib steak. Quarterly Farmer Series dinners bring local ingredients to the table.

Azure
$$$ **Hawaiian**
2259 Kalakaua Ave., Honolulu. 808-921-4600. www.azure waikiki.com. Dinner only.
This upscale restaurant in the Royal Hawaiian resort is one of the finest seafood restaurants on the islands. The dining room, with flickering candles and creamy white hues, overlooks Waikiki Beach, and the culinary creations of chef Shaymus Alwin match the exquisite setting. Signature items include smoked Hawaiian

Azure

© Starwood Hotels & Resorts Worldwide

moonfish tartare, and smoked swordfish poached in duck fat and risotto with lobster, clams and shrimp. Ultra fresh fish is a specialty and can be prepared Hawaiian style or high-heat roasted. Choices for meat lovers include island ribeye steak or island-grown porchetta. Reserve an outside table or book the private cabana, where the sound of waves provides background music.

Chef Chai

$$$ Pacific Rim

1009 Kapiolani Blvd., Honolulu. 808-585-0011. chefchai.com.

Longtime occupant at the Aloha Tower, Chef Chai Chaowasaree has brought his loyal following to a new location in Honolulu for his innovative Pacific-Rim cuisine. The popular eatery, which offers indoor and outdoor seating as well as live entertainment, serves a variety of creative dishes made with fresh local ingredients. Seafood dominates the menu, with items such as salmon and grilled spicy pineapple, and whole fresh fish with chili-ginger sauce. Pacific Rim cioppino blends in coconut and zucchini linguine.

Sansei Seafood Restaurant & Sushi Bar

$$$ Japanese

2552 Kalakaua Ave., Waikiki Beach Marriott Resort, Waikiki. 808-931-6286. www.sanseihawaii.com.

If you're looking for fresh, creatively prepared seafood and sushi, you'll find it at this lively restaurant, tucked into the popular Waikiki Beach Marriott Resort. Try the award-winning Japanese calamari salad, Asian shrimp cake, the Dungeness crab ramen with Asian truffle broth or mango-crab-salad roll. There are large plates, too, but most people —and rightfully so—come for the freshly prepared sushi.

Sansei Seafood Restaurant & Sushi Bar

© Sansei Seafood Restaurant & Sushi Bar

Sushi Sasabune

$$$ Japanese

1417 S. King St., Honolulu. Dinner only. 808-947-3800. Closed Sun.

This elegant little eatery takes its sushi and sashimi very seriously (please use chopsticks so as not to squeeze the rice!), and the result is culinary art for the taste buds. Bites of the freshest, finest fish—from California sea urchins to Boston halibut, and Japanese yellowtail to Pacific albacore—are nestled in warm rice, creating, arguably, the best sushi in Hawaii and beyond.

Giovanni's Shrimp Truck

There are plenty of shrimp trucks and small cafes along Oahu's East Shore, but this mainstay remains a favorite. The graffiti-covered white truck serves large platters of shrimp from local farms with lemon and butter or hot and spicy (very hot!) sauces, and the not-to-be-beat scampi comes with chunks of garlic. *The truck is parked along Hwy. 83, between Turtle Bay and Kahuku.*

Moderate

Duke's Waikiki
$$ Hawaiian
2335 Kalakaua Ave., Honolulu. 808-922-2268. www.dukeswaikiki.com.
You won't go away hungry at this restaurant, named after Duke Kahanamoku, the father of surfing. Known for its hefty steak and fresh seafood dishes and lively bar, the place is always bustling. The dining room is beach-bar casual—it sits on Waikiki Beach, with great ocean views—and is filled with surfing memorabilia. Appetizers include poke rolls and panko crusted calamari. Then it's on to prime steaks, mango-glazed barbecue ribs, and fresh fish plates, each offered with a variety of preparations and sauces. All dinners come with the legendary Duke's salad bar.

Hula Grill
$$ Hawaiian
2335 Kalakaua Ave., Outrigger Waikiki on the Beach, Honolulu. 808-923-4852. www.hulagrill waikiki.com. No lunch.

This beachfront eatery at the Outrigger Waikiki on the Beach resort is popular with locals and visitors alike for its tasty but simply prepared fresh fish dishes and melt-in-your-mouth steaks. Try the Hawaiian ceviche or kalua pork potstickers, before moving on to the fire grilled ahi steak or traditional standbys like BBQ ribs, steaks and stir-frys.

Roy's Restaurant
$$ Hawaiian
6600 Kalanianaole Hwy., Honolulu. 808-396-7697. www.roysrestaurant.com.
Renowned Chef Roy Yamaguchi and his talented staff fire up dishes such as kampachi smothered in macadamia-nut sauce, roasted duck with maple, blackened ahi, wood-grilled Szechuan-spiced ribs, hibachi salmon and more. The first of Roy's more than 30 restaurants around the world, this two-level dining room, with its open kitchen and casual vibe, overlooks the Pacific Ocean. *Roy's location in Waikiki is 226 Lewers St.; 808-9237697.*

Budget

Hukilau Cafe
$ Hawaiian
55-662 Wahinepee St., Laie. 808-293-8616. No dinner. No Sat lunch. Closed Sun & Mon.
This down-to-earth restaurant is a must-stop for hungry locals. It's best known for its hefty breakfast platters, including the beef stew omelette and homemade corned beef hash. Lunch plates are tasty, too; try the mahimahi or shrimp tempura. Or, opt for the hefty Hukilua burger, a hamburger patty

topped with teriyaki beef, fried egg and grilled onions.

Ichiriki Japanese Nabe
$ **Japanese**
510 Pilikoi St., Honolulu. 808-589-2299. ichirikinabe.com.
The Japanese version of hot-pot cookery is the offering at this serene restaurant near the Ala Moana Shopping Center. Guests are seated on low pads around a communal table. They select ingredients from a wide array of meats, vegetables, mushrooms and hot broths, and then cook their meals themselves in the hot pots set on the table. Service is discreet and exacting, the atmosphere subdued, and the food, of course, turns out just as you wish it.

Kaka'ako Kitchen
$ **Hawaiian**
1200 Ala Moana Blvd., Honolulu. 808-596-7488. kakaakokitchen.com.
There's nothing fancy about this local favorite across the street from Ala Moana Park—it's like a Hawaiian diner with a vast menu of comfort foods, including one of Oahu's best renditions of the lgendary loco moco. Fancier dishes called "couture entrées" on the menu include catch of the day and eggplant parmesan; but most go for the mixed plate, ahi sandwich or old-fashioned beef stew.

Leonard's Bakery
$ **Portuguese**
933 Kapahulu Ave., Honolulu. 808-737-5591. www.leonards hawaii.com.
At this no-frills, much-loved and longstanding (since 1952) bakery in Waimalu Shopping Center, the sweet, Portuguese-style *malasadas* are Leonard's claim to fame. These donuts with no holes are lightly dusted with cinnamon sugar and come with or without filling. The bakery also offers an array of cookies, cakes, pies and pastries, as well as fresh-baked pao doce sweet bread and wraps. Though it's open til 10pm, seating is minimal, and it's not truly a place for dinner.

Ono Hawaiian Food
$ **Hawaiian**
726 Kapahulu Ave., Honolulu. 808-737-2275. onohawaiianfoods.com. Closed Sun.
You can't beat this hole-in-the-wall eatery for traditional Hawaiian food. The local favorite for nearly 40 years, Ono is the place to go for luau-style kalua pig, steamed overnight in a wood-fired, underground oven. The signature laulau—ti-leaf-wrapped packets of taro leaves and chunks of pork—is another favorite. The heaping special plates come with big scoops of rice, poi, haupia, lomi lomi salmon and pipikaula.

Rainbow Drive-In
$ **Hawaiian**
3308 Kanaina Ave., Honolulu. 808-737-0177.
This classic Hawaiian plate-lunch cafe serves breakfast and dinner too. The popular eating spot offers a heaping dish of barbecued meat, fish, chicken or pork, piled high with scoops of the requisite macaroni salad and rice. Chili, loco moco and breakfast platters (for lunch, too) are among the other quintessential items here.

Lanai and Molokai

Luxury

Dining Room at The Lodge at Koele

$$$$ Hawaiian Regional
1 Keamoku Dr., Lanai City.
808-565-3800 or 800-450-3704.
www.fourseasons.com/koele.
Dinner only.

As the name implies, this top-end restaurant in The Lodge at Koele *(see Hotels)* offers an elegant dining experience, noted for its high-quality cuisine and impeccable service. The stately dining room is bathed in soft light from flickering candles and a glowing log fire. On the menu you'll find well-executed Hawaiian regional dishes, varying with the season and availability, ranging from Molokai venison to Big Island beef and Maui cheese and vegetables.

Moderate

Lanai City Grille

$$ Hawaiian Fusion
828 Lanai Ave., Hotel Lanai,
Lanai City. 808-565-7211.
www.hotellanai.com. Dinner
only. Closed Mon & Tue.

This warm and casual restaurant is under the auspices of Beverly Gannon, one of the 12 original founders of the Hawaii Regional Cuisine movement. Fresh and local—that's the focus of the ever-changing menu, which includes just-caught fish and island poultry and beef. The signature herb-marinated rotisserie chicken is a popular choice among patrons.

Budget

Kanemitsu Bakery & Restaurant

$ Hawaiian
79 Ala Malama St., Kaunakakai.
808-553-5855. Closed Tue.

This plain-Jane bakery is a great place to buy Molokai's distinctive sweet bread, known locally as "hot bread"—best eaten straight out of the oven. (The coconut-pineapple loaf is a favorite). Get it right out of the oven, to go, or nibble here, while you hang out with the regular breakfast crowd. Other plated dishes include such fusion comfort foods as kim chee fried rice and omelettes.

Kualapuu Cook House

$ American
102 Farrington Ave., Kualapuu.
808-567-9655. Closed Mon
morning and Sun. Cash only.

At lunch, this no-frills cafe sends out big plates of chicken, beef or pork stir-fry with eggs, rice and macaroni salad. The grilled mahi "burger" is a tasty choice. Things get slightly fancier at dinner time, when specials, like baby-back ribs in guava sauce or, on Thursday nights, prime rib, are offered.

Pele's Other Garden

$ American
811 Houston St., Lanai City.
808-565-9628. www.pelesother
garden.com. Closed Sun.

This tiny, bright bistro is the perfect place to stop for an overstuffed sandwich or burrito, organic salads, and homemade breads and soups. At night, order tasty, fresh-made pizzas and classic Italian dishes. The bistro has a full bar, too.

HOTELS

The properties listed below were selected for their ambience, location and/or value for money. Prices reflect the average cost for a standard double room for two people. Many hotels offer special discount packages; ask about them when you make your reservations. Price ranges quoted do not reflect the Hawaii hotel tax of 12%–13.5%.

Luxury	**$$$$$**	over $350	*Moderate*	**$$$**	$175–250
Expensive	**$$$$**	$250–$350	*Budget*	**$$–$**	under $175

Big Island

Luxury

Four Seasons Hualalai
$$$$$ **243 rooms**
100 Kaupulehu Dr., Kaupulehu-Kona. 808-325-8019 or 800-819-5053. www.fourseasons.com.
An elegant, bungalow-style resort on the water, this lush tropical retreat blends into the natural environment. Guests can swim in a saltwater pool (one of four pools) or a sheltered oceanfront lagoon or cool off in private outdoor showers after golf or a spa treatment. Every room has its own private lanai and ocean views. Other perks include a Hawaiian cultural program and three restaurants serving Hawaiian regional food, 75 percent of which comes from the islands.

Expensive

Fairmont Orchid
$$$$ **540 rooms**
One North Kaniku Dr., Kohala Coast. 808-885-2000 or 800-257-7544. www.fairmont.com/orchid.
Set on 32 acres surrounding a sheltered lagoon, the Fairmont Orchid exudes a hushed elegance. Guest rooms are beautifully appointed with island artwork, block-cut native wall coverings and palm-leaf pillow shams. The Fairmont uses chemical-free cleansers and practices organic landscaping. The resort's Spa Without Walls *(see p55)* offers outdoor massage. A bevy of restaurants, a kids' program, water sports, swimming pool, golf course and tennis courts round out the many amenities.

Four Seasons Hualalai

© Four Seasons

Hapuna Beach Prince Hotel

$$$$ 350 rooms

62-100 Kauna'oa Dr., Kohala Coast. 808-880-3000 or 888-977-4263. www.princeresortshawaii.com.
Only slightly less upscale than other area resorts, the Prince has spacious, airy rooms, excellent casual dining and a large free-form pool overlooking the property's amazing namesake beach. A famous golf course lies up the hill.

Hawaii Island Retreat at Ahu Pohaku Ho' omaluhia

$$$$ 10 rooms, 7 yurts

250 Lohaki Rd., Kapaau. 808-889-6336. www.hawaiiislandretreat.com. 2-night minimum stay.
This eco-friendly spa retreat seeks to revitalize the spirit and the land. The innkeeper and lead therapist has created a tranquil escape with Hawaiian-style rooms cooled by ceiling fans, each with a private balcony (no in-room TVs), and rustic yurt hales for two.
Most of the food is grown on-property. Spa treatments and yoga classes are top-notch. The property overlooks the ocean on north Kohala coast.

Hawaii Volcano House

$$$$ 33 rooms

Crater Rim Dr., Hawaii Volcanoes National Park. 808-441-7750 or 866-536-7972. www.hawaii volcanohouse.com.
Perched at the edge of the Kilauea Crater, this historic lodge (1941) reopened in 2013 after renovation. It is the only lodging inside the national park. Most rooms face out to the crater, as does the dining room. Furnishings reflect mid-20C style. Hiking trails lead along the rim from the lodge.

Rustic yurt, Hawaii Island Retreat

Lia Watkins/Hawaii Island Retreat

Moderate

Hilo Hawaiian Hotel

$$$ 286 rooms

71 Banyan Dr., Hilo. 808-935-9361. www.castleresorts.com.
Overlooking the ocean just outside Hilo proper, this classic mid-century hotel has been newly renovated and offers a great location from which to enjoy what locals consider the more authentically Hawaiian side of the Big Island. A large pool, nearby golf course, and famed Liliuokalani Gardens nearby entertain guests.

Hilton Waikoloa Village

$$$ 1,240 rooms

425 Waikoloa Beach Dr., Waikoloa. 808-886-1234. www.hiltonwaikoloavillage.com.
The Big Island's largest family-oriented waterfront resort whisks you to your room via monorail or boat, setting the tone for a wealth of on-site activities. Valuable artworks are displayed on the property, including a one-mile museum walkway. Kids can slide down a 175-foot waterslide, kayak in a lagoon, or swim with dolphins. The hotel's 13 different dining spots range from high-style Japanese to pizza. The Kohala Spa has landscaped outdoor facilities.

Waikoloa Beach Marriott Resort

$$$ **555 rooms**

69-275 Waikoloa Beach Dr., Waikoloa. 808-886-6789 or 888-924-5656. www.waikoloa beachmarriott.com.

With average room rates below $300 a night, this property offers loads of amenities, including a spa, children's activities and water sports galore. Six pools border ancient fish ponds and a swath of crescent sand on the Kohala Coast. On property, there's snorkeling, kayaking and windsurfing. Rooms are modern and clean, fine for a laid-back beach vacation.

Waikoloa Beach Marriott Resort

© Waikoloa Beach Marriott Resort

Budget

Kilauea Lodge

$$ **14 rooms, 3 cottages**

Old Volcano Rd., Volcano. 808-967-7366. www.kilauealodge.com.

Formerly a YMCA camp (c. 1938), this high-ceilinged, rustic lodge, adjacent to Hawaii Volcanoes National Park, is a cozy, inviting place to stay on a cool night. Some rooms have gas fireplaces, and all are adorned with fresh flowers. Rates include a full breakfast. The restaurant offers fine dining with an Old World, European flavor.

Waimea Gardens Cottage B&B

$$ **2 cottages, 1 studio**

Off Mamalahoa Hwy., 2mi east of town, Waimea; 808-885-8550. www.waimeagardens.com. 3 night minimum stay. No credit cards.

This homey alternative to the Big Island's resorts features two cottages set in the foothills of the Kohala Mountains. Cottages are nicely turned out with hardwood floors and French doors; one has a wood-burning fireplace; the other has a whirlpool tub. Attached to the main residence, a studio-type guest room (sleeps two) is available at a lower rate.

King Kamehameha's Kona Beach Hotel

$-$$ **460 rooms**

75-5660 Palani Rd, Kailua-Kona. 808-329-2911. www.konabeach hotel.com.

Standing where King Kamehameha once lived, this classic property (now a Courtyard by Marriott) overlooks a fine snorkeling bay. It is within walking distance of numerous shops and restaurants. The property sustained some damage in the tsunami, and repairs are on-going. Rooms are recently updated and reflect Big Island themes: lava, native flora and the Hawaiian tattoo. The lobby holds a priceless collection of Hawaiian artwork by Herb Kane. The feeling is friendly, casual, and a good value for the money.

Maui

Luxury

Andaz Maui
$$$$$ **297 rooms, 7 villas**
3550 Wailea Alanui Dr., Wailea. 808-573-1234. maui.andaz.hyatt.com.
Hyatt's new upscale boutique property in Wailea is distinguished by sleek modern design (ivory-toned rooms and angular wood furnishings), a four-level pool complex, five restaurants—and no resort fees. The 15-acre complex fronts directly on Wailea's famous golden-strand beach.

Fairmont Kea Lani
$$$$$ **450 rooms**
4100 Wailea Alanui Dr., Wailea. 808-875-4100 or 866-540-4456. www.fairmont.com.
Set on Wailea's Polo Beach, this distinctive hotel makes numerous "best" lists. Service is a true art form here, where valets literally sprint to your car to open the door for you, and guests are greeted with fresh leis. Each one-bedroom suite has a living room, master bedroom, and marble bath; oceanfront villas have two or three bedrooms, a kitchen, and a plunge pool. The hotel is bright white faux Mediterranean, set against the cerulean blue of sea and sky. The "plantation cuisine" at Ko restaurant has won several regional dining awards.

Four Seasons Resort Maui
$$$$$ **308 rooms**
3900 Wailea Alanui Dr., Wailea. 808-874-8000. www.fourseasons.com/maui.
This hotel offers all the subdued elegance you'd expect from a Four Seasons, with a colorful splash of contemporary Hawaiian art. Most of the well-appointed, spacious (600 sq ft) guest rooms offer ocean views from their lanais. Complimentary kids' programs are enhanced by amenities like baby gear and bicycles. The courtyard setting with three pools and gardens makes you feel like you're in your own world, not in one of a string of beachfront hotels. A sunset dinner at tiki torch-lit Ferraro's is a favorite with guests.

Ritz-Carlton Kapalua
$$$$$ **463 rooms**
1 Ritz-Carlton Dr., Kapalua. 808-669-6200 or 800-542-8680. www.ritzcarlton.com/kapalua.
Maui's northernmost major resort enjoys a breezy setting on a bluff overlooking the Molokai Channel. The signature Ritz- Carlton elegance (lots of brass and marble) and intense service ethic are evident throughout. The resort's dedication to Hawaiian culture and sustainability includes daily programs, peerless artwork and an alliance with Jean-Michael Cousteau's Ocean Futures Society. The adjacent golf course features stunning views of Molokai and the West Maui Mountains.

Travaasa Hana
$$$$$ **66 rooms**
5021 Hana Hwy., Hana. 808-359-2401 or 888-965-5890. www.travaasa.com/hana.
Bungalow-style suites and sea ranch cottages beautifully blend into the lush landscape at this elegant resort, with tropical forest and the ocean ever in view. A gentle, New Age spirit pervades this property: no TVs and no

Travaasa Hana

© Travaasa Experiential Resorts

air-conditioning (ceiling fans are ample in Hana). Guest rooms boast contemporary Hawaiian art, gorgeous shell sconces and wood countertops. The torch-lit pool and hot tub complex is spectacular. There's an excellent on-site spa, and Hawaiian cultural activities include lei-making and hula lessons.

Moderate

Inn at Mama's Fish House
$$$ 6 cottages
799 Poho Place, Paia.
808-579-9764 or 800-860-4852.
www.mamasfishhouse.com.
Behind the seminal **Mama's Fish House** restaurant (*see Restaurants*) stand six luxury cottages with tile floors and lanais, TVs, grills and—the best feature—access to the postcard beach. Cottages include four two-bedroom units and two one-bedroom units, each with Polynesian-style furnishings and full kitchens. With an open design plan, the cottages don't offer much privacy—but guests enjoy a discount at the famous restaurant.

Westin Maui Resort
$$$ 759 rooms
2365 Kaanapali Parkway, Lahaina.
808-667-2525 or 866-716-8112.
www.westinmaui.com.
One of two Westin properties at Kaanapali (the other is a condo development), this resort is famed for its massive, 87,000-square-foot tiered pool and waterfall complex, which easily absorbs the multitudes of families and adults seeking quiet relaxation. Guests with oceanview rooms are likely to see whales December through March. The adjacent beach has several times been rated best in the US.

Budget

Old Wailuku Inn at Ulupono
$$ 10 rooms
2199 Kahookele St, Wailuku.
808-244-5897 or 800-305-4899.
www.mauiinn.com. 2-night
minimum stay.
This restored 1924 former plantation manager's house evokes Hawaii in the 1920s and '30s, with ohia-wood floors and traditional Hawaiian quilts. A more recent addition features more modern rooms, with prints by fabric designer Sig Zane. The beach is a drive away (20min), but you can walk to Wailuku's historic district, where there are lots of antique shops and restaurants. A full gourmet breakfast is served in an enclosed lanai. The innkeepers will supply beach towels, boogieboards and a cooler for you to tote to the beach.

HOTELS

Grand Hyatt Kauai

MUST STAY

Kauai

Luxury

Grand Hyatt Kauai
$$$$$ **602 rooms**
1571 Poipu Rd., Koloa. 808-742-1234. www.kauai.hyatt.com.
The landscaped grounds surrounding this upscale resort on the south shore are beyond beautiful: a series of swimming pools snake through tropical gardens dotted with swaying palm trees and punctuated with cascades and waterfalls tumbling down over boulders.

Rooms have views of the ocean, hotel lagoons, gardens or the Haupu Mountains. No less than nine on-site restaurants include the award-winning **Tidepools** (*see Restaurants*), and the Ilima Terrace for dining outdoors. Also on premises, the Anara Spa is one of the best in the US (*see p103*).

St. Regis Princeville Resort
$$$$$ **252 rooms**
5520 Ka Haku Rd., Princeville. 808-826-9644 or 866-716-8140. www.stregisprinceville.com.

Considered one of the premier properties in the islands, St. Regis Princeville Resort commands a dramatic view of Hanalei Bay and the lush North Shore mountains. Most rooms overlook the beginnings of the rugged Na Pali Coast. Guests gather in the opulent lobby to sit and enjoy the views from its soaring windows; drinks and stunning ocean views are offered in the lobby's Library Room. Dining is world-class at **Kauai Grill** (*see Restaurants*).

Expensive

Kauai Marriott Resort
$$$$ **356 rooms**
Kalapaki Beach, Lihue. 808-245-5050 or 800-220-2925. www.marriotthawaii.com.
This lush 800-acre resort is set on 1.4 miles of south shore sandy beach, and surrounded by 51 acres of tropical gardens and two championship golf courses. The outdoor public spaces are impressive, with fine art, Asian-style statuary and sculpture and exotic flowers. The 24,000-square-foot pool features waterfalls and hidden hot tubs.

Koloa Landing

$$$$ **85 rooms**

*2641 Poipu Rd., Koloa. 808-240-
6600. www.wyndham.com.*

This luxury development, a
Wyndham Grand Resort property,
sits on 25 acres of lush landscaping
with waterfalls, meandering
walkways, tropical gardens and
two sprawling pools. Ultra-
spacious one-, two-, three- and
four-bedroom villas feature top-of-
the-line materials, furnishings and
appliances. Popular Poipu Beach is
a few minutes drive away.

Sheraton Kauai Resort

$$$$ **412 rooms**

*2440 Hoonani Rd., Poipu Beach.
808-742-1661. www.sheraton-
kauai.com.*

The Sheraton's location, on the
shores of Poipu Beach, is its main
selling point. A cluster of low-
slung buildings hugs the shores
of the sandy white beach, with
fine swimming and snorkeling at
the doorstep. Reserve a room in
the Beach or Ocean wings, where
views all face the sea.

Moderate

Hanalei Bay Resort

$$$ **134 suites**

*5380 Honoiki Rd., Princeville.
808-826-6522 or 877-344-0688.
www.hanaleibayresort.com.*

Set on the north shore, next to
the famed St. Regis Princeville
Resort, this value-packed all-suite
property is perfect for vacationers
looking for a destination resort.
Suites have wicker furnishings,
kitchenettes or full kitchens, and
a value-conscious price tag. The
property commands picturesque
views and a crescent of sandy beach.

Koa Kea Hotel

$$$ **121 rooms**

*2251 Poipu Rd., Koloa. 808-828-
8888. www.koakeahotel.com.*

If you're looking for warm, intimate
personal service with world-class
amenities, this upscale boutique
property lies just steps from Poipu
Beach. Rooms are contemporary
and all have a private lanai with
ocean or garden views. There's a
poolside bar and the hotel's **Red
Salt** (*see Restaurants*) is considered
one of the best on the island.

Outrigger Waipouli Beach
Resort and Spa

$$$ **350 rooms**

*4-820 Kuhio Highway, Kapaa.
808-823-1401 or 808-823-1402.
www.outrigger.com.*

Commanding a prime piece of
pristine oceanfront on the eastern
shore, this luxury resort condo
property is elegantly appointed
inside and out. Lush, landscaped
grounds include a two-acre river
pool with flumed water slides
and three sand-bottom whirlpool
spas. Condominiums are spacious
with high-end appliances, deluxe
bathrooms, and top-notch
furnishings in all the units.

Waimea Plantation Cottages

$$$ **44 cottages**

*9400 Kaumualii Hwy., Waimea.
808-338-1625 or 800-992-4632.
www.waimea-plantation.com.*

Waimea Plantation's charming
early 20C sugar-workers'
bungalows stretch out among 27
acres of coconut groves along a
black-sand beach on Kauai's west
side. Units with full kitchens and
televisions are perfect for families,
and hammocks for two invite long
naps by the sea.

HOTELS

Oahu

Luxury

Halekulani Hotel
$$$$$ **456 rooms**
2199 Kalia Rd., Honolulu.
808-923-2311 or 800-367-2343.
www.halekulani.com.
One of the top hotels in the world, the graceful Halekulani presides over Waikiki Beach like an elegant grand dame. Since 1917, this first-rate hotel has been a mecca for the rich and famous, who come for its Waikiki beach location, restaurant **La Mer** (*see Restaurants*) and excellent service. Rooms have elegant furnishings and amenities, such as marble vanities and deep soaking tubs, not to mention views overlooking the Pacific Ocean from towers as lofty as the clientele.

J.W. Marriott Ihilani Resort & Spa
$$$$$ **423 rooms**
92-1001 Olani St., Ko Olina.
808-679-0079. www.ihilani.com.
This sleek, ultra-luxe destination resort occupies 640 secluded oceanfront acres, 23 miles outside Waikiki Beach, on Oahu's sunny western shore. The 17-story hotel overlooks pristine beaches,

J.W. Marriott Ihilani Resort & Spa

turquoise lagoons and open ocean. Rooms are contemporary, with sweeping ocean views and private lanais. On-site you'll find a 35,000-square-foot spa (*see p143*), a golf course, a fitness club, pools and four restaurants.

Kahala Hotel and Resort
$$$$$ **345 rooms**
5000 Kahala Ave., Honolulu.
808-739-8888 or 800-367-2525.
www.kahalaresort.com.
Quiet, serene and luxurious describes this luscious resort tucked away on a secluded bay, 10 minutes from Waikiki. The oceanfront hotel features six restaurants, a full-service spa, a fitness center, a dive shop and an impressive 26,000-square-foot, dolphin lagoon. Rooms blend Old Hawaiian décor with Asian accents,

Diamond Head suite, Halekulani Hotel

MUST STAY

including mahogany furniture, teak parquet floors and grass-cloth wall coverings.

Moana Surfrider, A Westin Resort & Spa
$$$$$ **793 rooms**
2365 Kalakaua Ave., Waikiki Beach. 808-922-3111. www.moana-surfrider.com.
Dubbed the "first Lady of Waikiki," this 1901 landmark is the island's oldest hotel. Recently re-branded as a Westin luxury property, the large oceanfront resort combines Old Hawaiian charm with modern-day touches. The open-air lobby, boasts expansive Waikiki Beach views. Rooms in the newer tower are the most spacious. If you're looking for Old Hawaii ambience, reserve a room in the Banyan wing. Accommodations here are smaller but full of charm, decorated with antiques and rare koa-wood and custom furnishings.

Royal Hawaiian
$$$$$ **528 rooms**
2259 Kalakaua Ave., Honolulu. 808-923-7311. www.royal-hawaiian.com.
The sprawling, storied Pink Palace of the Pacific became a Hollywood playground after the Moorish-style hotel was built in 1927. It is now part of the Starwood Luxury Collection and recently underwent an extensive renovation of its rooms, lobby, outdoor areas, ✿ **spa**, and other areas. Modern conveniences and deluxe amenities blend with its historic architecture. The mai tai cocktail was supposedly created in the bar of the same name here, still a popular spot for sunset watching.

Royal Hawaiian

© Starwood Hotels & Resorts Worldwide

Expensive

Aulani
$$$$ **359 rooms**
92-1185 Ali'inui Dr., Kapolei. 808-674-6200. resorts.disney.go.com.
On Oahu's western shore, Disney's first stand-alone resort is poised above a delightful man-made lagoon, perfect for swimming. The usual Disney touches are evident in a lavish children's water-play area and "character breakfasts," where kids may meet Mickey and Goofy. Otherwise the resort is devoted to Hawaiian culture and includes a lounge where all staffers speak Hawaiian and guests are invited to learn the language. Hawaiian culture shows, lei-making and more entertain visitors of all ages. Rooms are discreetly elegant.

Hilton Hawaiian Village Beach Resort & Spa
$$$$ **2,998 rooms**
2005 Kalia Rd., Honolulu. 808-949-4321 or 800-445-8667. www.hiltonhawaiianvillage.com.
One of the world's largest oceanfront hotels stretches over 22 acres and features six separate guest towers. The complex includes some 90 fine shops, 22 restaurants and lounges, a fitness center and Mandara Spa. The immaculate

HOTELS

grounds wrap around a lagoon, with roaming wildlife and leafy botanical gardens; five pools include the largest one on the island.

Hyatt Regency Waikiki
$$$$ 1,230 rooms
2424 Kalakaua Ave., Honolulu. 808-923-1234 or 888-591-1234. www.hyattregencywaikiki.com.
Located across the street from Kuhio Beach and near Kapiolani Park, this large-scale resort is a lively spot. The open-air lobby, with its tumbling waterfalls and live music, is the center of action. Guest rooms, with private lanais, are modestly sized and decorated with light colors. The 10,000-square-foot **Na Hoola Spa** (*see p144*) and fitness center, oceanfront pool, supervised children's programs, and activities galore are added benefits.

Turtle Bay Resort & Spa
$$$$ 452 rooms
57-091 Kamehameha Hwy., Kahuku. 808-293-6000 or 866-827-5327. www.turtlebayresort.com.
Tucked beside its own sheltered lagoon on Oahu's northeast shore, near the Polynesian Cultural Center, Turtle Bay offers a resort experience far from the vacationing crowds on Oahu. A recent remodel has freshened the venerable property. Riding stables, surf experts and an on-site ukelele teacher lend distinctive elements.

Moderate

Ala Moana Hotel
$$$ 1,154 rooms
410 Atkinson Dr., Honolulu. 808-955-4811 or 800-367-6025. www.alamoanahotelhonolulu.com
Across from the Hawaii Convention Center, overlooking pretty Ala Moana Beach Park, this landmark high rise is popular with businesspeople and families looking for quality at a decent price. The towering 36-story hotel, with a fitness center, restaurants and bars, is also connected to the popular Ala Moana Shopping Center (*see p139*). Rooms (including 51 suites) are decorated with light, airy island colors and have private lanais, most with mountain or ocean views.

Aston Waikiki Beach Hotel
$$$ 644 rooms
2570 Kalakaua Ave., Honolulu. 877-997-6667 or 808-924-2924. www.astonwaikikibeach.com.
This two-tower high rise is one of the "best-value" properties in Honolulu. Located just off Waikiki Beach and within walking distance of major downtown sights and attractions, the hotel has gone from dowdy and non-distinctive to hip and lively. Wallet-pleasing prices, the hotel's wild and colorful Hawaiian décor and casual, friendly ambience appeal to young families and couples.

Coconut Hotel
$$$ 81 rooms
450 Lewers St., Honolulu. 808-923-8828. www.jdvhotels.com.
Decorated in cool ivory and lime shades with bright color splashes, this chic boutique hotel is on the "back side" of Waikiki and thus quieter and cheaper.
The rooms are spacious, and the service is user-friendly and low-key. Every amenity is present, and the beach lies just a three-block stroll away.

Hotel Renew

$$$ **72 rooms**

129 Paoakalani Ave.,
Honolulu. 808-687-7700.
www.hotelrenew.com.

Forget tropical prints and tiki
torches; this oh-so-sleek, elegant
boutique hotel is all about
sophisticated, modern décor and
stylish, hi-tech touches.
Monochromatic, earthy hues, soft
woods, and subtle lighting grace
the lobby and rooms of this nine-
story trendy hotel. Some rooms
have Waikiki Beach views, which is
about a half block away. All have
luxe bed linens, flat screen TVs and
WiFi access. A soothing, spa-like
ambience pervades, helped by
touches like scented candles
and fresh flowers. It's perfect for
couples looking for a quiet oasis in
bustling Waikiki Beach

Ilikai Hotel

$$$ **968 rooms**

1777 Ala Moana Blvd.,
Honolulu. 808-949-33811.
www.ilikaihotel.com.

Budget travelers flock to this
longstanding Honolulu 30-story
high rise, a prominent oceanfront
skyscraper for nearly four decades.
The old dame has been well-kept,
with white-glove clean and simply
furnished rooms. For more space,
opt for one of the suites or multi-
room condo units. The property
lies at the entrance to Waikiki
Beach, next to the Hilton Hawaiian
Village Beach Resort.

Outrigger Waikiki on the Beach

$$$ **524 rooms**

2335 Kalakaua Ave., Honolulu.
808-923-0711 or 800-688-7444.
www.outriggerwaikikihotel.com.

Outrigger Waikiki on the Beach

© Outrigger Hotels and Resorts

With a prime location on Waikiki
Beach and a slew of amenities and
activities, this beachfront hotel is
a top choice for Oahu vacationers.
Guests here can choose among a
host of water sports, boat cruises,
and shopping options. Be sure to
visit **Duke's Canoe Club** for food
and drink.

Waikiki Parc Hotel

$$$ **298 rooms**

2233 Helumoa Rd., Honolulu.
808-921-7272 or 800-422-0450.
www.waikikiparc.com.

Just off the Waikiki Beach
(across the street from Oahu's
famous Halekulani resort), this
contemporary property offers
the services and amenities of
a top-end resort hotel without
the beachfront price tag. Stylish
rooms are bright and airy,
decorated in neutral colors with
tropical accents. There's a fitness
center, and a small rooftop pool
overlooking the ocean.

HOTELS

Budget

Aston Waikiki Joy Hotel
$$ 94 rooms
320 Lewers St., Honolulu.
808-924-2924 or 877-997-6667.
www.astonhotels.com/aston.
Within walking distance of
Waikiki Beach, the 11-story hotel
provides a friendly oasis from busy
downtown Honolulu. Spacious
rooms have elegant touches, such
as marble-tile entries, in-room
Jacuzzis, private lanais and state-
of-the-art sound systems.
All come equipped with small
refrigerators; suites have full
kitchens, making it a money-
saving choice, especially for
families, who don't mind being
off the beach. There's an on-site
restaurant and pool, and breakfast
is complimentary.

Manoa Valley Inn
$$ 7 rooms, 1 cottage
2001 Vancouver Dr., Honolulu.
808-947-6019 or 808-256-5939.
www.manoavalleyinn.com.
This 1912 post-Victorian inn, set
in a lush and quiet neighborhood
near the University of Hawaii, is
filled with period antiques and
homey touches. Rooms have

Four Seasons Lanai, The Lodge at Koele

© Four Seasons

comfortable four-poster beds;
some share bathroom facilities.
It offers travelers an economic—
and less hectic—alternative to
Honolulu's extravagant high rises.

Lanai

Luxury

Four Seasons Lanai,
The Lodge at Koele
$$$$$ 102 rooms
1 Keamoku Dr., Lanai City.
808-565-4000. www.fourseasons.
com/koele.
Discerning travelers looking
for peace and pampering (and
willing to pay the high price for
it) favor this upscale, country-
style lodge, set in Lanai's uplands
among towering Cook pines and
banyan trees. The lodge's great
room features two massive stone
fireplaces, overstuffed chairs and
sofas, and an interesting array of
antiques, sculpture and artwork.
Rooms have four-poster beds
draped in crisp, fine linens, marble
baths and private lanais.

Four Seasons Lanai at
Manele Bay
$$$$$ 249 rooms
1 Manele Bay Rd., Lanai City.
808-565-2000. www.fourseasons.
com/manelebay.
Perched above Hulopoe Bay—
often rated the best beach in
the islands—this deluxe resort
boasts spacious, elegant rooms
surrounded by gardens and
waterfalls. A championship golf
course winds past homes owned
by mainland billionaires; the entire
resort was famously rented for
Bill and Melinda Gates' wedding.
Though island activities range from

MUST STAY

Four Seasons Lanai at Manele Bay

© Four Seasons

Jeep exploring to biking and even hunting, most guests just relax around the pool or on the beach.

Budget

Hotel Lanai
$$ **10 rooms, 1 cottage**
828 Lanai Ave., Lanai City.
800-795-7211 or 808-565-7211.
www.hotellanai.com.
This charming 1923 house, located in Lanai City, offers an economic and intimate option for lodging on the island of Lanai. Built by James Dole as housing for Dole Plantation executives, the restored plantation guest house provides small but pleasant rooms, with hardwood floors, ceiling fans, colorful country quilts and private baths.

Hotel Molokai

© Four © Hotel Molokai vSeasons

Molokai Pointers

- Rent a car. You won't really need a Jeep.
- If you want to be near groceries and eateries, stay in Kaunakakai.
- Consider a commuter flight; it can be cheaper than the ferry.

Molokai

Moderate

Hotel Molokai
$$$ **54 rooms**
1300 Kamehameha V Hwy., near Kaunakakai. 808-660-3408 or 877-553-5347. www.hotelmolokai.com.
Molokai's only hotel, this casual, beachfront property offers a taste of "Old Hawaii" with Polynesian-style bungalows adorned with island fabrics and cooled with ceiling fans. Rooms are clean and pleasant, but fairly basic, and guests spend most of their time around the pool and in hammocks strung between the palms. Though the lively bar is open nightly until 10:30pm or so, the hotel maintains quiet hours from midnight to 7am.

HOTELS

HAWAIIAN ISLANDS

The following abbreviations may appear in this Index and Star Attractions list: **BG** Botanical Garden; **NHS** National Historic Site; **NM** National Monument; **NMem** National Memorial; **NP** National Park; **NHP** National Historical Park; **NRA** National Recreational Area; **NWR** National Wildlife Refuge; **SP** State Park; **SHP** State Historical Park; **SHS** State Historic Site; **SRA** State Recreation Area.

INDEX

INDEX